To Kev
nope !
Joe

C000065571

War Trials

War Trials

Investigation of a Soldier and the Trauma of Iraq

Will Yates

Pen & Sword
MILITARY

First published in Great Britain in 2021 by
Pen & Sword Military
An imprint of
Pen & Sword Books Ltd
Yorkshire – Philadelphia

Copyright © Will Yates 2021

ISBN 978 1 52679 602 8

A CIP catalogue record for this book is
available from the British Library.

Typeset by Mac Style
Printed and bound in the UK by CPI Group (UK) Ltd,
Croydon, CR0 4YY.

Pen & Sword Books Limited incorporates the imprints of Atlas,
Archaeology, Aviation, Discovery, Family History, Fiction, History,
Maritime, Military, Military Classics, Politics, Select, Transport,
True Crime, Air World, Frontline Publishing, Leo Cooper, Remember
When, Seaforth Publishing, The Praetorian Press, Wharncliffe
Local History, Wharncliffe Transport, Wharncliffe True Crime
and White Owl.

For a complete list of Pen & Sword titles please contact

PEN & SWORD BOOKS LIMITED
47 Church Street, Barnsley, South Yorkshire, S70 2AS, England
E-mail: enquiries@pen-and-sword.co.uk
Website: www.pen-and-sword.co.uk

Or

PEN AND SWORD BOOKS
1950 Lawrence Rd, Havertown, PA 19083, USA
E-mail: Uspen-and-sword@casematepublishers.com
Website: www.penandswordbooks.com

Contents

'I am young, I am twenty years old; yet I know nothing of life but despair, death, fear, and fatuous superficiality cast over an abyss of sorrow. I see how peoples are set against one another, and in silence, unknowingly, foolishly, obediently, innocently slay one another.'

Erich Maria Remarque, *All Quiet on the Western Front*

'I was just living and breathing and wanting to die, every day … the trial itself, that was just like the war, that was like seven weeks of hell.'

Former Guardsman Joe McCleary

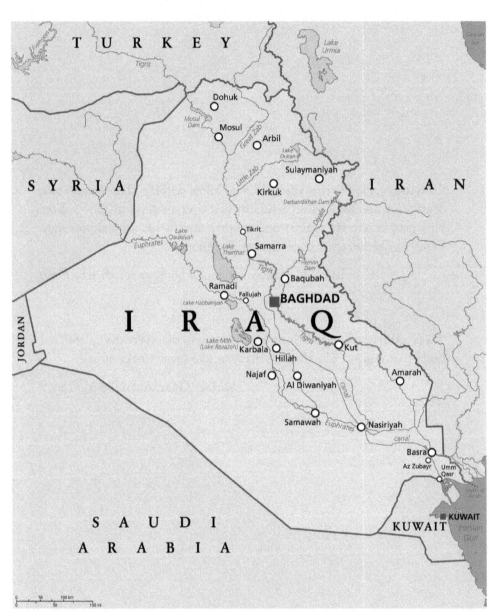

Iraq Map. (*Credit: Peter Hermes Furian/iStock*)

Part I

Investigation

Chapter 1

Water's Edge

The boy stands by the water's edge, that's the last place he is clearly seen before he drowns. The soldier will have nightmares about these moments over and over and over again.

The boy, Ahmed, is 15, with dark caramel complexion and can't swim. He is loved by his parents, has a brother Mohammed and two sisters. The family's financial situation is bad, even worse now than it was under Saddam. Ahmed shuffles in terror, just a couple of feet from the deep channel, ever closer. The swell of fear he feels and surge of adrenaline causes his asthmatic lungs to involuntarily constrict. Grey, discoloured boulders litter the ledge that mark the divide between land and the water. Loose rocks dig uncomfortably into the tender bare skin of the boy's feet. Below him the slopping sound of the dirty mauve-green water, the Al-Zubair in spring, its current cutting through the Shatt al-Basra canal. Next to Ahmed is another lad, Ayad, and although their fathers know of each other and trade at the Basra market, the boys met only this morning. Ayad is slightly older and he clutches a ruptured, bleeding cut along his forearm. Already in the water are two more guys who have swum with ease across to a pale concrete pillar that holds up Bridge Four, the busy arterial road and recent checkpoint into the city of Basra. The sloping bank beneath the bridge is where Ahmed, Ayad and the other two are brought. When the doors of the military personnel carrier open, the terrified boys see the canal and seem to know what's expected of them. When the rags used to tie their wrists are unbound, they head towards the water. Ahmed inhales a struggling breath, experiencing a wave of queasiness. He shivers, even amid the heat of a day like this one in early May.

Giving a nervous backward glance, Ahmed sees the bulky British guardsmen wearing tattered and battle-worn fatigues. There are three of them standing on the dusty ground; they're still young, not much older than Ayad, and their presence casts shadows in the harsh mid-morning light. Just a few feet away, the dust-coated mustard-coloured Warrior vehicle waits, humming on twelve wheels, six on each side, encased in tracks. The machine's heavy engine growls impatiently, almost like its commander, who sits atop in the commander's position of the hulking armour-plated vehicle.

The nearby soldiers clutch their SA-80 rifles and the two Iraqi lads linger, looking at the murky dark liquid below the jagged ledge. The infantry soldier says something that neither Ahmed nor Ayad can understand. Ayad steps out over the chunky rocks first and then into the canal, his arms splayed as he first makes contact with the water. Descending unsteadily, up to his waist, he seems to find no footing. The lad bobs up and down, splashing bubbles as he struggles against the flow of the river. Ahmed watches a moment as Ayad's exertion of will finds him an awkward rhythm, doggy-paddling, seemingly safely in the direction of the bridge's concrete supports.

Distant guns fire. Black smoke still hangs on the horizon. They are miles from anywhere here.

Ahmed, his wrists still sore from being tied, body hurting from a beating and shoulder still aching from being forcibly shoved, angles himself towards the canal's ledge. Hesitantly, he takes a half-step into the water. His foot causes crumbling and eroded rocks to scatter down the embankment, which are quickly swept away. Water reaches up against the thick rocks, the trace of the liquid staining them dark. As he enters the water, muscles in Ahmed's legs tighten, trying to steady his feet on the slippery rock surface. The water isn't cold, but not being able to feel the canal bed fills the boy with instinctive terror. Self-preservation kicks in and he thrashes his legs beneath the surface. It is like being weightless but with panic.

Ahmed flails his arms, doing battle with the thick presence of the water. At the splash against his face he fights, expending his energy to stay afloat. A lot of the kids here can swim. The other lad, Ayad, has swum some distance off by now.

Ahmed dips under water, he can still see the soldiers shimmering above on the shore as if through frosted glass. Brackish water is in Ahmed's nose and mouth now as the river threatens to swallow him. There is the raging soreness in his nostrils as he gags. Then a taste putrid from the black polluted viscosity as the boy gags and gasps for air. This is water that has begun its journey in the north at the Euphrates, where some faiths think life began. It is there where Saddam long ago drained marshes to punish and persecute the Shiites of Ahmed's home town. The Brits were meant to bring hope and freedom to the boy, his family and the people of Basra. That was weeks ago, before life in the city descended into anarchy.

The boy sees one of the soldiers, up on the dry bank, peeling off a layer of clothing, stepping towards the canal as if to help. But then the man atop the tank waves his hands in a frantic manner. Following orders, the men retreat to their army vehicle. Struggling in the water the Arab teenager sees the vehicle disappear. The soldiers are gone.

And Ahmed's young, spindly body bobs repeatedly above the water – until the canal's contents envelope him. His arms flap vainly, the useless fight against drowning. The water engulfs his adolescent form. The last image he sees is the bleached blue sky above disappearing.

*   *   *

A year later in England and the memory of that day continues to haunt the soldier. The ghosts of what happened dredged up by army investigators. In the night-terror, the soldier is lost in the thin periphery between night and consciousness. The edges of the room seem blurred, woolly. Textures of colour and lines of shapes bleed into one another. The man becomes aware of being in a bath. The only source of light is a single bulb suspended high up from an unseen ceiling. The tepid water is dark; his skin wrinkled from long exposure there. All is still for a moment. There isn't peace.

At the far end of the bath, a tap drips. A sudden single capsule of water plummets towards the milky bathwater. The click of its impact echoes a warping and loud sound. Perspective seems to distort and in his state of mind it's as if the bath stretches on out of all proportion, the tap far off beyond some distant Gulf.

A ripple slowly seems to form; a disturbance beneath the water. The soldier becomes aware of the shape in the bath. Somehow it is there with him, invading his space. Gradually its features break the surface. Human hair emerges first, like some slow-motion birth from within coagulated fluid.

The soldier is still a fit, bulky form, but he can do nothing but watch, in shivered paralysis of fear. It seems now like there is hair everywhere. The hair is dark and short, and seems to him an afro-style. It covers a slowly emerging, brown Middle Eastern head.

There is the face of the teenage boy.

He recognises the face instantly. Its glare has a force that makes the soldier desperate to escape but his muscles don't respond. He feels claustrophobia's inhibition.

And then hands grip from beneath. A clamp grasping around his still-toned torso, arms and legs. He tries to think, his training at a loss, then flails. And struggles. More hands now are on his shoulders. They dig into his skin and other dark Arab fingers like talons clasp at his forehead and cheeks. They claw the soldier down and it's as though the floor of the bath has melted away. His arms slowly respond and he tries desperately to pull off the hands.

His strength is now ineffective.

Down, down, drown they drag. The surface of the bathwater covers him. The distant light bulb gives way to darkness. He awakens sharply.

His breathing and pulse are rapid. A wave of sweat coats him and nausea and exhaustion tremor through his body. He wants to cry.

He tries to breathe, feeling raw and exhausted as he tries to remember where he is.

Chapter 2

Bootle Boyhood

Raw gusts often blew off the bleak horizon of the Irish Sea and battered Bootle, a defiant town despite its history. Bootle, three miles north-west of Liverpool, was where Joseph John McCleary was born among people hardened and broken by history and circumstance. Joe grew up here in one of the long rows of terraced houses and played on streets that ached with the grimy scars of a place once pummelled but that had resisted and rebuilt from the ravages of war.

Joe's family, like most souls here, came from hardworking stock, used to enduring. Bootle's character and its people embodied its name, given by long-forgotten Anglo-Saxons to mean a bold dwelling. The industrious folk who first made their home here hundreds of years ago had looked out over Bootle Bay and taken in its pleasant sandy shoreline. It had been water that had drawn people here; not the nearby Irish Sea, but Bootle's source of spring water, which would supply Liverpool and power its watermills. Bootle's settlers embraced the early industry of bleaching, tanning and paper making. Progress soon sliced through the town as the Liverpool to Leeds Canal bisected Bootle, weaving its slow 127-mile course eastwards. The railway had brought tourists and prosperity. A spur of land protected glorious golden sands from tidal forces. The Strand Promenade was a pleasant stroll to the shore. Rows of bountiful gardens dotted the landscape beyond. As a seaside resort in the early eighteenth century this was Bootle Bay's heyday. It didn't last.

The twin goliaths of the Industrial Revolution and Bootle's booming city next door, Liverpool, would change everything. The city at the end of the Mersey soon overshadowed Bootle as the Atlantic slave trade made its merchants rich. The dirty docks became an international port of departure for coal, cotton and emigrants chasing hollow dreams of better things. Like a domineering neighbour, Liverpool's port expanded north. The new Canada Dock was built, concreting over Bootle's former bathing beaches. Only the ghosts of long-departed holidaymakers haunted the town as it turned to industry.

Arriving here instead were starving, desperate itinerants, fleeing the famine in 1845 from across the Irish Sea. Malevolence seemed to drift in like salt on the air. On one street alone, prostitutes were brutally murdered by two seamen, another woman had her brains bashed out by a disturbed fireman and a 6-year-old was callously slaughtered by a killer who went uncaught. To cover the memory of the grisly killings, the town renamed the road, but the dark thread of fate remained. Four workmen born in Bootle proudly found short-lived employ aboard the HMS Titanic. And as a town under siege, fires broke out and troops guarded the docks from deadly attacks by Irish Republican guerrillas in their War of Independence. For all the endurance and prevailing of Bootle's 75,000 people, it was the Second World War that brought drastic change and altered the landscape of the town.

Growing up, Joe McCleary's granddad, Arthur Hartley, was his best mate. Hartley was a young lad when the first bombs rained down on Bootle. He remembered it was a night swollen with dread in late August 1940. Hundreds of Luftwaffe planes inflicted a summertime bombardment of Sprengbombe Cylindrisch 250 high explosives. Gas masks on, hiding under tables, climbing out of rubble. For young Arthur Hartley and other families here it was the first of more than fifty raids, an endless terrorising three months, as Joe's home town bore the worst of the Blitz.

As a small suburban town just outside Liverpool's boundaries, Bootle was inseparable from its neighbour's docks and it suffered as strategic collateral. War-weary Allied naval vessels moored here. Eager, death-bound soldiers off to engage the enemy on the Atlantic departed from here. Seventy-five million tons of war materials were offloaded here, 90 per cent of all the supplies urgently imported into England. With 11 miles of quaysides, Liverpool was the target, but Bootle bore the brunt of the bombardment.

When the government's man, Minister for Home Security Herbert Morrison, the bespectacled Baron, braved a visit to war-torn Bootle he saw the damage. Rescue workers tramped through sodden ash. Flames still smouldered. Survivors scowled as they picked through what remained of a destroyed house front. To this wrought crowd, Morrison declared his glib pride in the town and its defenders.

'They have faced the blitz, and believe me,' he said, 'when the story of this great war comes to be written, one of its brightest chapters will be written about this civil defence army ...' But his chorus of encouragement was ignorant of the chilling prophecy he spoke over the town. 'We've had a rough time but we can take it and we can take more.'

Take more they did, as the nerve-shattering onslaught of aerial salvos stormed down, Bootle bore the brunt of German bombers. In the first week of May 1941, the towns along the Mersey endured their worst. The sinister buzz of 680 attacking bomber planes levelled the town. Eight hundred and seventy tonnes of high explosives erupted night after night. Frightened families knit themselves closer while cracks burst from the sky. Throughout the darkness of that torturous week, the horizon ignited with an unforgiving cascade of 112,000 incendiaries. German bomber crews overhead marvelled at the 400 fires burning around the Mersey.

Out of the caves of their ruins, Joe's then young grandparents surveyed their shattered town. Half of Liverpool's docks destroyed, hulking skeletons of steel smouldered on the quayside or sunk into the river. Streets ruptured as 500 roads were now impassable, strewn with jagged brick and debris. Trams and railways were a twisted mass of metal and canals caved in.

In that week alone, the blitz on Bootle cost the lives of 257 women, children and men and left an equal number bleeding, broken, agonised. Those who survived could only pick through the rubble of their brutalised town. More than 8,000 of the town's 17,000 houses were destroyed or damaged during the first eight days of May. By the month's end a full 74 per cent of Bootle's haggard and jaded inhabitants' homes were wrecked almost beyond repair.

In the summer of 1941, the beleaguered town that had faced down the attack began to rebuild. Charred remains were cleared. Unsalvageable homes pulled down. Defiance marched through the town. Like a pitiless judge, the autumn of 1941 brought more – this time a daylight bombing of Bootle. Nazi planes screamed again through a battle-weary sky, parachuting landmines to inflict greater destruction by exploding at roof-top level. On a crisp October day, homes left standing on Surrey Street were blown to pieces. The raid snatched the lives of another fifteen husbands and wives, sons and daughters. Demoralised residents gave up on their government, who sought to downplay all the damage done to protect its propaganda machine.

When the long war was over, Joe's granddad Arthur signed up as a Merchant Navy seaman, setting sail for adventure. The land he left behind was fighting, shifting, changing. Setback after setback, pounding after pounding, Bootle rebounded in grim defiance to circumstance. Its people clung to the town's motto: *'Respice, Aspice, Prospice'* – 'look to the past, the present, the future'. This future took the form of transformation and redevelopment of the scarred war-torn town. Planners redesigned the centre of Bootle, built office blocks and homes. The Bootle Corporation boasted of its potential as a post-war new town. The Strand shopping precinct, a new computer HQ and acres of factory space were all built. A national newspaper advertisement showed an illustration of a sideburn-wearing lounge singer captioned with the words: 'It's a long time since you could say Bootle and get a laugh.' The laughter choked a quick death by tides of change that eroded the hopes of the town. In working men's clubs, Bootle's blue-collar dockers bemoaned politicians' merging of their borough with another suburb. The consolidation of councils put a Conservative clique in charge and the bitter decay was only beginning.

Into this new world Joe's mum Lynn moved from Ford, a village at the eastern part of town. She wanted to be in the heart of Bootle, closer to her Nan. Family was, still is, everything, and blood thicker than water – even as depression sank over the struggling dock-working community. The new modern container port needed fewer and fewer men, and in the late 1970s Bootle's docks began to close. Every industry and every family felt the creeping crisis of unemployment. The Thatcher government's policy of cutbacks doled out only despair on the town. Hope deteriorated and pessimism surged for the 23 per cent of the town left unemployed. The sour decline was epitomised by Tate and Lyle. The company had made the world's first sugar cube here in 1875; they closed down their factory and left town in 1984, laying off 1,570. This was Bootle.

Into this town, Joe – or Joseph to his mum, was born in 1981. He was lean, lithe and tall even in his early years. His chiselled face, slightly narrow, with brown eyes and crop of brown hair often bore the cheeky, sheepish smile of a young boy. Joe was a few months old when his parents, Lynn and John, moved into a modest three-level house. It was in the middle row of terraced houses, a mile from the shipping port. This was home and where Joe and his brother, David, eleven months older, shared an attic bedroom. Their elder sister, Helen, had the room below. She'd glare at her brothers and complain, as siblings do, that they were ganging up on her.

'It's the pair of them. It's not fair,' she'd tell their mum. 'You always stick up for them.'

Her protests felt like spray on the ocean; their mum lavished love on them all but doted on her boys. She savoured cuddling her kids, weaving into their lives the bonds of maternal protection.

'You're mollycoddling me, mum,' Joe would say, feigning the faint sting of embarrassed self-consciousness; a young boy veiling what he really felt, his honest affection.

'Stop it, they'll grow up like sissies,' their dad would growl. John's harsh scowl shot a hardened look of disapproval on his wife's warmth. His calloused, angry manner was often oiled with his love of the drink. John came from nearby Kirby, a one-time slum that Liverpool also tried to redevelop into a post-war new town to settle those desperate for housing. He worked hard as a fabricator welder and then put in long hours at the pub. Hot flames fusing together steel while the fabric of his family untangled.

'You're always out, never in,' Lynn complained after another night of being alone with the three kids, tucked under the wing of her arm. John stumbled in, beer on his breath and another argument ignited. Argue, argue, argue; Joe heard it behind the stage-managed domesticity of marriage.

The worst was at Christmas; Lynn hated Christmas. Joe would jovially lob a snowball, but the presents and celebrations for the kids couldn't decorate over John's absence as a father. He'd go out, get drunk and return in a mood that spoiled the celebrations. There'd be more arguments. The shouting shattering the silent nights. Violent ruthless words.

Each winter brought the same thing at Christmastime. Lynn and her brood of three; John and his horrible side, busy at the bar. In the glistening sparkle of tree lights, she was alone and mulled over leaving. But resilient, defiant, weary, she wouldn't do it; didn't want to curse her kids with coming from a broken home.

As a lad, lanky and energetic, Joe often escaped down the streets to explore the docks with mates, oblivious to factory closures, workers' strikes and protest picket lines. Over industrial fences, behind tangled wires and in among the shadows of ships and trucks. The nature here was trees of steel cranes. The leaves were curls of ginger rust. Hedgerows were the long lines of blue, orange and red metal cargo containers. Streets on windy days littered with industrial polythene, ring-pull coke cans and discarded faded plastic crisp packets. Joe was a good lad in a grim town. Fishing; football; thick as thieves with his brother David and best mate Michael. Michael was always at the McCleary household. They were like The Three Amigos their mum used to say, watching with a ringside seat their childhood antics.

A knock on the front door. There stood the very big woman who lived at the top of the street. Fat Jackie they called her.

'Where's your boys?' she demanded haughtily, a crease of wet hair strung over her furrowed forehead.

'I'm sorry?' their mum shot back, 'They're not here, why?'

'Someone's just threw a water bomb and it hit me on the head.' Fat Jackie raged accusingly in thick Scouse accent.

'Well, no, no. I'm sorry, no it's not them!' Lynn stood her ground defensively, protectively, till Jackie retreated, disgusted and unconvinced, from the doorstep.

The door closed, Lynn traipsed with predicted expectation up two flights of stairs.

'Joseph ...' she chided, opening to reveal him sitting on the bed, laughing with Michael. Nearby, the attic window was ajar; the two boys had damp hands, and devious, cheeky grins splashed across their faces.

Joe and David usually headed to school with Michael in tow after another sleepover, their friend practically living in their house to escape the instability of his own. A band of brothers in the same year at Sacred Heart Catholic School. When all the other kids picked up books and read, Joe turned the pages and saw only disconnected letters. Words that wouldn't structure meaning. Sentences a mystery beyond comprehension. His boredom and rage simmered on a low heat.

The only salvation was Joe's growing friendship with Father Michael, their determined Catholic priest who was a father figure even when their dad John wasn't. Father Michael made Joe a proud altar boy. He'd get adorned in ill-fitting robes, but as a young lad was encouraged by payments of 50p pieces, a small boy's fortune. Before church duties, Father Michael with comb in hand, parted Joe's hair to the lad's great discomfort. Father Michael's attention elsewhere, Joe would restyle his hair in his own cocky way before he reached the altar.

'He's too headstrong, that one,' said Father Michael to Lynn, casting a weary sideways glance in Joe's direction.

'Aye, Father!' Lynn replied. 'And so are you. Both of yous are alike.'

For a while, as a young lad Joe would serve at weddings and at funerals until, caught skipping down the solemn church, was chided by his mum with a remark: 'Joseph! You have to be sad. It's a funeral.'

Kept off street corners, protected from the gangs, Joe was well-mannered and caused his mum little worry growing up in Bootle. Yet this was a town where heartache often came to dock at its ports.

Chapter 3

'Suspicious Death'

In the port city of Basra, Iraq, Jabbar Kareem Ali El-Hamoudad and his wife's heartache is just beginning. Their son Ahmed is missing. Early morning 9 May 2003, Ahmed's father, Jabbar, attends the local market and his friend's son, Ayad, comes over. He explains that something happened yesterday, an incident involving Ahmed; the British took the boys to the Zubair Bridge and they ended up in the canal. Ayad can swim, but Ahmed …

Jabbar Kareem knows what this means and starts to collapse. His son had left their house on 60 Street in Basra around 9am, in his black trousers and white fallila that he wore under a black shirt. Ahmed had been expected home for lunch and when he did not arrive Jabbar Kareem had asked his wife about the boy's whereabouts. By the evening they were worried.

The man grabs at his clothes, tearing, overcome. There have been so many deaths here. Composure comes slowly for the father after the eclipse of grief. He turns away from Ayad, half in a solemn and defeated daze, to find a taxi home where he quickly gathers his brothers, relatives, neighbours and friends to go immediately to the Zubair Bridge and look for the boy. One brother, Fadel Kareem Ali, goes directly into Basra to a place they know as a British complaints centre where he reports his nephew's disappearance. A British army official keeps Fadel Kareem's Iraqi identification and tells him it will be given back if they find a body.

Elsewhere in Basra, the British army's regiment of the Irish Guards, to which Joe McCleary belongs, is packing up to leave the city. Trucks, tanks and 25-tonne armoured Warrior vehicles prepare to roll out of the city that has been their home for more than a month.

At the concrete crossing that stretches over the wide canal and down by the Zubair, Jabbar Kareem's family members and friends stop people on the bridge and along the shore begging them to tell if they have seen Ahmed. The father keeps watch by the river all day; he continues to hope that people have seen that his son could not swim, maybe even the soldiers, and pulled him out. The man's attention is taken by movement. He sees the blocky shapes of a convoy of army vehicles barrelling at speed towards the nearby bridge. They are leaving town, the line of them like Solenopsis worker ants as they speed down the four-lane highway, a flag of dust cascading in their wake. The old bearded man stares towards Basra, 8 miles to the northeast of the canal. It is Iraq's second city and Basra, the place whose name means the *overwatcher*, seems to stare back, helplessly.

The landscape is dotted with flat-roofed buildings, the carcass of the Technical College and the domes of mosques. The horizon is pale and faded, a washed-out watercolour smeared over with hanging black of still-smouldering oil wells. Down beneath the man's tattered well-worn shoes is the dry earth. It withholds slick black riches, its reserves the second largest in the world. Scattered around are sticks of palm trees and poles holding up pointless power cables that now fail to bring electricity to the more than one million residents of the once proud city.

Basra and its trading port had a millennia of rich history as a cosmopolitan centre for intellectual advancement. During the Golden Age of the Abbasids, all the greats were birthed here: the mathematician Ibn al-Haytham, the literary giant al-Jahiz, and the Sufi mystic Rabia Basri. Sanad al-Dawla al-Habashi, a governor of the city, built an impressive library of 15,000 books. Some of the world's most sought-after pearls were named after this city.

But none of this is important to Jabbar Kareem, looking for his missing son. Besides, the former glories pale next to the repeated betrayal of history. The fourteenth-century Mongol invasions maligned the port city and pillaged all that was good and valuable. The city was rebuilt and English, Dutch, and Portuguese traders came here, along with goods destined for Baghdad, 340 miles to the north. Basra's valuable position saw the city bloom from its strategic value during the world wars, receiving British protection and the building of a new harbour. The people here remember prosperity like the oasis that it once was. By the 1970s, the Baswari people were able to educate their children at schools and universities that were among the finest in the developing world. The hospitals had state-of-the-art equipment and air-conditioning. Basra's banking and infrastructure made the city the jewel of the region. The vast network of canals earned the city the nickname of the Venice of the Middle East. However, in the 1980s, a treacherous turn of fate caught Basra in the crossfire of a protracted and pointless war. Iraq's Sunni Muslim President Saddam of the Ba'ath party took power in July 1979. The same year, across the border in Iran, less than a dozen miles to the east, the Islamic Revolution brought Shiite Muslim Ayatollah Khomeini to rule. For eight long years the two egos fought their bloody war of attrition and bombardments of shells rained down on Basra.

Jabber Kareem thinks about his son. Ahmed will be 16 in three weeks. He was just 3 years old when another conflict began and Saddam's troops breached the border with Kuwait to invade their southern neighbour. As an infant, bombs are things his parents worried most about to begin with, but then the sanctions started. Iraq's economy crumbled and the food supply dried up. Little Ahmed's hunger was his growing pain while American forces hammered his country from the skies. Hundreds of oilfields burned, carcasses of 2,000 mangled military tanks littered the Tarīq al-mawt, the Highway of Death, and the Americans encouraged an uprising against the bully Hussein.

From the US-patrolled skies leaflets floated down like confetti. 'Iraqi people, peace' they read.

'Saddam is the cause of the war and its sorrows. He must be stopped. Join with your brothers and demonstrate rejection of Saddam's brutal policies.'

Basra's streets soon swirled with the imperialist Airborne PsyOps' message of insurrection.

The rebellion began here in Basra, the first city to rise up. An Iraqi tank commander lit the fuse as he fired a shell through a prideful portrait of Saddam, hung in Basra's city square. Anti-Saddam Shia forces came out of hiding to graffiti the walls. The radio broadcasts called for overthrow. At the rallying cry, resisters' forces attacked the apparatus of their dictator.

The words of Bush the First exhorting Basra's revolt came from the skies; would not also American weapons come to their aid from the skies, the people wondered? They would not. It was Bush's betrayal. His F-15s patrolled the heavens, watching on as Saddam's armed helicopter gunships unleashed hellfire. Reprisal by the Republican Guard brutalised Basra's women, dissidents, babies, by the thousands. The once fertile 5,000-year-old marshlands were drained by the dictator's vengeance. In his suppression, Saddam's loyalists slaughtered the young on Basra's streets, in homes, in hospitals. The Baswari locals remembered 1991 in vivid angry detail. Brush-strokes of dark oil smoke painted the darkening horizon then as now.

Like a solitary night watchman, Jabbar Kareem sits through the evening long after family members return to their homes. Water in the Shatt al-Arab moves along, part of Basra's network of canals like veins and arteries, its dirty inky waters moving slowly as if it's coagulating. The contents of the canal quicken with the new day. On into the next morning, Jabbar Kareem scours the water's edge, up and down the shoreline. Around 2.00 pm he sees a shape, undefined and rising to the water's surface. Treading reverently closer to the water line, the father somehow knows this is his family's fear. Jabbar Kareem peers sadly at a dark-skinned mass with a small, malnourished pair of legs trailing off behind. As water replaces air in the human lungs, a body quickly sinks; bacteria in the gut combines to make methane, hydrogen sulphide, and carbon dioxide that fill up the chest cavity. Like an inflating balloon the body rises to the surface, a grim resurrection. The body is some way off and appears, deceptively, to move, cradled by the current of water. A local man with a boat who has stayed nearby goes closer and approaches the body to place a rope around the neck and pull it nearer the river bank.

Events move quickly during the rest of the day. The family arranges a grave and a burial service, but first they need a death certificate. Dr Nadeem Shea'a, a specialist in family medicine at Basra General Hospital, issues death certificate 210782. She observes a body that has been in the water for some time; it is swollen and has blood coming out of the eyes. That is the extent of her quick examination; the family's faith motivates them to act quickly so a burial can occur within twenty-four hours of Ahmed's discovery.

Elsewhere, Ahmed's uncle visits Ayad and the lad explains his account of Ahmed's last moments. Ayad, Ahmed and two others were looking for work near al-Sa'ad Square when a British patrol came, he says, arrested them and put them in an armoured personnel carrier. The lads were beaten and driven to the Zubair Bridge. They were all frightened, Ayad explains, and promised to tell each other's families if anything bad happened. Beneath the bridge, soldiers with guns made them get into the water.

Uncle Fadel Kareem Ali goes with Ayad to give this story to the British and in response the army sends out a team to begin an investigation. Jamie Piscopo, with the Royal Military Police – the RMP – rushes to the scene near Bridge Four, taking along Sergeant Turner and Flight Sergeant Boyce. They want to see the site where the alleged offence took place at the hands of unknown British soldiers.

The Irish Guards leave Basra behind and now spend two days at Shaibah Airbase, a former staging area, where they were based earlier in the war. Shaibah is just outside the city of Basra and the troops are busy here for two days, stripping the ammo out of their Warriors, which are to be put on boats and shipped out back to Europe by sea.

On the Irish Guards' final day in Basra, the last packet of vehicles to depart received a visit from an RMP investigator.

'Did your company have a patrol down near the river?' he had probed.

'No, we were the last packet out,' Pat Geraghty, a company sergeant major with the No. 1 Company Irish Guards had answered. 'Go find the Ops

Officer; ask him, he might know,' Geraghty had advised, before he joined his company commander aboard a convoy of vehicles, one of the last to withdraw to Shaibah.

Two days later, the Irish Guards soldiers are bound for Kuwait, from where they fly to Hanover, Germany.

Despite initial setbacks and being snowed under with work, RMP Investigator Piscopo continues looking into the allegations of British involvement in a young Iraqi boy's drowning. He has discussions with legal officers, conducts research and questions troop positions. Within ten days of the incident, Piscopo establishes which regiment and which company are his prime suspects: key to this discovery is finding out that the victim and three others were at Basra General Hospital and so was an Irish Guards Warrior vehicle. By 18 May there is a running document headed with the ominous words: 'Suspicious Death'.

The only witness the military police can find is Ayad and in the days that follow he is interviewed and taken back to the bank below Bridge Four, where investigators take photos and video. There are still doubts that a meaningful prosecution could stand up without medical evidence. Piscopo discusses the matter with Colonel Nicholas Mercer, the highest British legal authority in Iraq, Brigadier Hart Robinson and Colonel Graham. Graham asserts that they must obtain and examine the deceased to look at the lungs to confirm if the cause of death is drowning. The colonel is unsure about the qualifications of an Iraqi pathologist so they must find a British pathologist. But this being Iraq, they must wait for the forty days of mourning to pass.

For Joe McCleary and the other members of the Irish Guards back in Germany, they quickly find that while they have left Iraq, it is a country that will not leave them. There is a cursory question from a young welfare officer who asks all the soldiers passing through his small tent if they're alright. Everyone is fine. No one admits anything to the contrary. Apart from the odd sardonic comment from the likes of one Irish Guards sergeant who jokingly says, 'yeah, I want to go and kill puppies.'

At Oxford Barracks in the town of Müenster, Germany, there are early reminders of what has been lost in Iraq: Jonny Stranix entering his room and seeing the empty bed space that once belonged to his friend Muzvuru, who did not return.

Joe's company commander, Major Peter MacMullen, tells him that he intends to put him forward for a corporals' course because he's been impressed by his soldiering in Iraq. About a month after their arrival in Germany, in June 2003, Major MacMullen receives a visit from the RMP, telling him that they are investigating a civilian drowning in Iraq. MacMullen asks his platoon commanders and senior NCOs if something happened, but they answer no, nothing did. That evening, a guardsman who was there at the water's edge says he is visited by a fellow soldier who tells him, 'I have a family to worry about; don't share anything with anyone.'

In Iraq, young Ahmed is ready to share his sorry final moments. The boy has been in Iraq's holiest city of Al-Najaf, for the required forty days. Al-Najaf is about 275 miles north-west of Ahmed's family home in Basra. Najaf's name is said to owe itself to the legend of a young boy's drowning. The Biblical Noah's disbelieving son had, it was said, looked out from a mountain spot near here to see if the flood waters would really rise. When the waters came, the mountain crumbled, giving way to a wide river, drowning the doubting boy. In time the waters receded and the place was named 'Nay-Jaff', meaning dried river. Now Najaf is a city of crusty browns in the heat of late June 2003, almost three months on from the liberator's invasion. Much of the city still lies in ruins.

Al-Najaf has long been built and broken by its religious history. For a millennia the city has been the holiest site for the Shiite Muslims, one branch of the fractured faith. Al-Najaf owes its notoriety to Ali ibn Abi Talib, cousin and son-in-law of the Prophet. Ali was the first male to accept the faith and whom the Prophet, in his final sermon at Ghadir Khumm, pronounced as his rightful heir. Upon the Prophet's death, Ali was forced to wait as leaders of the Islamic community named another, Abu Bakr, as caliph. Bakr's followers became the Sunni and the battle over succession became the heart of Islam's division. Twenty years and four caliphs later, Ali finally got his chance to lead, but his rulership was cut short. Within five years he was martyred by a poison-tipped assassin. The disciples of Ali, who called themselves the Shia, placed their leader's body on a camel, another legend says, and let it wander. Its desert roamings came to rest in Al-Najaf. The town grew up around the holy burial site of Ali's body in the tomb beneath the revered Imām 'Alī Holy Shrine. The mosque became the sacred place of pilgrimage for Shiites and Najaf's fortunes fared through the steady stream of the faithful. The dry city that skirted the edge of a vast desert also found its fate anchored to the changing course of the nearby Euphrates.

Water and faith have always been entwined here. A mighty thirteenth-century Mongol governor came from Baghdad and dug the first canal connecting the Euphrates River to Najaf. Two and a half centuries later, the Shah Esmā'il Ṣafawi, founder of the Safavid dynasty, cleared the canal of sediments and made pilgrimage to the city. As access to water expanded, so did the city. It grew like the palm trees that lined the canals as more and more pilgrims poured through. But a shift in the course of the Euphrates and raids by Wahabi-Sunni extremists led to decline and drought in the Shia holy city. Najaf was all but abandoned until the 1800s when the Hindiya Canal was dug, channelling the river, and prosperity, back to the city.

In this place, water and the swells of religious sectarianism are death or life. When Najaf was revived, it again became one of the most important Shia sites, a place of fervent trade, great libraries and wise religious scholars, until Saddam's Sunni-led rule. After 1991, Saddam's growing suppression of the Shiites was felt here in Najaf, just as in Basra. The Shia Ayatollah, Mohammed Sadeq al-Sadr, defied Saddam, calling for the release of imprisoned clergy and inciting sedition against the president. The cleric al-Sadr paid with his life when he was ambushed and gunned down while leaving mosque with his two sons on a prayerful Friday in 1999. In response, rebellion stirred in the air of the city until the great boot of Saddam's troops stamped down hard. They stormed into Najaf, adorned with threatening gas masks accompanied by units commanded by the dictator's son's brutal Fedayeen armed forces.

Now Najaf, the city just 100 miles due south of Baghdad, finds itself reeling from being stormed again. In the dying days of March 2003 and the American invasion, the city and its strategic location were surrounded. Najaf is on the highway leading north to Karbala and Baghdad, so the invaders had cut it off to prevent the Iraqi army from assaulting the US army supply lines. The sky swarmed with vast Black Hawk and Chinook helicopters that dropped brigades of young Americans with guns to surround the city. The fierce fighting slaughtered hundreds of Saddam's soldiers. Trying to halt the invaders, the Iraqis detonated a weak cache of explosives on the city bridge but the Americans' mighty tanks made it across the river. The foreign forces isolated Najaf, cutting it off as its population of half a million endured a week of hell. Saddam's Fedayeen soldiers tried coercing Najaf's local militia members to fight. They gathered families and threatened their execution unless their men opposed the Americans. Using a frightening new tactic, an Iraqi army NCO made himself the first suicide bomber of the war. The man sped his taxi at a checkpoint outside of Najaf, blew himself up and took out four American soldiers. His martyrdom would inspire hundreds, but for the invaders it was the final straw.

With intelligence that the area's Ba'ath party leader was dead, the Americans made their last assault. First they attacked Iraqi forces at the Agricultural College, south of the city. Next Najaf's airfield fell. Then two 2,000lb-JDAMs, Joint Direct Attack Munition missiles, pulverised Saddam's Ba'ath party HQ. Coalition cluster bombs rained down with frightening force, trying to take out Iraqi radar trucks, a deadly collateral nightmare for civilian neighbourhoods whose homes collapsed around them. Apache helicopters hovered noisily overhead, eyes in the skies. Three American battalions landed south-west along Highway 8 and the 101st Airborne surged through the city. Across the market squares, through alleyways and past the magnificent gold-domed mosque they came.

Iraqi Sunni forces, disregarding the sanctity of the Shia shrine, holed up in the ornate Imam Ali Mosque and picked off Americans with rocket-propelled grenades (RPGs). But as the invaders thunder runs advanced, tanks cut through the streets and mechanised beasts bombarded from the air. Hours of fighting, attacking from the ground and from the heavens until the victor emerged.

Najaf is free. It is the first major city to feel liberation. People thank their occupiers for breaking the chains of the Ba'ath party. Grand Ayatollah Sistani tells his Shia followers not to interfere with the Americans. Cheers go up as American tanks tear down the emblems of the old dictator, this city the scene of the first Saddam statue of the war to be toppled. But at a cost. The holy mosque is divinely spared damage, but the dead pile up in thousands.

The bodies of the fallen, a couple of hundred a day, fill Najaf's cemetery at an unforgiving rate. The Wadi Al-Salam Cemetery, famed as the holiest burial site for devout Shiites in Iraq, is also the biggest cemetery in the world. Bodies have been interred here for over 1,400 years, since the days following Shia's founder, Imām Ali, himself. This is a city of the dead. The war has been fuelling its expansion. It now covers almost 1,500 acres and stretches across the valley as far as the eye can see. This is a massive sprawling maze of winding lanes, baked brick graves and endless block mausoleums, the colour of faded sand. The bodies of more than 5 million are separated from their souls here. Beggars and prophets, servants and sultans, kings and children. No matter their status in this life, millions of Shia seek rest here. This cemetery city's name – Wadi Al-Salam – means Valley of Peace, but there is no peace for young Ahmed.

It is forty days since the boy's body was laid here in the ground, the time that Muslim tradition determines. The British wanted to cut open and examine his body straight away but the father said no, his son had to be buried within twenty-four hours of being found; they respected his faith. Jabbar Kareem Ali brought the boy's body here in the early hours of 11 May and at around 1.30 am performed the sacred rites in darkness. The Islamic funeral prayer of Salat al-Janazah was said and Ahmed's limp body was laid on its right side facing south and slightly west, qiblah, towards holy Mecca. Jabbar Kareem Ali placed three handfuls of soil upon the body, an act of consecration that Abu Hurayrah, a companion of Allah's Messenger, once described seeing the

Prophet do. The grave was filled in; no flowers were placed, nor wreaths, nor offerings nor ornate grave headstones, merely a small stone marker above the mound. A father should not outlive his son; it is not the nature of things. But Mawt, Wafat! – اللّٰهُ يَتَوَفَّى الْأَنْفُسَ حِينَ مَوْتِهَا وَالَّتِي لَمْ تَمُتْ فِي مَنَامِهَا, Allah takes the souls at the time of their death. By sunrise, Jabbar Kareem was well on his way back to Basra, the sun slowly tearing through the horizon like a seeping wound. As a devout Shia Muslim, his son should rest in the cemetery, waiting there in the hopes of being raised up from death with Imām 'Alī on Judgement Day.

Yet for 15-year-old Ahmed Jabbar Kareem Ali, judgement day is now; raised up not in resurrection but in exhumation. His body is taken from the ground and to the American hospital set up in Najaf. Tearing the child from the sanctity of the earth and cutting him open compromises Jabbar Kareem's most deeply held beliefs. This desecration of the body goes against much of what a Muslim believes, for in the Qur'an the Prophet said كسر عظم الميت كسركه حيا, 'we are honoured children of Adam and fracturing the bone of the dead is the same as breaking the bones of the living'. Tampering, cutting, mutilating the body is unlawful. But after the forty days of mourning, Jabbar Kareem Ali permits the foreign investigators to conduct their post-mortem on his son to find out the truth.

The air-cooled medical room is grey and stark, bare but for a concrete table against ashen walls where Ahmed's body – or what remains of it – rests. His corpse, still partially wrapped in plastic is a contorted blackened mass. It only just resembles a human body. After forty days in the heat of Al-Najaf cemetery, decomposition has had its way. The state of decay and the loss of the young life is still appalling, even to the British pathologist, Air Commodore Tony Cullen, the 64-year-old veteran. His autopsy process is always the same. X-rays are taken, looking for anything lodged inside the body, measurements are made and then the corpse is photographed from all angles, with close-up details that might reveal the circumstances of death.

For Ahmed, pictures taken of his body, and in particular his legs, reveal areas where much of the boy's flesh and tissue has gone from beneath the right femur and the left tibia. The bones of the lower legs are clearly visible, though some stubborn remnants of flesh still cling to them. This stench of rotting human still causes revulsion, even for pathologist Cullen and his forty years' experience of medicine and the military. He examines the body, its midsection and slightly swollen chest, skin twisted, grey and taut. He looks for injury to the skull; fracture to bones or ribs. Then up to the face. Ahmed's head is twisted back on his neck, eye cavities are vacant holes and his mouth is locked open wide as if frozen static in some final howl of death. The man peers in the juvenile's jaw at a row of fine Arab teeth, useful for identification. Who was this child when he was alive? What were his dreams? And how did he die? The pathologist looks for evidence of injuries in particular. There have been accusations that the dead boy was beaten, perhaps by British soldiers, before he ended up in the water. Air Commodore Cullen is meticulous in a search for any signs that Ahmed has been hit. However, any wounds have been covered up with post-mortem discolouration. The time that the body has spent in the water and its decomposition in the ground in Al-Najaf means finding bruises is almost impossible.

Even now, more than two months on from the fall of Saddam, the country is bruised, the body of its landscape still simmering with violence and death. North of Baghdad, American troops kill twenty-seven in a pitched battle with Iraqis. The week before, US troops shoot dead two former Iraqi soldiers who were complaining that they had not been paid since their country was occupied. And a few days before authorities exhume Ahmed, an Iraqi shepherd in Ramadi brings the first claim against the Coalition forces, seeking $200m in damages because he says seventeen of his family and 200 sheep have been killed in a missile strike. This man's case is the first of many in this modern, litigious world of war.

After completing his external examination, Cullen gathers the tools: electric saw for cranium and rib cage, the short-handled scalpel and scissors to cut out the internal organs and delicate tissue. He takes out what's left of the liver, spleen, kidneys and heart for weighing. With a drowned child a pathologist would expect the lungs to be bloated, but with the passage of time that's hard to see. It takes two or three gruelling hours for Cullen to complete his examination of Ahmed's corpse. On his clipboard he has Dr Nadeem Raheem Shea'a original death certificate from just over a month ago – with the cause of death as drowning. On his own pathology report, Cullen fills out the paperwork with the date: 21 June 2003. There are a series of tick boxes, listing the head, neck, chest, abdomen and then room for conclusions and cause at death beneath.

Commodore Cullen heads out of the room to see RMP investigator, Staff Sergeant Daren Jay. Jay is taking over the investigation, the files being handed over by Jamie Piscopo who is leaving Iraq. Jay, along with an undertaker, supervised the exhumation and now receives the pathology report. It tells him that the decomposition of Ahmed's body is so severe that the pathologist can't ascertain the cause of death from his autopsy. Staff Sergeant Jay is there as Cullen fills in the box at the bottom of his form with the unsatisfying word: 'inconclusive'.

Chapter 4

Elephant And Castle

As a teenager, Joe McCleary found solace from the unfulfilling and unsatisfying belittlement of school by spending time at the edges of the waterways around Bootle. On a Saturday, like many before, he was dropped off by his mum, Lynn, late in the morning with his permit for lake fishing near Ince Blundell. The village, near Thornton in Merseyside, was just a few miles drive from home, on the rural outskirts north of Liverpool. The vantage points gave impressive views across Clieves Hill towards Rivington Pike and beyond the fields to the Ince Blundell Estate. Trees and bushes dotted the far side of the lake and cast blurry blue-grey shadows on the silvery water. The curved distant hills were a backdrop to thick bilious clouds that collected together like bruises in the sky. Moist cold air had augurs of rain as Joe reached for a soggy sandwich, made by his mum, and took a bite from the wilting white slice. Lynn had been bringing her son here since well before he was a teenager. Hours would be absorbed, sitting with rod cast, content, even when the lake failed to yield its lazy lurking carp, roach and perch.

Joe was glad to escape the deteriorating brokenness of Bootle's streets, with hopeless betting shops, men ill-at-ease sitting on doorsteps, and plenty drinking their despair at the local. The town had been declared the most disadvantaged area in Britain. There was an accuracy in the accolade and a fear that Joe's prospects could mirror those of the town.

His place by the water's edge was also a sanctuary from the miserable and frustrating days spent at Sacred Heart Catholic School. He'd sit in secondary school lessons and in every book, on every page, saw just a kaleidoscopic scattering of senseless letters. They ran backwards without coherence. The teachers seemed to revel in displaying his teenage incompetence.

'Joseph, it's your turn to read,' the English teacher would say, in a voice seeming to teem with vindictiveness and glee.

Listlessly, he'd stand up, traipse the way to the front of the class, clutching a dog-eared copy of a curriculum paperback. He would leaf open the battered book and see an incomprehensible jumble, letters shifting around in a giddy dance. They refused to construct meaning. A tall beacon for the mocking attention of his class, he'd squint, his brow contorted in concentration until his head ached. The class sniggered until permission was given to return to his place. It was a Catholic school ritual humiliation.

In the classroom, Joe larked about, dodging what he didn't know and holding the simmering rage. He would lean over towards his brother and classmate, David, to make a joke and laugh disruptively. A pestered teacher's shortened temper often shot a scowl at the disconnected student. When everyone's head was down, a flurry of blue biros set about their dance; the fuzzy out-of-focus words of the text book returned to taunt Joe. Away from the teacher's glare, he'd slide his workbook secretly on to David's desk and seeing his vulnerable younger sibling, David would scrawl an imitation of his own work into Joe's book. Throughout lessons, Joe's young mind would wander off, consumed with boredom, an acidic bile of fury, barely suppressed.

There was the annual indignity of parents' evening. Joe and David, still dressed in school uniforms, while mum listened as the teacher praised David's efforts. She paged through the elder brother's workbook and then on to Joe. The yellow-bound textbooks were almost mirror images of one another, the handwriting the same in both.

'Oh, it's identical?' Lynn had said, disturbed as she held out Joe's English workbook towards the teacher accusingly.

'Yes,' the teacher replied plainly. 'David's finishing his work and doing Joe's as well.'

Out of the corner of his eye, Joe saw his mum gaze at the hapless teacher with a furrowed frown of dissatisfaction. Joe turned to stare out of an adjacent window, lost in adolescent lustful musings and the empty impotence of this place.

'I really think Joseph's struggling, he's having real difficulties and he needs some extra help, some support,' pleaded Lynn.

'Oh, don't be worrying,' the teacher uttered to an unconvinced Lynn. 'They're young. Everything will be okay.'

Joe stewed in bitter boyhood embarrassment, unarticulated contempt at the confrontation. The family paraded on to repeat the ordeal in a room adorned with tricolour flags of vertical red, white and blue. A small plastic Eiffel Tower sat on a rough wooden desk.

'His French …' the accented teacher began. 'Joseph's not good at French.'

The man's pale skin bore the same emulsion complexion as his faded beige jumper.

'But then, if he can't understand English,' the Frenchman had continued caustically, 'he can't likely understand French!' The man seemed to swallow down a grim chuckle.

'How dare you say that,' Lynn shot back. 'When he wants to learn!' Her cheeks reddened with protective rage. The fuse of a mother's fury was ignited, while Joe felt the mocking shame in muffled silence.

Shuffled along, Lynn dragged her way to another appointment, this time with an art teacher. He began with a tale of Joe being incensed with anger in his class.

'Recently, your son nearly picked up a chair and threw it at me,' the man explained.

'Excuse me?' Lynn retorted, incredulous at what seemed like slander against her son, her gentle giant.

'I had asked him to draw a subject,' the infuriated lecturer continued. 'And he draws me a bloody fish.' The man paused. 'A bloody fish,' the teacher echoed for emphasis.

'Well that's probably the only thing he can draw,' Joe's mum snapped back in her son's defence.

'But do you know what?' the teacher said in a husky dry voice, 'I gave your lad what for – and the very next day he comes in bright as day, and says, "Hi, sir, how are you?" I'd nearly wanted to throttle Joseph. And there he is saying, "Hi sir".'

'See, it just shows the forgiving nature of Joseph,' said Lynn proudly. Her face lit up at the chance to display some other emotion beyond her anger and resentment at the school's lack of help and diagnosis. All the while, Joe felt wound up defensively, a taut coil of adolescent anxiety.

That evening at home, Joe's frustration at his academic inability and feelings of disappointment formed itself into a violent flow of tears.

'Joseph, sit down,' his mum begged.

He crumpled on to the sofa and Lynn held her youngest son. David was confident, strong in learning and sport – yet Joe struggled, shy, ashamed.

'There's something not right, son,' she'd said in muffled tones and uttered that she'd call the school for some kind of support.

'Mum, do not!' Joe begged forcefully. 'Or I'll never tell you nothing again in my life.' Joe clenched and tried to hold back the indignity of a mother's intervention.

Joe was the joker, always up for a laugh in class. But the disruptiveness was a deflection.

'Yer' can't barely read or write!' the other teenage lads would laugh and taunt.

Soon the reputation stuck. The stigma made Joe the obvious target. Each time the teacher made him stand in the middle of class, forcing a public struggle through some maze of text. And each time the echoes of laughter would amplify a rising anger.

Again and again the English teacher ordered Joe to the front of the class and again the boy battled to read the assault of words on the page. In unspent fury, the motor of the lad's pulse raced. From the back of the room he was conscious of student sniggering that started like muffled sniffles. Pockets of laughter broke out like random raindrops before a torrent and the tide of anger surged up in Joe.

'Alright, alright. Now then,' the teacher shouted, a cruel judge requiring order in a court of humiliation.

Then something snapped.

Joe shot a glance across at the man, his expression betrayal. On that teacher's face seemed an evil, gleeful smirk; that churlish chuckle that shoved Joe over the edge. A swell of adrenaline streamed hot through his veins. Testosterone and rage took hold as he clasped a chair and raised it at the teacher's head. In a dizzying instant, the tall lad beat down the seat, smashing upon a defenceless man. Joe's fury finally unfettered, he grasped the chair a second time and hit the cowering teacher again.

Fucking arsehole, the horrific rage seared through Joe's mind. *I'm sick of getting laughed at.* Unleashed, unstoppable, it was a typhoon of teenage anger. *You fucking made my life a hell.* Two dozen acne-blotched faces gasped a hissed intake of breath and stared on at Joe's crime of frenzy.

The aftermath of the incident was a series of fractured half-remembered moments. The teacher rose, bloodied, from the floor and barked the order for Joe to march to the school's office. The doctor was called in to attend to the victim teacher, and a police car arrived, blue lights flashing. Joe sat alone, still shaking but his anger spent. Outside the austere headmaster's office, there were the baritone murmurs of adults within. From across the hall, a door scraped open and Joe looked up for just a moment before dropping his head in solemn shame.

'Joseph. What have you done?' Lynn uttered, dragged away from her work as a hospital nurse to care for her own. Devastation was etched across her features. They waited moments before being led into the familiar office. Inside Joe sat, resigned, while Lynn went on the defensive, a final volley.

'My son is struggling. He's got dyslexia and he's not to blame for this,' she implored, her soft Scouse shrilled to a defiant pitch. 'Yer were not helping him; you're singling him out.'

'Oh no.' The denial was resolute; there were no more warnings or last chances. The school headmaster's words rang with solemn shameful finality. 'He's expelled, take him home.'

Joe's future became uncertain, uncomfortable after he was kicked out of school. Soon after expulsion he'd spied his mum, her head down, rubbing creased temples, balancing the weight of her youngest son's unfulfilled expectations. The shaming sting was amplified by moody adolescence. His dad, John, had been gone for several years and in his place, Lynn had met Carlos, a warm and calm presence from Portugal. Awakened to a replacement, John wanted to come back into the family's life, but the ruptured relationship was too far gone. John had left and set up a life in London. Idle weeks into Joe's enforced exclusion and John had called to discuss his troubled son.

'He wants hard discipline; that's what the lad needs,' John barked down the phone to his ex-wife.

'I don't know how to control him; what am I going to do?' Lynn had retorted at his affront to her single parenting.

'Send him down to me and he can get a job,' John demanded, plotting out his son's future, one that led to London.

The days in south London's Elephant and Castle area working a market stall for his dad would be many the same. Joe traipsed suburban streets, a boy of 15, expelled with no results or report card. Instead he was in London and felt as out of place as the emblem he walked past each morning: the bronze statue of the pink elephant mounted 10 feet up on a platform with its back painted yellow and blue with a white castle strapped atop it. Joe's route to work took him past where the Metropolitan Tabernacle colonnades stood, down the A3, Newington Butts, already clogged. The dense early morning mix of cars, red double-decker Routemasters and vans that expelled their toxic fumes as they waited to head their different directions. Walworth Road, St George's, Newington Causeway and London Road all collided here into a roundabout. This region was a wasteland of concrete and outdated architecture built around an intersection.

Early morning and already the thickening of foot traffic poured past to descend into the underground. Joe always headed against the stream, beyond the Tube stop and skirting the corner edge of the big junction. A slope took him down towards a cacophony of foreign voices and Caribbean complexions, a mini-city of canvas market stalls, awnings and steel frames. Here, south of the Thames, was a place now contemptible in its faded illusion of post-war progress and prosperity. The Elephant and Castle area was, like Joe's home town, a product of a history battered by war. Once a cosmopolitan hub, the Elephant and Castle had been the Piccadilly Circus south of the

River. A bustling tram link had run through here; the Trocadero boasted the largest Wurlitzer organ in Europe, and the art deco Coronet picture house accommodated 2,000 patrons.

Then war struck. In May 1941, while Luftwaffe bombers loomed low over Liverpool, residents of London evaded death in Underground Tube tunnels as the skies came alive with the drumbeat of the Blitz. Unremitting air raids targeted London's south side, its factories, its warehouses, and its railway interchange. Out of the ashes and masonry and craters, urban planners brought forth the mammoth regeneration for the Elephant. At its heart was a double roulette wheel of roundabouts that would send traffic to their destinations. Surrounding them, the high rises of hopes and architectural aspirations surrendered to Goldfinger's stark 1960s' Brutalism. Metro Central Heights and Heygate Housing Estate were hubs for crime and poverty as they smothered the skyline. The buildings were temples to soulless utilitarianism, concrete ziggurats. Down below was a warren of subways where the high street of yore gave way to Europe's first American-style mall. From the ashes of a bombed-out site was built the Elephant and Castle Shopping Centre, a windowless box with the promise of consumerism's dream. From its opening day in 1965, when many of its shops were vacant, the decline began, another failed dream. A gaudy pink paint job on the shopping precinct's frontage helped secure its status as one of London's ugliest eyesores.

Outside on the shopping centre's piazza, entrepreneurial traders now pitched their market stalls and it was here that as a teenager Joe took his place among them. In the damp he performed his morning ritual: walking to the big blue doors of the metal storage, unpadlocking the deadbolt and carrying the cardboard boxes of handbags over to his assigned stall. Joe's already tall frame wheeled out the metal skeleton display tree and hung the bags, a daily discipline of decorating the stands. He then laid out the dense array of 100 knock-off Vuittons and Pradas and purses, clutches and Kappa-brand backpacks. With the mindless distraction of tasks done, he'd perch on a stool and settle into a lonely despair. Joe hated it here, a teenager stuck in the certain monotony of selling bags on a street stall. He and his father clashed like flint on flint. The elder man, his breath still stained with beer, chided Joe for being aimless. He then took all but £50 of the £250 that was the result of his son's long market-stall labours. As clouds descended, they spat rain that landed like bullets on the blue canvas awning. Joe huddled into a jacket against the chafe of the wind and thought back to Bootle as the day passed by.

Hours slipped away and the stall taken down, Joe headed for the now dreaded flat where he stayed with his dad. Dragging himself into the hollow concrete underpass, Joe emerged on to St George's Road as rain still seeped from the early evening sky. He pulled up a hood as he passed the College of Printing, with fag-smoking kids on the corner. Their purposefulness taunted as they stubbed out their smokes on the wall and retreated from the wet. Joe went on towards the junction, beyond the bus stop and down the pavement littered with leaves. As he moved on past spindly barren trees, he couldn't help but be struck by the dome-topped majesty of the Imperial War Museum. The structure had once been a mental asylum. Insanity was entwined with conflict. Even in the shadow of the grey dying light of dusk the glorious Greco portico that adorned the building's frontage could still be seen. Beneath the entrance aimed the pair of 15in-thick and 54ft-long naval guns from the Royal Navy's HMS *Ramillies* and *Resolution*. These 100-tonne relics from the Dreadnought era of great British battleships pointed up in parallel at 45 degrees towards the skies over Lambeth. They sat guarding the grounds of the museum, seemingly targeting Joe with their purposefulness as he passed by.

He arrived at the flat, walked to the door and let himself in. He flipped on a switch, extinguishing the silent shadows. The place was absent of John, his dad, and his new missus shouting at each other. Slumping into a chair, Joe's attention fell on a newspaper. On its back page were players uniformed in the familiar blue strip of Everton, his team. They were on a losing streak, pissing away the promise after coming in sixth place in the league just last season.

After a moment Joe let his grip slacken, dropped the paper and picked up the phone. He pressed the familiar area code and heard the crisp chirp of the dial tone, then 'Hello-?'

'Y'right, mum?' he uttered down the phone.

'Y'right, Joe?' Lynn replied.

'Yeah,' her son lied. 'Dad's out. Down the pub again.'

'You sound down …' came the mother's concern.

'It's horrible here.' Joe sniffed, blinking away moisture from the inner corner of his eyes. 'I feel like you got rid of me to me dad,' the lad said with familial honesty, bringing truth to the surface.

'No. You know it wasn't like that at all,' Joe's mum soothed. 'It was yer dad trying to get you a job.'

'I wanna come back to Bootle; I hate it here with dad. I wanna see you and Carlos. I hate it here mum. I wanna come home.'

Chapter 5

The RMP

They are coming home. They have experienced the horrors of war, but they are not infantry soldiers or cavalrymen. They are Royal Military Police, the RMP, and six of their fallen bodies are being repatriated to the UK.

Only three days after pathologist Air Commodore Cullen conducted Ahmed's autopsy, six military policemen faced slaughter in an ambush in Iraq. In the country where its deposed dictator was still at large, the tragedy was the largest single loss of life of a British unit from enemy fire since the Falklands War.

On 24 June 2003, in Majar al-Kabir, the Shiite town north of Basra, townspeople gathered, jeering with weapons jutting upwards. Their furious discontent and disaffection was with the British, they say, for breaching a signed agreement. The invaders had said they'd cease their heavy-handed searching of Arab houses, but the locals didn't see this happening. The people here had had enough of the violation of their homes, of soldiers seeing wives and daughters unveiled, of their livelihoods of farm animals killed. Their rage boiled over, as a group of Iraqis faced-off against Coalition soldiers in the town square in the middle of Majar al-Kabir.

There were British troops in the town centre, members of the 1st Battalion of the Parachute Regiment, unprepared for the tension of the stand-off. They fired warning shots at the massing crowd. British rubber bullets incited an abrupt cascade of deadly live ammo from angry Iraqis and their AKs. The crowd surged and Chinook helicopters hovered and mounted a rescue mission of the stranded Paras. Yet the mob still sought an outlet for its rage.

In another part of town, unaware of the malevolent throng of people in the town square, six British RMP were leading the training of some Iraqi policemen within the brittle shell of the Majar al-Kabir police station. With the Para's evacuation, the mob marched the 100 metres through the town and surrounded the police building. Holed up in the garrison, the half-dozen RMPs are soon deserted by their Iraqi security guards. Outside, the braying, swollen mass of 500 Iraqis encircles the occupants, their Occupiers, in their concrete refuge. The mob stole the British military police Land Rover that contained the radios and link to call for support. The vehicle was driven to a bridge, looted, burned and tipped into the river, washing away the military policemen's hope of escape.

Simon Miller, Russ Aston, Paul Long, Ben Hyde, Thomas Keys and Simon Hamilton-Jewell – some of the RMP's finest – made their last stand. In their final inglorious ninety minutes, the red-cap wearing men were pierced, blood ran scarlet as they replied with all they had. SA-80 rifles had fifty rounds of ammo each; they should have had three times that amount. They were lacking satellite phones too, no chance to signal for help from inside. This lack of supply had been the plague of the invasion force since the beginning. Here its military men paid the horrific price of policing the volatile post-conflict country as the angriest members of the mob stormed through the building.

Afterwards, amid the shards of glass, empty shell casings and burnt pieces of plaster, was a grim scene that helped piece together the final devastating firefight. The debris and bodies were evidence of a desperate struggle. The RMP had attempted to surrender, the fearful men so desperate that they held up photos of their families. Begging for mercy, their fate was imminent, inevitable. Overrun and then the aftermath. Signs that some of the RMP men, as they still clung to life, faced execution. This dark cloud of a day hangs over nearly half a century of the RMP's proud history.

Shattered bodies of the fallen make their final flight. The corpses of the six RMP victims, all young British casualties of the emerging Iraqi insurgency that marks mid-summer 2003. Nine light brown wooden coffins heading home for burial, each draped with the brightly coloured curse of the Union Jack.

In Iraq, throughout the incendiary heat of the Middle Eastern summer, the RMP work intently to untangle the mystery of who was behind the death of the drowned Iraqi boy. In mid-July, more than nine weeks after Ahmed's death, they are still no closer to identifying the perpetrators. David Spence, Daren Jay's senior officer, agrees to a more detailed furtherance of enquiry, or FOE, to be conducted as soon as possible. The priorities are to identify the suspects and Jay re-interviews Ayad Hanon, the only witness that they know of, to obtain a second witness statement. There were two other lads who were allegedly picked up and ended up in the water, but amid the post-war fog no one can track these possible witnesses down.

In his statement, Ayad maintains that four British soldiers rounded him up along with three other Iraqis, including Ahmed, and they were taken from the Basra hospital to the canal. Ayad says there were Iraqi police officers near the hospital when the soldiers took them away, but when RMP investigators take him to various police stations near the hospital he is unable to identify the policeman. The lad claims Ahmed's drowning was because some of the British soldiers forced them into the canal and threw bricks at them, but all he remembers are 'four soldiers', 'two more aggressive than the others' and a 'vehicle with tracks'. With no real description of the soldiers and a multinational force of 46,000 in the area in May, the RMP can't be sure who it was or even confirm what platoon the suspects are from; all they can determine is that it was an Irish Guards' vehicle because they were guarding the hospital that day. Tracking down suspects from the mass of military personnel is the RMP's steepest challenge. The army is an anonymous entity, a swelling angry body of soldiers with individuality indistinguishable in uniforms hidden beneath helmets and berets. It is their asset on the battlefield or when avoiding vengeful martyr-hungry militants but unhelpful for military investigators. It is a fluid beast on its own schedule, the army disperses from one tour to countless other countries.

Staff Sergeant Daren Jay oversees obtaining statements from the Irish Guards' platoon commanders and by the end of the first week in August 2003 the investigator receives details from a platoon commander named Daniel O'Connell, describing the procedure for dealing with looters. It says: 'If no weaponry or munitions were involved, the looters were escorted out of the area. If, however, weaponry was present, the individuals would be taken to company HQ and processed by the company sergeant major prior to being conveyed to a central location.' What Jay and the RMP don't know is why, if this was the policy, did four young Iraqis end up in the water and how did one drown? Ahmed's father wants answers too, but also more: in mid-August, Jabber Kareem submits his claim for compensation from the British over the loss of his son.

A grim background to the ongoing investigations is the liberated country sliding into insurgency's grip. On a simmering hot Saturday in Basra, eight weeks to the day since the six RMP were massacred in Majar al-Kabir, the RMP again are targets.

On the scene, one of the RMP's unmarked four-wheel-drive Fords has careered over the pavement and into a wall. The dark cavities of bullet holes perforate the vehicle's back end. The four-person car was attacked with grenades, rocket launchers and automatic-weapons fire. After the car's crash the assailants kept shooting without mercy at the wreck.

The deaths continue but some of them may be due to the British soldiers. In September 2003, Staff Sergeant Jay investigates the suspicious death of Iraqi man Baha Moussa. Moussa has been badly beaten while he was in coalition custody and later died. Jay video-tapes Moussa's post-mortem at the RMP base in Shaibah Airbase. He questions the soldiers suspected of causing Moussa's asphyxiation while in custody and care of the British. The deaths on all sides leave the RMP too with scars that cannot be seen.

At the end of the summer, Britain is a country consumed with a different Iraq-related death inquiry – that of the strange and tragic suicide of a former UN inspector, found having bled to death in an Oxfordshire forest. Dr David Kelly, a man who loved Iraq, had briefed a BBC journalist, off the record, about his suspicions surrounding the government's use of intelligence to justify the push for war. His unauthorised discussion discovered, the private scientist was hauled before a televised public committee investigating 'The Decision to go to War in Iraq', which forced him to answer testy questions over his interactions with the media. Two days later, Kelly set out on his final walk in the woods, took pills to thin his blood, and a knife with which he slit his wrists. An inquiry quickly convenes to examine the weapons inspector's death, putting the Iraq war on de facto trial, at the end of which even its wearied and emotional QC admits that 'somewhere along the way we lost a summer. I hope we exchange it for understanding.'

Through autumn and into winter of 2003, Joe McCleary and his brothers in arms of No. 1 Company Irish Guards prepare to leave Germany for deployment in Northern Ireland. Their posting is on the border at Crossmaglen Barracks in South Armagh: a British base for over thirty years of the Troubles. The locals here despise the presence of the armed forces. This is a land still known as bandit country with strongly nationalist inhabitants violently in favour of the IRA, where the blood of deadly action is still soaked into the boggy ground. British soldiers were shot here, blown up by bombs, British army helicopters engaged in pitched battles with armed trucks down these narrow roads. Joe and his company are seven months out of Iraq, this green, damp land looking every bit a contrast from Basra, but 50 miles south of Belfast, their mission at this border town isn't too dissimilar. They are here on peacekeeping operations, part of Operation Banner, already the longest continuous campaign in British military history. At the end of 2003, there are 9,000 troops in Northern Ireland, less than a third of what there once was. Five years on from Good Friday, the animosity remains rife from agitated locals who feel that intimidation is still a way of life. Out patrolling the streets, Joe sees pissed-off locals sticking two fingers up in indignant 'fuckyouse', bricks being thrown by resentful youths, and tombstones bearing the inscription 'Murdered by British Troops'. The majority Catholic residents in County Armagh have grown up with the harassment and suspicion of traffic checkpoints at Cloughogue on the outskirts of Newry. They unwillingly accommodate the Bessbrook base and its heliport, which is one of the busiest in the world, choppers irritating neighbours by taking off or landing every eight minutes. Such is this region: considered so dangerous that the military cannot safely use the roads so move about by helicopter – and Joe, for one, hates flying.

While the company is in Crossmaglen, news comes on the television from Iraq that gets a cheer from the soldiers: Saddam is captured. American Special Forces from 1st Brigade Combat Team of the 4th Infantry Division follow intelligence gathered from a suspect captured the previous day on a raid in Baghdad. Embarking on Operation Red Dawn, the information leads to a small orange grove on a farm near the village of Adwar, 10 miles from Hussein's home town of Tikrit. There, late on the evening of 13 December, the forces discover the fallen dictator hiding in a hole, an ultimate indignity for a man known for his opulent extravagances and extreme brutality.

'We got him!' The civilian leader of the US-fronted Coalition proudly gloats. 'The tyrant is a prisoner.' The American president declares that 'A hopeful day has arrived.'

The soldiers celebrate, but Iraq and what is happening there is still too raw, buried things they don't want to deal with. Christmas approaches and families send their soldiers presents from England. While the other lads are opening CDs and new shirts, to Joe's embarrassment he unwraps a pin-the-bra-on-the-boobs game and some kids' sweets from his mum. At an evening meal, the company sergeant allows the lads a drink, but sets a two-can limit. As Joe peels open a can of Fosters, about to take a sip, a call comes in and he's part of a team to deal with the aftermath of a horrific fatal crash on South Armagh's winding roads. Joe, always feeling as though he's one of the first out, leads as some guardsmen attend the scene of the crash. Its female culprit is a suddenly sullen and dazed drunk driver. Joe sees her crying and feels no pity, desensitised to the remorseful girl, now cuffed and an unintentional killer after too many Christmas drinks. Returning to base, Joe finds the cans still there, untouched. He drinks up as their tour settles into the cold of winter months.

Chapter 6

'You're In the Army Now'

Anew season's autumnal breeze blew down James Street, Liverpool, as Joe's lanky frame climbed the concrete steps of the army careers office. He crossed the greying threshold, his mum Lynn in step behind. The recruiting office door was held open in welcome by an imposing figure wearing green fatigues. The man was decked out in a beret marked with a rectangular flag of deep maroon sandwiched between two bars of navy blue. He seemed wide eyed and energised at Joe's appearance.

It was 1997 and there was a palpable sense of invigoration that pulsed through Cool Britannia. The country was high with the hopes that the idealistic new government had heralded. Labour had triumphed after the tenure of Tory rule and found in Bootle its safest seat in the country. Blair's party rose to the crest of power on the exhilarating promise that 'Things Can Only Get Better'. And they did. Lynn had witnessed how the long, hard years had hit Liverpool when from 1984 to 1996 employment in the city region fell by 12 per cent, but in 1997 the recovery began and employment increased. The IRA, who'd placed a coded message to Bootle police station and threatened a bomb at the 150th Grand National at Aintree as recently as April, had declared a full renewal of its ceasefire in July. Newly installed Prime Minister Tony Blair shook hands with Gerry Adams and became the first British premier to meet a Sinn Fein delegation in seventy years. Optimism was rising like a cresting wave. And Joe too felt alive with the hope that purposefulness provides.

'You okay, son?' the bulky recruiting sergeant asked in ebullient thick Scouse.

'Well, Joe here's really interested in joining the navy,' Lynn answered. A lively thrust of pride like electricity permeated her tone. 'His uncle was in the Royal Navy, yer'see, and fought in the Falklands so he wants to follow in that,' she added proudly.

Lynn beamed, overjoyed to have her son home again. Since he'd returned to Liverpool from London, he felt like a different person, as if he'd turned a corner in late teenagehood. Joe's former school mates were off starting college and sixth-forms, but he'd been booted from school without qualifications. The sour taste of life on a London market stall seemed to have been the tonic of a life he didn't want. Just a few months earlier, Joe's elder brother David had joined the army and it left an impression. Joe was adamant and told his mum that he wanted the same.

The recruiting sergeant led mother and son over to four coarse fabric office chairs and they sat down amid an array of patriotic posters. Joe craned his head admiringly to look up. His attention was drawn by the all-action photos of stylishly lit heroes. They were the handiwork of marketing maestros at Saatchi and Saatchi, the two brothers born in Baghdad during the middle of the two decades of rule by the Sunni monarchy in Iraq. On one wall of the recruiting office was an image of two tense-looking army soldiers in combat dress, clutching SA-80 rifles as they stared off at some unseen target beyond their sights. The poster bore the challenge in block capital letters:

OR PERHAPS YOU FIND A NIGHT IN FRONT OF THE TELLY MORE EXCITING.

On an adjacent wall, another rugged lone warrior, his face camouflaged with brown and green paint, cradled his rifle. The fighter, frozen in time, was emblazoned with the solitary word:

Infantry

Its promise was enticing:

If you are looking for a worthwhile job with good pay, adventure, travel, sport and a training for life – try the infantry. Pay after training £179.63 per week.

On the table in front of Joe and his mum was a folder headed with the red, white, blue of Cool Britannia's flag, the Union Jack that exhorted direction in bold text:

ARMY BE THE BEST.

The recruiting sergeant sat opposite Joe and hunched over, engaging. The thick fingers of his hands interlocked together between his knees.

'Well, our naval officer's out. On his lunch,' the sergeant began.

Joe held back a flicker of disappointment, averting a gaze and noticing the colours and stars and insignias that decorated the recruiter's uniform sleeves.

'But,' the man continued, leaning in, his shirt stretching revealing more of his tattooed arms, 'I think you wanna join the infantry, dontcha, son?'

A moment of blankness in the young lad's eyes was taken by the officer as opportunity.

'How old are you, son?'

'Sixteen, sir.' Joe uttered with deference.

'Well, you're just the right age for the infantry. The infantry are the real soldiers. We're yer boots on the ground. I'm Irish Guards infantry, me. Us Scousers – we make up half of the Irish Guards.' He paused a moment; letting Joe dream.

'His brother David's in the Irish Guards as well,' Lynn McCleary added.

Family recruitment was a common staple of the Irish Guards, the distinguished infantry regiment with a proud history dating back to the beginning of the twentieth century. It is not the oldest regiment, like the Coldstream Guards, nor most senior, like the Grenadier Guards; but the Irish Guards displayed their renowned grit and bravery on the fields of battle in nearly all the UK's conflicts from the First World War to the Middle East. At home the regiment is part of the Household Division that protects Royal palaces. Perhaps to return the favour, a member of the Royal family presents members of the regiment with a fresh shamrock each St Patrick's Day, a tradition begun by Queen Alexandra in 1901. Strong was the sense of the regimental family, with Irish Guards soldiers known as 'Micks' or 'The Fighting Micks'. All proudly share a bond from service, familiar with the phrase 'Once a Mick, always a Mick'. Irish Guards are colourful characters from all places and all walks of life. They're marked by an indomitable spirit, panache, rugged strength, deep gallantry, and wry, sly gallows humour. Their motto, *Quis Separabit*, inscribed simply as 'QS', is Latin for 'who shall separate us?', words penned at the dictation of St Paul in his letter to the Romans which asked 'Who shall separate us from the love of Christ? Shall trouble or hardship or persecution or famine or nakedness or danger or sword?'

'Well, that's a sign is that!' said the recruiter brightly upon hearing the family connection. 'Does that sound good?'

Joe nodded, wide-eyed.

'Alright, well yer need to do a test, son,' said the recruiting sergeant, leaning in even further and narrowing his eyes.

Joe's chest tightened, unprepared, and he experienced a palpitation of adolescent panic.

'Jill's faster than Tom,' the recruiter said with strained seriousness. 'Who's faster?' mock earnestness maintained.

'Jill!' Joe said quickly, a smile of recognition that he was being toyed with.

'Congratulations! You're in the Irish Guards, kid!' said the recruiter, meeting Joe's smile, swollen with pride and grasping his hand to pump a firm shake. 'You've passed! You're okay, son. You're in the army now!'

Elation erupted across Joe's face. He felt he'd finally found something he really wanted – and been accepted. *Whoa*, he thought, *fecking hell, this is dead exciting.* Next to him, Lynn beamed: hopes fulfilled and a mother's pride. *He'll work out okay*, she thought to herself, *he's got David, his brother, there in the army as well.* This was finally getting her youngest son on the path for a good career. The recruiting sergeant strode over to a desk and brought back some paperwork and sat back down.

'Alright, we'll have you fill these out,' the sergeant said.

'You'll get a driving licence, too, son.'

'Driving licence!?' The recruiter had Joe fully hooked now. 'Sign me up!'

Some of the words on the forms were a jumble and his mum helped him fill some of the paperwork. Joe was told that this was the beginning of a process, to be followed by an appointment for a medical and fitness in a few weeks' time before going on to basic training. This was how the army would manufacture its soldiers. After signing his name, Joe's decision to serve monarch and military was sealed with the Queen's Shilling.

'This is for you, son,' said the recruiting sergeant, handing out a crisp £10 note. 'It's the Queen's Shilling. The Queen's Shilling means you're agreeing to serve in the army. Think of it as an advance on your first day's pay!'

To take the King, or Queen's, Shilling meant to agree to serve in the sovereign's army. Joe felt as if he was just being given his bus fare back home, not realising he was partaking in a tradition going back to the English Civil War and the era that followed when the daily pay for a private was the sum of one shilling. It was a tradition crooned about in the First World War recruiting song, 'On Saturday I'm willing, if you'll only take the shilling, to make a man of any one of you.' Its acceptance was a symbol of commitment, the dowry consummating his allegiance to the army.

This small token paled next to the huge surge of excitement he felt about what lay ahead.

Lynn and Joe left the recruiting office and afterwards he felt like celebrating. He went out with a couple of mates and found the proceeds from his Queen's Shilling were enough to buy a round of beers at the local pub, the Queen's Hotel. Out that night Joe was made up, jubilant, underage yet abuzz on booze and the new prospects he had. A fit girl in a low-cut top, tight over smooth skin and perky breasts, asked what he was celebrating.

'I went to the recruiting office and signed up in the army.'

'Really?' the suddenly attentive, fulsome teenage girl answered, stretching out the middle syllable of the word with instant interest.

'Yeah, I'm a soldier,' Joe said proudly smiling.

The girls loved it.

Back home that night, he turned in alone in his room. David had gone on ahead, already serving in the Irish Guards. Joe looked down at his admission papers, surfing the high crescents of wonder and excited about what lay ahead. His teenage head was dizzy with drink, but he also felt exuberance at a future that seemed assuredly structured. He'd serve, embraced by the motto of the Irish Guards that nothing can separate them, one from the other, part of a lifelong brotherhood of loyalty and belonging.

Chapter 7

QS

For the Royal Military Police investigators their biggest frustration is how soldiers stick together; QS is the Irish Guards' brotherhood and creed that creates, it can seem, an often-impenetrable wall against the investigation into the death of young Ahmed. The interviews with witness Ayad Hanon are the bedrock of the case, but identifying the soldiers responsible, the possible suspects, proves anything but straightforward. By January of 2004, Daren Jay is trying to focus his case, confident that the suspects are members of the Irish Guards regiment though he cannot determine which Warrior fighting vehicle, designated by a numbered call sign, was involved or who the occupants were. The investigator learns that No. 1 Company Irish Guards is on a peacekeeping tour at the British base in Crossmaglen, County Armagh, so in February he travels to Northern Ireland.

Jay speaks with the platoon commander, Daniel O'Connell, whose acts of heroism in Iraq earned him a Military Cross. The investigator presses him over which vehicles may have been in the vicinity of Basra's General Hospital around the time the Iraqi boys were allegedly taken to the canal. O'Connell says that the Warrior would have only been at the hospital for static patrol, meaning they should not have moved from the position; it wouldn't make sense for them to take anyone near water. O'Connell examines the Orbats, the orders of battle, that describe the organisation of the units and narrows the list to two possible call signs and their respective commanders who may have been near the hospital: Darren Beech in Call Sign One One and Sergeant Carle Selman in Call Sign One Two. Two call signs still means up to twenty people but Staff Sergeant Jay determines to speak to all senior members. The only member of Call Sign One Two around at Crossmaglen is Martin McGing, a 19-year-old guardsman who is on surveillance duty while others are on patrol. Jay, with his colleague Warren Hatton, takes McGing's statement. The soldier seems fragile, confused and withdrawn, even when they explain that an Iraqi boy has drowned. Jay introduces himself as being from the Special Investigative Branch and asks how the young soldier is doing. The lad has been on medical leave before Christmas; Iraq was a stressful time, there's just a lot of pressure at the moment, he explains. McGing has seen an army psychiatrist who has decided that he is not capable of handling weapons so has limited his duties. There may be more below the surface but Jay has to turn the conversation to Iraq. He doesn't caution the soldier, seeing him just as a possible witness not a suspect. McGing denies being involved in any incident where local civilians were detained, or civilians detained in his call sign vehicle nor is he aware of any incidents where anybody was forced into the water. Jay feels the case could be reaching a dead end. Several other members of the call sign have gone on to postings overseas, scattered like pebbles into the tide. The staff sergeant investigator leaves Northern Ireland with copies of the company log from May 2003. Examining the documents, Jay makes a breakthrough when he sees in the radio log a reference to Call Sign One Two being at the hospital. The commander of that call sign, Sergeant Carle Selman, has transferred from the Irish Guards to the Scots Guards but Jay tracks him down to a posting in Germany. Jay puts in a call immediately and Selman answers. Jay doesn't outline the reason for his call but Selman tells him to call back later. After a couple of hours, Jay rings again.

'I'm from the SIB and I'm investigating an incident that happened in Basra on what would have been your penultimate day there,' says Jay. 'I'd like to ask you some questions.' Again, Jay doesn't caution the sergeant, presuming he is simply another witness.

'Well, I'm on duty, but what do you need to know?'

'Do you remember an incident involving looters at Basra General Hospital?' Jay asks.

'It's nearly a year ago now, but I did try to protect some looters that came into my control, yes.' Selman says. 'I was the senior and responsible NCO that day.' Sergeant Carle Selman is 37 and has extensive experience serving in the infantry since he was 17. In Germany he skilfully oversaw the maintenance of the Warriors as part of the Coldstream Guards when the army headed to Iraq.

'Where were you when the call sign moved from static guard with the looters?' asks Jay.

'I was in the Warrior when it left the hospital,' Selman replies. It occurs to Jay that, contrary to being a suspect, Selman may in fact be a key potential witness to whatever happened at the canal bank. But being at the scene doesn't make someone a suspect. From the call there is nothing to suggest to Jay that Selman is even aware that someone has drowned. Jay believes now he is closing in on his suspects and thinks they must be the infantry soldiers – or dismounts under Selman's command. The RMP investigator asks Selman to prepare a statement detailing what happened at the water's edge and who else was there.

While he is in Northern Ireland, Joe McCleary hears that the SIB is investigating a drowning that took place in Iraq.

He realises then.

It is an incident he tried to blot from his mind, but it now starts to gnaw inside him.

When Joe leaves Crossmaglen to join his corporals' training course back in England, it is with a sense of growing disquiet over what might be brought up about the things that happened in Iraq. It was over there where Joe's company commander, Major MacMullen, had seen and been impressed by the young infantryman's skills. Joe's superior had noted the potential for leadership and arranged for him to begin the six-week course.

It is held in Surrey and being there brings back memories for Joe of the brutal basic training he'd gone through at Pirbright, where he attended the Army Training Centre. These are not the only memories the course dredges up. The course is physical and Joe is proud of maintaining his fitness, but it is also theoretical and he struggles still with dyslexia just as he did at Sacred Heart School in Bootle. Joe's difficulty with reading and writing batters his confidence and when it comes to standing in front of troops, leading them forward, he becomes flustered. *I'd be the first to climb a mountain*, he thinks, always stronger at the physical demands but to stand up, encourage others makes him hesitant and self-conscious. The pressure builds and lingering is what he left behind in Basra, Iraq.

Sergeant Carle Selman's statement about the incident in Basra is revealing. RMP Staff Sergeant Jay reads the details of the day almost a year ago. It's an account of looters, routinely dropping them at the edge of the city, being 'on stag' or on guard duty, with his Warrior vehicle near the hospital along with Martin McGing and the driver, a lance corporal named James Cooke, and three or maybe five looters being detained. Selman says he was concerned about the amassing crowd so he decided to put the looters in the Warrior to remove them from the scene. He is confident that two guardsmen, Wayne Sampat and Joe McCleary, were in the rear of the vehicle because he saw them get out at the other end. Selman says:

> 'At no time did I sanction or instruct personnel to force or otherwise make detainees enter the river. The looters had clearly already had a harrowing ordeal. The sole purpose was to make them walk back to Basra under their own steam.
>
> 'The dismounts were at the water's edge, couldn't hear me so I jumped down, walked over and said "come on"; I motioned that we were leaving.
>
> I didn't see anyone struggling in the water.'

With this new information in Jay's possession his net is tightening. Witness Ayad has said that four soldiers got out of the warrior but two were more aggressive than the others. Jay's two suspects are McCleary and Sampat.

Jay moves as quickly as he can. The investigator must track down his key suspects and contact new and old witnesses. He approaches the men's company commander, Major Peter MacMullen, for his statement. Martin McGing also receives more questions, answering that he is now able to recall but had little to do with the Iraqis' detention. He was in the Warrior but remained in his position, the gunner's turret, throughout. He did not know where they stopped nor does he look out of the turret. McGing also says that he was hesitant to share more previously because he doesn't want to get anyone in trouble. Other members of the call sign are questioned but seem only to provide a limited account. Regimental amnesia, Jay thinks. He speaks by phone with James Cooke who is now serving in Canada, explaining what he is investigating, but the soldier too seems reluctant to provide a statement. Jay isn't surprised. He assumes that, like others, Cooke is acting out of loyalty to his dismount section. Jay makes plans to fly and formally visit Cooke in North America.

The following day, 20 April, the RMP arrest Wayne Sampat for manslaughter. He is cautioned and questioned at Bulford Camp, Wiltshire, the SIB HQ. Jay can see that Sampat finds the interview stressful. The young soldier doesn't want to be there, what soldier would? He acts confused, as if he doesn't understand why he's there. He is initially uncooperative and his replies are seething with resentment.

'There's nothing I can remember about the 8 May 2003,' Sampat says early on. 'It's nearly a year ago. I can't pinpoint the day,' Sampat lies.

'The incident took place at the Basra General Hospital,' reminds Jay, tersely. 'Some looters were taken from there to a canal outside of Basra.'

'I'm sorry, I don't know what you're on about,' Sampat says.

'There was a drowning.' Jay continues, clarifying the event. 'A teenage Iraqi boy drowned.'

'Drowning doesn't ring a bell. I'm sorry.' Sampat looks genuinely shocked.

Jay suspects that the soldier's loyalty to his colleagues is really what is making him maintain a wall of silence. He intends to bring that wall crashing down.

'I've been told, by two of your colleagues, that you were there at the river,' returns Jay, determined in his questioning. The faces of wounded and dead Iraqi civilians, the bodies he's seen likely lodged in his mind.

Wayne Sampat's face is suddenly a portrait of realisation and disgust and he slowly begins to cooperate.

What he knows, he says, is limited. In his account he says he was present when the Iraqi looters were arrested and taken to the hospital. They left in the Warrior, but he makes clear that he wasn't in the vehicle when the looters were taken. There were conversations about something happening afterwards and then again in Oxford Barracks back in Germany. He says he had no idea of what actually happened, but he knew he wasn't there at the water's edge. He is desperate to persuade Jay that he wasn't there.

Staff Sergeant Jay's dogged pursuit of the case pisses off members of No. 1 Company, who speak to their commander. They feel pressured, alone and unsure whether they are being asked for information or being accused. To a man they feel beaten up by the experience and don't know what to do. They're being asked to recollect details of events that happened in a conflict zone. MacMullen feels the confusion of his men is fair and makes a report to his commanding officer, complaining about SIB officer Jay's conduct. When he's told, Jay doesn't initially understand that he is the person being criticised. Spence, Jay's senior officer, receives the complaint and feels fully justified in their course and actions. He is also frustrated. He too feels that regimental loyalty means that the soldiers are remaining loyal to colleagues rather than to the truth.

Joe McCleary has yet to be approached by the RMP for questioning, but he experiences a different pressure as he nears the completion of his corporals' course. He has gained a lot from the weeks of physical training, shouting, running and the planning of orders, organising drills and planning queen's marches. He'd had a taste of stepping into a corporal's shoes, calling soldiers on the right leg to stop, to halt, having to stand in front and march the troops.

Yet soon the pressure becomes overwhelming. Tearing apart and reassembling a general purpose machine gun is something Joe can do without a thought, but he struggles to mentally process as quickly as others and his inability to read holds him back. He has also heard the rumours that the RMP are talking to a lot of people from No. 1 Company and Joe starts to struggle with fears and memories of Iraq. It becomes too much.

Joe goes AWOL from the course in Surrey and, fuelled by insecurity and growing anxiety, decides to return to London's Wellington Barracks where his regiment is based. Joe jumps in his car with its broken exhaust pipe and races desperately up the motorway. A speed camera clocks him and flashes as he heads at 79mph north towards London.

Chapter 8

Basic Training

Ared flash, the West Coast InterCity train, shot fast through the landscape. Like the crease of dawn, it carried Joe south towards London, the countryside beyond the window a blur lost to speed, and he felt a swell of excitement. This feeling of excitement had been surging inside since even before he'd pulled away from Liverpool Lime Street Station.

It had been several weeks since Joe had undergone the army's routine medical and fitness testing. For that he'd headed the two hours south-west of Bootle, reporting as ordered to Whittington Barracks, near Lichfield, Staffordshire. Whittington was the home of the Army Development and Selection Centre (ADSC), the first stage assessment and screening. Overnighted here, Joe was away from home and family for the first time and placed in a room with five strangers.

'Alright, lads?' he had declared, cocky youthful exuberance boosted at finally being free from Bootle.

Together Joe and the other new recruits went through the same process – facing their medicals, all in their boxers with their gangly bare and pale legs. The lads lined up in a hall as military doctors invaded, with the intimacy of testicles touched and hearts listened to for murmurs and signs of sensitivity. There were hearing tests and sight tests, sifting through the specimens of barely post-pubescent men. The following morning, Joe flew through the basic fitness test – a mile and a half run in ten minutes or less. Sixty press ups in two minutes, sixty sit ups, and three pull ups. He was always fast. Finally came a strength test involving pulling a handle mounted on the floor like a young Arthur pulling forth the sword from stone. The army's first round of filtering completed, Joe went home where a letter arrived a few days later that told him he'd passed. Joe would be welcomed to the next intake of basic training, ready to be moulded into a soldier.

From London Joe changed trains and journeyed the 30 miles south-west of the capital towards the Army Training Centre (ATC) Pirbright into what seemed like another country. Seen from a slower rolling train, meadows and grassy commons of Chobham Ridge unfolded, the patchwork quilt of damp green that had been acquired by the British army in 1875. His eyes consumed the approach of Surrey's wide-open sand hills and heaths. The terrain was fertile, emerald in the wet of March, yet the landscape was freshly scarred. Two months earlier, at the start of 1998, a freak winter tornado had blown destruction through the neighbouring county. Its destruction like 'Dresden after a raid' was how one local witness described the explosive and unexpected ferocity of the storm.

Joe was the youngest of the 127 mostly teenage recruits, raw material for the drill sergeants to manufacture into men. The army expected selfless commitment of its soldiers, subordinating them even to the point of death of body and spirit. Joe's fourteen weeks began with a pledge of honour, soul and service swearing the formal attestation that marked admission into the British army.

'I swear by almighty God that I will be faithful and bear true allegiance to Her Majesty Queen Elizabeth II ...'

Joe proclaimed in unison along with the other lads, all unaware of the extent of their declaration.

'And that I will, as in duty bound, honestly and faithfully defend her Majesty, her heirs and successors in person, crown and dignity against all enemies.'

In 1998 there were few enemies. It had been sixteen years since the British action in the Falklands and active military engagements were few and far between. A unit of the Irish Guards, which included Joe's brother David, was in Kosovo, having crossed the border from Macedonia, but they had little need of their intensely honed infantry skills. Elsewhere, despite Saddam's defiance of UN weapons inspectors, the Middle East was mostly calm. Only the bombing of the US embassy in Nairobi, an early act of terror by al-Qaeda and Egyptian Islamic Jihad, was indication of the brewing storm. Elsewhere, the West was still sheepish about the consequences of intervention post-Mogadishu and even the IRA were around the negotiating table.

'And I will observe and obey all orders of her Majesty, her heirs and successors and of the generals and officers set over me.'

The attestation was concluded, their commitment, hopes and service declared. In those first days, Joe and the others were issued their own kit, began the exercise regime and were instructed how to shave and wash with military precision.

Later in his first week, Joe lined up with the rest of the recruits for inspection. Spencer, a burly boot sergeant from the Coldstream Guards with a streak of masochism, reprimanded a lad further down the line. The kid had the audacity of not shaving to army standards, for in the military, appearance is everything. Joe sniggered in disdain at the rollicking. Like an owl, Sergeant Spencer overheard and swooped. At the sniff of laughter, he targeted his angled jawline and scolding eyes. The man marched double time. He stood nose to nose with Joe.

'You think that's funny, do you?'

'Yeah. I think it's funny, mate,' Joe uttered back, defiant and naive of the superiority of rank.

'I'm your mate, am I?' roused the shouting sergeant. 'Go 'round the back of that shed!'

'Fuck off,' came Joe's cocky nuke of disregard.

Spencer's face bled red hot at the insubordination.

In a stabbing flash, Sergeant Spencer unleashed the thrust of his fist. It punched Joe hard in the plexus of his stomach. He felt the wind forcefully deflate him. In its wake was nausea. Involuntarily Joe's splayed palm clutched his chest as he leaned forward.

'Listen, you think you're a cocky little fucker?' Sergeant Spencer spat in Joe's ear lobe. 'I tell ya, I'm gonna break you. I'm going to fucking break you. You hear me?'

'Yessir, sir, sergeant, corporal,' Breathless from adrenaline, Joe grasped at the vagaries of ranks, in panicked pleas of understanding the army's discipline.

The next day Joe knew what to do. He was on time at 6.00 am with scraped smooth skin red raw. Shoes polished, with shine like they were glazed. Weapon assembly was memorised till it could be done blind. Joe, the scrawny kid, body not yet filled-out, lifted, trained, ran endless miles. Through the first weeks of training, Sergeant Spencer kneaded, pounded, punished. Joe was his favourite runt on which to inflict insignificance.

After each day of relentless dawn drills, cold water swim tests, and frigid night marches in open fields, Joe and the other depleted recruits trudged in. They were assigned twenty to a room, beds stretching a few feet apart like a youth hostel. Joe's bunk was the second bed by the door and first in the firing line for Spencer's inspections. The drill sergeant marched in, arms straight behind his back, hands clamped tight together. In front of him stood testosterone-tanked recruits, erect to attention. Spencer looked at the neatness of the lads' beds, the straightness of their uniform, the flawlessness of their presentation. On each inspection he always detected some flawed detail as he rifled through Joe's locker. Unbearably, he looted through it in full sight of the room.

'What's this McCleary? This isn't regulation!' Spencer steamed petulantly. 'Trainee Jones, empty out McCleary's locker!'

Impotent but to stand to attention, Joe's locker was emptied of its contents on orders. Shirts and personal items were flung to the floor and Spencer's steel toe-capped boots poked and flicked them around.

'McCleary! Your fucking shirt's on the floor.' Spencer's fire breathed, alive with radiant anger. His fury stoked, the drill sergeant would inflict collective punishment on the whole section of soldiers in the room.

'Trainee McCleary's not working for his section, is he?' Spencer taunted.

'No sir,' the others replied in unison. As a singled-out soldier, Joe was obligated to obedience or else face the humiliation and anger of the group.

'I'm gonna fucking change things,' Sergeant Spencer roared. He shoved Joe's head against the wall. *This is what he lived for*, Joe thought.

'Get that picked up. Now!'

Joe bent down to replace his spilled clothes, glimpsed the sergeant's medals; *unlikely that they were ones awarded for conflict*, he mused. Spencer marched down the line of beds. Lucky were those whose beds were at the far end of the room by which time the drill sergeant had become bored of his game.

Spencer was as tough and disciplined as a disappointed father. Joe retaliated and found his rhythm. The sergeant, a devil on the lad's shoulders screamed for more and administered a brutal slap or a punch. But the discipline made them.

Among the others there were dropouts, the attrition rate of lads not tolerating the humiliation, having had enough and they were gone. It was for the good of the group. For men under fire, the last thing that they needed were dropouts by their side on the battlefield if they couldn't even hack the training.

Joe showed his worth; resolute even when paying the penance for ill-appearance. The colour sergeant had called him out, he said, for not shaving properly. His penalty was forced laps up and down Concrete Hill, a brutal 3-mile slog up an ascent of rough muddy earth. This was known by recruits as an ultimate test of mental and physical resilience. Joe ran, always the runner, up and back. And he repeated the gruelling scramble then returned, Sergeant Spencer yelling from behind him. Around the lad turned for another leg, then another, his young face drawn, strained, pale with fatigue.

'Are you finished? Are you tired now?' the sergeant yelled, patronising, pushing and punishing. Joe kept on taking it; his home town had sown endurance into his sinews.

'Get on up that hill,' the sergeant screamed as Joe commenced his fifth march upwards. Fingernails were covered in blood as he climbed, but Joe wouldn't submit.

He stumbled up to the summit, knees buckled, his body gave way to exhaustion. He tumbled to the floor, smashing his head, arm, face, blood streaming over cheeks where once might have been tears. Joe got back up, to run again.

'Are you finished?' demanded the sergeant.

'No, sergeant,' Joe replied, defiant.

He held the course, thinking of the poor prospects there were to go back to in Bootle, few jobs, drinking, hanging around betting shops. There was nothing.

The sergeant leaned in and grabbed Joe's shirt, growling in his ear.

Legs burned with pain, body drained from the exertion, but Joe was willing to go on. His face was flushed with adrenaline, painted with sweat.

'You're fucking finished! Fall back in now.'

Joe summoned strength to stumble back to barracks, vision blurred with eyes hot and heavy with unspent emotion and rage. *Sergeant Spencer, the vindictive fucker*, Joe thought. The weaker chaff of the recruits were gone; gone too was Joseph McCleary and in his place was Trainee Guardsman Joe McCleary.

The next day, the trainees and Joe lined up for morning inspection and he stood firm as tempered alloyed titanium. The tough as nails sergeant moved down the row of men and reached Joe.

'You know what McCleary? Well done yesterday,' Spencer uttered.

In the days afterwards, the sergeant walked straight past Joe's locker during inspection.

'Yep, okay,' he'd say and moved on.

Every two weeks Joe collected wages from the pay clerk's office.

'What's your number?' he was asked.

'Trainee Guardsman McCleary #25093081,' Joe replied.

'Okay, you've got £200 for these two weeks. Spend it well,' the woman said.

Feeling minted, Joe and some fellow newly pressed trainee recruits were like weekend millionaires. Heading off for two days back home, he picked up four beers with some other lads and they rode the train back for a long weekend in Liverpool. Joe walked in through the doors of his home back in Bootle, was welcomed home and gave his mum £50, as she celebrated her young soldier in training.

For the rest of the training the routine was the same. Up at 5.00 am for early parade, uniform inspection at 7.00 am on the grounds and then their names were called.

'McCleary?'

'Here, sergeant,' he obeyed with diligent attention.

'Peterson?' and so it went on.

There was locker inspection; this time the next lad along from Joe got his locker trashed. And bloody Spencer was strict – if one messed up it was still collective punishment for all. At 8.00 am physical training began: swimming, weights, sprinting back and forth. Joe built up his strength power walking with all his kit and heavy Bergen pack on. Runs got quicker, Joe able to make a mile and a half in seven and a half minutes, then forcing his stamina doing longer distances.

The drillmasters followed the Common Military Syllabus, the CMS, a course drenched in discipline. It was hard and Joe hated it. And it made him.

He became fit, strong, and loved it. Joe went through the basics of infantry weapons training at the range, learned how to load and then live fire the SA-80, the army's workhorse 5.56×45mm NATO small-arms rifle. He received Chemical/Biological/Nuclear/Radiation training; was sent into a mock gas chamber where a lit pellet of CS gas simulated chemical agents. The instructor, now immune to the gas's effects, watched while the lads' eyes stung horribly with tears as they coughed hoarse with salty phlegm and they demonstrated getting their respirator gear on, then exhaling to scrape the chemicals from their lungs. There was dinner in the canteen, with food in tins from the Royal Logistics Corps. Pasta bake or potatoes slopped on a plate, the lads all sat in rows. Then doing the bed and kit for the next day.

The training at Pirbright was hard. In the final weeks there were training exercises in freezing fields of Wales. All recruits debased themselves as they crawled on bellies in the mud and plodded in wet green uniforms and shivered through life-sucking streams. Then came the physical fitness tests, the Combat Marksmanship Test and four nights in the field on Exercise Final Fling, practising all the skills they'd learned at boot camp. This was where the army manufactured soldiers, aiming to infuse character into every tendon and muscle.

In the fourteenth week, the surviving recruits paraded proudly in front of family at the Passing Out, the ceremony to mark the end of training. The prestigious Pirbright grounds were massive, and Joe's mum in attendance stood beaming at her son on display in his uniform. As he marched by in formation, headed towards final inspection and dismissal, Joe caught her eye.

Hours later, bags stuffed ready to leave, Sergeant Spencer shook Joe's hand.

'He's a good kid, him,' Spencer told Lynn.

When it was finished Spencer turned towards Joe.

'You know what, McCleary. I've given you some shit, but you're tough as old boots aren't ya?'

Chapter 9

Arrest

Joe doesn't feel tough, not since Iraq. He puts miles between himself and the corporals' course he has been attending in Surrey. Something is starting to crack. He is not where he is supposed to be and is being searched for.

The Royal Military Police learns that Joe was at Crossmaglen and that he then went on to his corporals' training course. With his unexplained absences the RMP call Lynn McCleary in Bootle. She takes the call and is asked if she knows where her son is. She is told that the military police plan to take her son in for questioning. It crushes her, the knowledge that her son is heading back to London where he'll be immediately picked up by the RMP.

Joe drives through the south of London, slowly among the trawl of late morning Tuesday traffic, passing Battersea, the Thames and into Westminster. He arrives at Wellington Barracks, the London headquarters of the Foot Guards. Joe's regiment, the Irish Guards, is one of the five, along with Grenadier, Coldstream, Scots and Welsh Guards regiments, that make up the Foot Guards of the Regular Infantry of the British army's Household Division. Their barracks are a block away from Buckingham Palace and No. 1 Company of the Irish Guards is here after their posting in Northern Ireland.

At Wellington Barracks David Spence, the senior RMP investigating officer, arrests and cautions Joe. The young soldier barely knows what is going on, shock not even having time to settle in. For a start he thinks that he's in trouble for walking out on his corporals' course training. Investigator Spence tells Joe that he is going to be interviewed regarding his suspected involvement in the alleged manslaughter of an Iraqi civilian in the vicinity of Bridge Four. Joe's mind wanders to that day in sun-scorched Iraq almost a year ago and what happened at Bridge Four.

In an anonymous interview room with Joe is Spence and another lead investigator named Warren Hatton. Hatton has been with the RMP since the start of 1988. He's conducted criminal and internal investigations around the world, from the UK, Northern Ireland and Germany, to conflict zones like Bosnia, Iraq and Afghanistan. As well as being a lead investigator on this case, Hatton's recent investigations include the photographs of alleged abuse by British soldiers of Iraqi detainees that were published in a national newspaper. The *Daily Mirror* had printed the damning images in early February 2004, purporting to show abuse of Iraqis by members of the Queen's Lancashire Regiment, the QLR. The story was Piers Morgan's major scoop for the consistently anti-war *Mirror*. The black and white photos smeared the front pages, blazoned with the headline 'VILE'. In one photo, a soldier appeared to urinate on a hooded man and in another the hooded man in the back of a military truck is being hit with a rifle in the groin. It was the British abuse scandal just months after Abu Ghraib. In response, Hatton and the RMP diligently investigated the accusations and found the truck shown in the photographs was never even in Iraq and that aspects of uniform and equipment did not match those of the QLR. It proved the images were fake, a staged scenario, likely contrived by a 25-year-old Territorial Army soldier. The *Daily Mirror* was victim of a twisted joke and forced into an embarrassing headline retraction admitting: 'SORRY. WE WERE HOAXED'. A former commander of the Queen's regiment, denounced the damaging photos as a recruiting poster for al-Qaeda. 'It is time that the ego of one editor is measured against the life of a soldier,' he says. The paper owns up, its editor, Morgan, though unrepentant to the last, is fired and ejected from the paper's offices. To supporters of the war and battle-scarred soldiers this is the snide, liberal media coming home to roost.

During his interview Joe is legally permitted an impartial observer and legal guidance with him so is joined by a Unit Observer named Doherty and provided with a young army legal advisor named Green. The young man doesn't inspire Joe's confidence. Joe is struck by the terror and confusion of the arrest and hopes to take comfort from this army-appointed advocate.

'What do I do? What's going on?' Joe asks.

'Just speak to them,' the young solicitor tells Joe plainly. The air fills with emptiness. Joe waits for silence to be filled with words about his rights or consequences or protection. 'Tell them what happened so you can go.'

'Are you sure?' Joe questions with uncertainty. He's feeling like his footing is falling away. *This advisor seems like he's fresh out of school*, Joe thinks of the young military solicitor.

'I think … It's probably best,' comes the anaemic response.

A thousand dizzying thoughts swirl around Joe's mind. Mostly he feels unsafe with this military-provided legal by his side. *It's as if I'm back on the battlefield but with a gunner I can't trust*, he thinks. Before he can protest further, Hatton launches into his questioning.

'Right. Can you then tell me in your own words, what you know of that day and what happened?'

Joe looks in vain for support from his army advisor, but the man seems mentally elsewhere so the young guardsman searches the half-forgotten thoughts to describe the events of 8 May 2003. They are on guard at the hospital, looters, Iraqi police, an angry forty-strong mob and Sergeant Selman says to get into the back of the wagon with the four Iraqis. Then the Warrior drives to Bridge Four, en route one Iraqi with afro-type hair becomes hysterical, panicked and has to be calmed by Joe. They reach their destination, the Iraqis get out and end up in the water.

'Right so you're saying the reason why they went into the river was reasons beknown only to themselves,' Hatton probes gently. 'They, they made that decision?'

'They made that decision,' Joe assures.

'Did you force them into the river?'

'No,' the guardsman says adamantly.

'Right, so they've gone in on their own accord?'

'Yes Sir.' Joe replies.

Joe answers questions about what he had said to another soldier when he returned from the water's edge and the claim that Sergeant Selman told him to 'forget about it.'

'Yeah? Right, that's quite detailed.' says Hatton. 'The allegation against … why you're here today is …' says Hatton, halting in his speech as if trying to determine his best approach.

'There has been one person drowned, they subsequently underwent a post-mortem examination and were found to have drowned. One chap in that incident who complained about it, said that he was beaten whilst he was travelling from the hospital to the river.'

'No one was beaten inside there.' Joe pleads and looks to his legal advisor for help before continuing. The young man is glancing just over his shoulder, staring away. His absent expression seems to say to Joe that he is bored – *it's as if he's been dragged out of his bed to come and fix another fucking army lad,* Joe reasons. Joe holds a glance at the disinterested lawyer until his distraction is noticed and he responds with a raise of his eyebrows as if to say, Yeah, Yeah, I'm listening.

'And to be fair, an Iraqi who says that, that he's been beaten, you know, to believe that, you know, is unreal like because you know, he's not going to turn round and say we gave him biscuits and cake.' Joe goes on. 'He's not going to turn round and say the best things about us. We just dropped them off in the middle of nowhere.'

'Right,' says Hatton, diving deeper, asking about Ayad's allegation. 'Did you point your rifle at him?'

'No, my rifle's at my side.'

'Right. And you definitely didn't force them into the river?'

'No.' Joe replies firmly.

'Okay. And in the river, he says that they were forced back into the river by soldiers throwing stones at them.'

'Probably find that hard like cos there was no stones, like. There was all sand or, I don't know whether there was any stones anyway,' Joe answers, quickly wearying of the questions.

'Did you do anything to help him at all?' Hatton pursues.

'No Sir.'

'Right. But you were concerned for him. Why didn't you then help him or inform your crew?'

'We get the order: to mount up, mount up.'

'Right.'

'Once you get that signal, I've been trained to do so, in that, especially in an area like Iraq when you come to mount up like and that's it, I don't argue the case and stand at the side of the wagon. For all I know, there could have been a shot fired.'

'Regardless of whether somebody's drowning in the river?' demands Hatton.

'When I get told to mount up, I mount up.' Joe states with finality.

Over the course of more than two hours, Hatton takes Joe through the details of that day in Basra, unpicking the avalanche of memories. Joe is told that he may be interviewed at a later date and the questioning concludes.

On the same afternoon, questioning is about to get underway of another suspect, 4,000 miles away in Canada. Staff Sergeant Jay flies into Calgary, Alberta; it is the first time that he has travelled across the world to take someone's witness statement. From the city at the confluence of the Bow and the Elbow Rivers, Jay heads 150 miles south-east to the isolated hamlet of Suffield. He's visiting a training facility known as BATUS, The British Army Training Unit Suffield, which has used this sparsely inhabited region for massive training exercises since 1972. Drills in this remote region take place between spring and late autumn, what is called 'prairie season', before the chill of northern temperatures descend to their lows of minus 30C degrees.

Jay is here to spring an unannounced visit to James Cooke, the driver of the Call Sign One Two Warrior, which the staff sergeant knows transported the four Iraqis boys including Ahmed. The investigator has deliberately decided that Cooke should not be told he is coming, hoping to ensure that his quarry will be untainted by talking to others in his regiment and not confused by anyone else. He also doesn't want regimental allegiance to taint the soldier's responses.

James Cooke enlisted in the British army in 2001, at just 16 and like Joe, completed his basic training at Pirbright, followed by specialist infantry training and then moved to join his regiment in Müenster, Germany. Cooke was an 18-year-old guardsman in No. 1 Company, 1st Battalion Irish Guards when they were sent to Iraq. Following the traumatic tour Cooke was proudly promoted to lance corporal and, after the posting to Northern Ireland, sent to BATUS. When Cooke is led in to meet Staff Sergeant Jay, the RMP officer introduces himself and explains what he's investigating and what is going to happen. Jay doesn't know what Cooke has been doing in recent days, when he's last slept, eaten or if he feels able to be interviewed. These are often key considerations when preparing for an interview, but Jay feels there's no reason to think that Cooke isn't up to an interview. Jay also has no plan for this meeting, relying only on his years of training, and as this is only a witness interview, not a suspect interview, he feels that he doesn't need someone with the young soldier. There is also no requirement to record a witness interview, but Jay has two separate notebooks keeping a running record of the investigation. Cooke, on hearing the focus of Jay's enquiries, seems reluctant to provide a statement. Jay isn't surprised and thinks that, like others, Cooke is holding back out of loyalty to his dismount section.

When Cooke hesitantly starts sharing, he tells Jay that he recalls the incident that led to the drowning and that he was the driver. He says that he called in using the radio and was told to take the looters to Bridge Four. When they arrived, he exited the vehicle and the looters were acting up, thinking they were all about to be shot. Guardsmen McGing and McCleary each had a looter near the water's edge and forced them down the embankment into the river while Cooke had hold of the two remaining looters. He starts to tell Jay his perspective of what then takes place.

'At the same time this was happening, I pushed …'

'I'm going to stop you there,' Jay interrupts quickly.

Immediately the investigator realises the gravity of Cooke's words. He immediately brings the session to an abrupt halt. The lance corporal across from him is now a suspect.

Jay leaves the room and hurriedly finds a phone. It's late afternoon in Alberta, but in the UK it is well into the night hours when he reaches his senior, Warrant Officer David Spence. It's the first time that Jay has had contact with the office since the interview with Joe earlier that day. Jay explains that he stopped the interview as Cooke seems about to say he pushed the looters. Spence tells Jay that he must arrest and caution Cooke before he continues the interview. Otherwise the evidence risks not being admissible in a court case. Spence adds that McCleary's interview that afternoon in London didn't suggest that Cooke was a suspect. He didn't say Cooke pushed anyone in. Jay returns to Cooke and proceeds to arrest him and read him his rights. Jay presents him with the handwritten notes, rehearses them and has Cooke sign the notebook to the effect that the statement thus far was true, allowing it to be considered a Section 9 written statement that's admissible to the same extent as oral evidence.

Jay asks Cooke to confirm two key parts of his statement again: that Martin McGing and Joe McCleary each had a looter and pushed or forced the prisoners into the water until they were waist high.

'And who pushed the other two into the river?' Jay asks squarely.

'I did.' returns Cooke.

Cooke goes on to talk about the insufficient training in dealing with prisoners and claims that when he radioed through his plan to go to Bridge Four he was given the instruction to 'Throw them off the top deck', a term he was unfamiliar with but one he took to mean get rid of them as the company was leaving Basra the next day. He further details the moments at the water's edge saying that McGing and McCleary threw their prisoners in the river first, shouting at them, 'Get in the river'.

'You constantly think about it,' Cooke says sombrely, as the two and a quarter hour interview concludes. 'As we drive off, I was aware that someone had just drowned.'

Seven time zones away, Joe McCleary cradles a phone, that's small in his large hands. The chirp-chirp of the telecom dial tone seems to draw at his impatience. Then, a click and the inestimable relief of a familiar voice.

'Hello?'

'Mum, it's Joe here. Listen, I've been arrested. They've arrested me for manslaughter and ...'

Another click sounds and then comes the ongoing drone of a phone having been hung up.

Joe's eyes become rinsed as he sniffs away moisture and repeats the process again. *Oh fucking hell*, he thinks, *all these years of practical jokes have come and bit me right in the arse.* This time the answer to the phone is fast and sharp.

'Joe …' Lynn starts off down the phone.

'Mum.' The weight, the burden, the memories thunder into that precise moment and steal words. In the shared silence he knows she senses something is wrong; this is not a prank call.

'I've been arrested …'

'Son, you have to tell me what's going on. Have you done something wrong?'

There is nothing between them but a maternal bond and a catalogue of experiences she can never understand.

'If you've done something wrong, son. You can tell me I'm your mum,' she says sympathetically.

'Mum, I haven't done nothing,' Joe pleads back.

'You must've done something, they've arrested you. I'm not saying you've done it but just please let me know what's going on.'

'I have no idea, mum,' Joe says with a harsh sniff to clear away his emotional debris.

'Okay, I'm on my way to London.' Lynn says.

'Don't come to London. You won't be allowed to see me.' Joe hears down the phone a handset rattling, shaking of a mother's panic and her sniffling.

'Don't.' he whispers, 'Don't. Mum,' Joe continues to say, 'Mum, I need help. I need a solicitor because this fellow they given me here is … it doesn't feel right, Mum.' Then there is silence that he knows are her tears.

Chapter 10

Beasting

'You a'right, son?' Lynn said through tears, separated from her caged son by the barrack's green chain-link perimeter fence.

'No, I wanna come home ...' Joe answered from the other side. 'It's horrible here, mum.'

Joe was a week into Phase 2 of infantry training. He'd left Pirbright and, after a few days' break, travelled to Catterick Garrison Infantry Training Centre, the ITC, in North Yorkshire. The super garrison covered over 4,400 acres, set in rugged landscape between the Dales to the west and the desolate Moors to the east. For those working to become a boots-on-the-ground frontline soldier, this was the next stop after basic training.

At infantry training the army was quicker to administer strictness and severity. Early on, Joe and his fellow guardsmen had been denied the privilege of going home for the weekend. It was their punishment for not cleaning their rooms well enough, as though they were petulant 10-year-olds. Instead, Joe's mum had visited and stood on the outside and wept, wire cutting her off from her son as it spiralled the endless length of the fence. Stories of the punishing conditions at the training camp had driven Lynn to her knees in divine petition. She was often sleepless and her belly empty from anxiety, making the cosmic plea, 'God, please make him be safe.' In his first weeks, Joe had phoned her with stories of the army's almighty grinding down of its young men. She absorbed these tales of beatings, demeaning, and abuse. Lynn believed the army discipline was tough and good for her sons, but what she'd heard compelled her to some kind of intervention.

'Please mum, please, do not ...' Joe implored with strained words. 'Do not phone up the army mum, please do not. Do. Not. Do. It.' Less than a year since he'd signed up and Joe knew already there were consequences to violating the military's sacred code of silence. Instead, Lynn accepted with muted heartbreak to passively watch what the military machine methods did.

The army had busted Joe on his first day, even before he'd arrived at Catterick Barracks. He and another lad, Michael Duffy, had cracked open a couple of beers on the long cross-country train journey from Liverpool, via

Manchester and York to Darlington. On the way, Joe had met up with Duffy, a mate and fellow trainee from Liverpool who was heading to Catterick. It was the heat of late August 1998, sweaty and stuffy in the carriage. The early months of that year's summer had been one of the wettest of the decade, but the heat had finally made it and the cold cans of illicit beer went down a treat. Joe, still one of the younger trainees, had just turned 17 and was still riding high from passing-out at Pirbright a week before. He'd got a nice gentle youthful buzz by the time the train pulled into Darlington, close to the town of Catterick and where an army minibus was picking them up.

Catterick was first home to a military base almost 2,000 years ago. Romans settled a fort where a road crossed the River Swale, said to be the fastest flowing in England. This close connection to water helped the Romans name the settlement Cataractonium, from the Latin word for 'waterfall' or 'cataract'. It was here that early sixth-century Anglo-Saxons were victorious in their fight against Celtic-speaking Britons at the Battle of Catraeth. And here the Domesday Book's great eleventh-century survey of Britain mentions Catrice, soon to evolve into Catterick.

Joe and Duffy, along with a handful of other recruits from around the country arrived and piled on to the army minibus, hauling their rucksacks on their shoulders. At the front of the bus, a severe-looking corporal, with markings of an MP, the Military Police, introduced himself as the lads settled in for the 16-mile journey to the Garrison. Walking down the narrow aisle between two rows of seats, the corporal gauged Joe and Duffy with particular disdain, as though there was something wretched and off-putting at their presence on the bus.

'I can smell beer on someone's breath,' the corporal said disquietingly, words barren of emotion. He turned his head sharply toward Duffy. *We aren't even on the fucking base yet*, Joe told himself with the aftertaste of foamy, malty-dark liquid.

'Yeah, I've had a drink,' Michael Duffy owned up.

'Anyone else?!'

'That'll be me, sir,' Joe volunteered, both a bit sloshed and unable to feign a mistruth. 'Me. I had a beer, sir.' *I'm not gonna let Duffy just take the flack for it*, he thought.

The MP corporal turned his head back around quickly, faced the front of the bus and was wordless. His reaction, silent and deadly, like nothing had happened, spooked Joe as he settled and they barrelled down the motorway. The lads took in the big black and white road sign pointing to 'Catterick A6136' and beneath it, a red rectangular sign almost warned: 'Catterick

Garrison'. A few minutes down the road and they passed a dominating dark-green sign that told the trainees where they were:

Infantry Training Centre Catterick
HELLES BARRACKS

The mis-spelt thoughts of a place of ultimate torment were not misplaced. All the barracks at Catterick took their names from major British military offensives. Cape Helles was where the British and French attempted to invade the Gallipoli peninsula in 1915 during the early years of the First World War. Mismanagement by a British commander of the landing led to a costly bloodbath on the beaches. After two months of mixed fortunes trying to gain a foothold on Turkish lands, the Ottomans repulsed the Allies.

As soon as Joe and Duffy's boots set down on Helles' hallowed ground the tone changed. The corporal snatched their bags and threw them against a nearby wall.

'You. And you, fucking MARCH!' The MP corporal erupted in a throat coarsening roar. His voice revved like an engine's angry revolution of its crankshaft. He spat orders like sparks at Joe and Duffy

'LEFT, RIGHT, LEFT, RIGHT, LEFT, RIGHT. About TURN!'

While the few other arrivals shuffled their way inside the barracks, Joe and Duffy, singled out, marched 800 metres double-time to the base's jail.

'You two, you're arrested for drinking!' the MP corporal yelled.

'WAIT HERE!' He headed inside the jail office and Joe saw him confer with another man, standing within the shadows. The corporal was crew-cutted, blocky and moustached. *Built like a brick shit-house*, Joe thought as he stood to attention with Duffy, the two of them anxiously waiting outside.

Moments later the corporal returned and pointed to two old wooden barrels on the ground outside. They reminded Joe of the beer barrels with steel pins around their circumference that he'd seen at the Queen's Hotel pub back in Bootle.

'GUARDSMEN,' the MP corporal boomed, 'Pick that barrel up, NOW! Hold it up. STILL! Don't let me see you drop it.'

Joe and Duffy each leaned down, tilting the thick barrels to grasp either end, top and bottom, and straining to heft the object from the ground. *What the fuck?* Joe thought, his facial muscles contorted as he locked arms at right angles, a demand to every bit of his strength. Braced, spines becoming rigid, fixed to hold the barrel tightly against their young chests. Soon Joe's upper arms, forearms, wrists and shoulders began to burn with the bulk of the thing. The constancy of its weight made him ache, but he held it out of defiance and fear. Joe shot a look over at Duffy, straining hard in the same way. His mind simmered a warning to his body: it felt as though his arms would snap or his knees would buckle. Which would be first? He steeled his frame and clenched his jaw hard. They held for an hour, maybe more, or so it seemed and sweated from the exertion and the climbing temperatures of the sun approaching its zenith, a sun god raining down scolding vengeance.

'Put the barrel down and give me twenty press-ups,' the corporal screamed 'NOW! DO IT!'

Joe and Duffy both did as instructed, unsteadily returning their barrels to the ground and placing palms flat, feet on splayed toes. Joe's arms shook and trembled, his lower body tried to tense. His muscles, stiff from holding aloft the barrel, ached and struggled at the exertion. *Fuck*, he screamed inwardly, forcing himself to rise from the press up.

'You're slow. LIFT YOURSELF!' the corporal barked.

The ground burned, gravel dug into the boys' hands. *The smack in the gut on the first day at basic training was nothing next to this,* Joe thought. His shoulders ached as he lowered and lifted his torso. The beer he'd drunk swilled in the gut. The towering statue of the Military Police corporal stood in silhouette. His presence a monolith and his constant glare the only thing preventing Joe from collapsing. When his set was done, he slowly crawled back on to his feet.

'It's hot. You're thirsty – have some water.' The corporal barked with a smirk, holding loaded cups of clear, cold water. Joe and Duffy reached, sweat spread on their faces and the roof of their mouths barren. They tried to clasp the cups, but their hands shook uncontrollably, muscles worn and arms still locked. Water cascaded to the floor. The corporal overflowed with laughter, a sick joke to him.

'Now both of you, MARCH! LEFT, RIGHT, LEFT, RIGHT.'

They weathered the assault of forced marches inflicted on them through the sticky afternoon. The corporal was someone with nowhere else to be; an oppressive shadow that trotted alongside and cursed them with 'March! MARCH!' He spat the words quickly, his outburst one of disgust.

What is going on? Joe thought, the mercury of his rage rising. *This sadistic fucker.*

With each laboured step the day's heat sapped strength out of the two lads as they were forced uphill. Their throats were dry-sore, stomachs raw from the coating of beer, acidic bile of exhaustion vibrating in their guts.

'Back, forth, back, forth, left, right, left right!' After interminable hours, the MP corporal marched the hungry two down to the 'Scoff House'. Dropped in front of them were chips, beans and a pie, amid grease like a river, congealed, sliding on a plate. Joe looked down, fighting the collision of hunger and dehydration; a battle of nutritional need and a throbbing stomach. The lad lifted the fork limply and stabbed through the crust, chewing some brown creamy mass and dry yellow chips. At the salty taste of meat and texture of fat, a rolling wave of nausea claimed decisive victory. He broke for the door and outside the Scoff House vomited.

'Clean it up,' the MP corporal said from the doorway as Joe was forced to use the back of his hand to wipe a string of saliva from dry crusted lips. After Joe was done came more marching and finally he and Duffy were led to a cell inside the guard station where, long past exhaustion, they spent the first part of their first night.

The young guard on duty at the jail took in Joe and Duffy's collapsed forms.

'You two was beasted good and proper, mate,' said the lad with a laugh.

'Beasting', he told them, or being 'yakked' or 'thrashed', was the army's form of discipline to scold a soldier for their misdemeanours. Joe's mind meandered in exhausted agitation: *fucking day number one, you're joking me?* He thought of this cruel initiation. This was worse than being in prison. Shattered from the beasting and his body shutting down, he let tears sluice his face and cried in the Catterick Barracks cell.

A mask of impenetrable clouds blotted out the sun on the infantry trainees' first full day. Joe and Duffy had been in the cell till ten or eleven their first night, then were sent to their rooms to sleep but awoke too soon stiff, aching. The roll call at 5.00 am introduced them to the one who'd be the author of their pain. Sergeant McGowen, their new drill instructor, was a member of the Scots Guards and was made like a machine of muscle. He had round stocky arms, big shoulders, and a thick neck. His default expression seemed a scowl of disapproval. To Joe, McGowen looked like GI Joe action figure brought to life. He overheard another trainee say that McGowen once broke his leg on a march and still managed to carry 60lbs on his back and finish the run. McGowen inducted his new recruits with a rigorous march, grinding them up with a blitz of physical training. That evening, a Friday night, the trainees, drained like flat batteries, were polishing their dusty boots when McGowen entered and raged.

'Everyone in that corridor now!'

They all lined up as commanded, to be made into the military's image.

'Haircuts!' McGowen declared. Joe and the others each handed over £4 and sat in a chair for their trim.

'What do you want?' the sergeant said, almost a scoff of sarcasm.

'I'll have short back and sides,' Joe answered.

In an instant, McGowen raised his hand, his fist clenching a battery-powered razor. He buzzed over Joe's head shaving off the hair to the skin in several quick swaths.

'Perfect. Next. What do you want?' said McGowen.

Within half an hour there were forty heads all shaven the same, like newly released convicts. *We look awful,* Joe thought, at the alien appearance of his new hair-shorn scalp in the polished reflection of a metal locker.

He and the rest of his trainee platoon were told that they hadn't marched back to barracks for dinner correctly. The military's violent discipline was still as simple as ever: If one messed up, they were all in for it. It was what was known as 'negative reinforcement'.

'Out of combats and into drill kit,' McGowen screamed, his temper lost.

The platoon changed and stood in formation before McGowen emerged. He punished them with inevitable forced sit ups, press ups and running that took the place of dinner. It was beasting to the trainees; physical training to the army sergeants. The instructors trained recruits hard, their job to turn the lads into frontline soldiers because they knew that what they faced could be fiercer if they were sent to a conflict zone.

In the dark art of beasting, Sergeant McGowen inflicted more and longer than Joe and Duffy and had been dealt on their first day. From 5.00 am each day there were forced marches, climbing strenuously uphill, pushing them beyond themselves. McGowen would kick, jab, punch to force them forward.

The sergeant's standards were ruthless. McGowen's inspections were an obsessive quest. He measured the symmetrical neatness of lad's clothes. In Joe's locker all the shirts had to hang with mirror image uniformity, individually ironed and lined up with seemingly pointless precision. White T-shirts folded and aligned in parallel to each other. Socks folded as though they had a smile on them. Water canteens were polished to glistening perfection. Boots on bottom shelf, clean without question but also waxed to new car black. They had to convince their sergeant that the display was Moss Bros Knightsbridge perfection. McGowen would make sure each soldier's bed was squared away meticulously. He'd test trainees' work with the 'twenty pence bounce', the shining heptagon coin dropped on the beds had to bounce off the well-made and tightly tucked-up sheets. If not, McGowen would strip the room apart.

'Why's your locker a shit state?' McGowen would rage.

This was Sergeant Spencer all over again, but worse. If McGowen went ballistic he'd pick up the locker and throw it on its side; lift up the bed, throw it, once out of the large window of Joe's fourth-storey barracks room. Joe had to haul it up three flights of stairs, dragging the metal bed frame back with sheets, mattress, pillow. Like at Pirbright, if one soldier messed up once it was the catalyst for more collective punishment. It was after such an infraction their first weekend's leave was lost.

Catterick hosted the School of Infantry and Infantry Training Centre and each infantry recruit in the British army underwent instruction there. For sixteen weeks they'd advance their fitness, McGowen and other instructors forcing the trainees through ferocious regimes of marches. Wearing 50lb-Bergen backpacks, armour and weapons, Joe and the others were made to endure bruising obstacles. Forced over high walls, the butt of his weapon slung over his shoulder would slam into his face, blacken his eye. The mass of men on mandatory incline treks until the dehydrated combatants collapsed hard and weary in the rough Yorkshire dirt.

Catterick was cradled in the River Swale floodplain, from beneath which 250,000 tonnes of valuable aggregate and gravel were mined in abundance. Gravel was the loose quarried foot soldier of the geological world. The action of rivers piled up large accumulations of loose stones, worked them, pounded and refined them, smoothed them over time. Repeated abrasion compacted and lithified the sediments, solidified it under extreme pressure, the material expelled fluids, gradually became solid rock. It's what happened below the surface here. The scape of the land was as blistered and gritted and calloused as the men's bodies became. The instructors mined the lads into men and towards madness for all they were worth. Exercises that trained through thorny wooden terrain tore up soft juvenile skin till they got used to the pain.

The drill sergeant's regime pushed some of the young soldiers past what they could handle. One evening, Joe walked into his room and saw a fellow trainee, his face saturated with desperation, at the end of the dormitory. His leg was up on a chair and in his hand he bore down a steel shovel, caught in the act of slamming the tool on his own knee cap. Unimpeded by the interruption, the lad achieved what he set out to, a shattered bone exchanged for freedom from the torment of training. He roared in agony, twisted with the sound of merciful relief as Joe stared across the distance between them. *All that just to leave*, Joe thought, *people were dropping like flies*. The lad's story wasn't spoken of, he was hustled away and he wasn't alone. Still the might of McGowen's regime drilled deeper, further until a desperate suicide note floated up. Was it genuine? Weeks later, the same anguished author tried to make good on his threat, a rope coiled around his neck in the soldier's shared bathroom. This lad, with a necklace of scarlet scorch-lines, couldn't hack it, was sent to spill all in a psychiatrist's office. He was said to be 'soft' but told the counsellor that he felt trapped, had missed the window to leave, was exhausted and beaten; battle was not for him.

Pushing and pounding, Sergeant McGowan saw highly prized soldiers in the rough, but they would be hewn through swift kicks and sharp punches. Beasting was embedded as part of the institutional way at Catterick and Deep Cut, and wherever else it was torturously employed. Yet so severe was McGowen's harassment that even his superiors told him to relent.

'You better ease up on them boys,' McGowen was warned by two senior officers who'd dragged him into a garrison office after they observed the brutality, belittling, yelling, beating of the lads. McGowen marched back, stung by the rebuke muttering madly.

'You wait, just you fucking wait, you boys.' *He was acting as though we'd done it, dobbed him in,* Joe thought, *but we didn't even open our mouths.* Now the senior soldiers had unleashed McGowen-the-Bastard, an even more totalitarian regime to his young trainees. They panted and sweated, bruised and ached even more.

Joe McCleary had been tall and lanky but the army manufactured him into muscle and provided an arena to use it. The military tradition was called 'milling', soldiers stood toe-to-toe, punching one-another. They'd have to fight fist-to-fist encircled by fellow soldiers for thirty seconds or a minute or until they or their opponents were knocked out and bloodied. This was the ring where Joe learned to stand up for himself.

'Alright, who's going to go up against McCleary?' thundered McGowen at the start of one milling session. The only rule was picking someone of similar height and weight. A herd of lads came forward with a charge for the opportunity to face off against Joe, the youngest of the pack. He peered over his shoulder and saw McGowen lock eyes; his expression that seemed to say, 'Fucking hell, everyone's going for Joe.'

'I want him,' said one square-jawed lad in his early twenties with fashioned forearms and scabbed knuckles, seeing Joe as his easy prize. McGowen nodded in assent as the other lads made a ring around the two opponents.

'Go on Joe, go on Joe,' like a choir chanting for the underdog.

Shit, Joe thought. Square Jaw beamed a Cheshire cat look that said: 'I'm gonna have you'.

Joe edged forward, fists up, hovering around his chin. After a moment's dance, he hooked a damned clenched fist. Square Jaw dodged easily, responded with a jab that impacted hard in the kidneys. Joe collected a pained breath while fury and adrenaline flooded his veins. He squinted and something mechanical took over. He leapt up and pounded with dual fists thrust in volleys, hit upon hit. Square Jaw swayed to the side, shocked at the unleashing, the unceasing aggression. Joe punched, punched, a deluge of rage. Hit upon hit pummelled Square Jaw, tore at his balance until he toppled. Joe followed him down and struck with hard thumps unremitting until a hand scrunched the material of his back collar.

'Let go of him, you fucking lunatic!' McGowen yelled.

Joe's heart pounded, fists yearned as he was hauled apart. He drank in air.

'You know what son,' started McGowen. 'You know what? There's something in you, isn't there, McCleary?'

Joe was too breathless to reply.

'Go on, get over there,' said the sergeant. Square Jaw jumped to his feet, nursing bruised pride.

'I was just about to knock you out,' he said.

'Yeah,' course you were.' Joe muttered with a cocky, bloodied smile.

McGowen ground the trainees down. The lads were booted, punched, thrown into water and shaken by the sadistic smiling sergeant. A variety of infractions – having gloves on when shooting, pointing the gun down in case it ricocheted, recruits not hearing an instruction – all unfettered the ferocity of their instructor. Anyone who thought of standing up to him knew they'd be battered twice as badly as before. They hated McGowen who screamed and swore, forced lads through bayonet training, pushed them to perfect field-craft, navigating their way through the vast youthful lostness.

Their infantry training practised 'bugging out', packing up their gear and moving as if under 'attack'. All training at Catterick was for combat. This infantry was not made for peacekeeping; it was for bloody-minded battle. They all learned fighting formations, were lectured in explosives use and fostered skill in live firing. There was no training for urban combat or house-to-house hunting for rabid insurgents, instead they yelled ferociously across the Yorkshire Moors. They shot rifles on the range over damp Dales of green fields as if their lives depended upon it. They received a single session of prisoner of war handling, a four-hour course in the training wing at Alma Barracks of Catterick, run by an external training group known as OPTAG. They were all told that in a conflict scenario, captives were to be treated as prisoners of war afforded rights of the Geneva Convention. Their instructors talked to them about securing the prisoner, showed handling techniques, hooding and plasticuffing for security purposes.

At every step, McGowen was there, relentless and testing the steel of the men. He peered into the soul of his recruits, dissected and determined whether they could handle the pressure of whatever battle may come. They were frontline men in the forming, but Joe questioned: was this the life he wanted? The final window of escape was two weeks before the end of training. Joe made a decision, mentally rehearsed writing his discharge letter and met with McGowen.

'I don't think this is for me, sir,' he said, the 17-year-old, mustering defiance and determination.

'Come here, son,' beckoned McGowen from across his desk. *Was this with perhaps a whisp of understanding?* Joe leaned in and McGowen clobbered him sharply across the head with his rigid wooden paystick. Dizziness hit with blinding slow-motion speckles for just a moment.

'What do you want me to do? Give you a fucking hug? Tell you everything's okay?' raved McGowen.

'That you're a good soldier? Well, I'm not gonna do that! Now fucking get out of my office, you're not signing out. You're doing well.' The final three words buoyed Joe with their unexpectedness, their clarity. He left the sergeant's office not registering a bruise but with some adolescent pride.

Catterick was the crucible that made precision instruments, pliable and prepared to kill. McGowen, the despised inflictor of all the months of torment, was the man that made Joe disciplined, reinforced his politeness, obedient to authority. In his final days at ITC he settled into a realisation and told himself: *That McGowen's an arse, but if I can't take him giving me stick, throwing me into water and punching me, then I'm not gonna handle it as a soldier in a real scenario. He put me through hell, I hate him, constantly picking on me, but the fucker's gone and made me a better soldier.* Joe rationalised the abuse. The instructor was feared and to be respected. He was the blade Joe despised yet he sculpted the young trainee. McGowen was hated but the one he learned to honour, loathed and yet yearned for recognition from like a son. Through it all, the only thing that got Joe through was sheer ferocious aggression.

The exhausting routine continued and Joe became a stranger to his bed. It felt as though it took hours to meticulously make and he hated McGowen, so adapted to sleeping in a sack on the hard floor.

Recruits were roused to the brutality of pre-dawn for battle drills. It was 4.00 am. A filthy flick of the switch doused the basalt grey room with acidic bile yellow light. The blur of a camouflaged corporal rattled across the room.

'What's bayonet for?' a voice bellowed hard to the dozen murmuring young men and on the march toward Joe's bed.

'WHAT'S A BAYONET FOR?!' the corporal yelled now close up in Joe's face.

'To put on the end of your rifle, sir,' he slurred in reply.

'NO! To KILL!' The corporal punched Joe hard in the ribs.

'What's a bayonet for?!' A repeated scream, in his space.

'To kill!' Joe shouted correctly, coarsening his larynx.

The corporal stood.

'Up! Up! Up! Fucking get dressed. Bayonet training. Everyone!' the corporal yelled, spitting chaos and fire. Scrambled outside their block, the platoon braced against the nauseating dregs of cold January. The corporal regarded the line-up with loathing and threw buckets of ice water onto them. Soaked, shuddering to their pants, the trainees were sent for six hours solid of icy marching. Then the corporal led them to a course, forcing the group on bellies through squalid streams dragging their guns and bayonets behind. Joe crawled through the jaundiced water, the gravel grazing and slicing cuts on elbows as he slithered in the dirty pool. At the end of the course clothed figures were waiting. As they'd been trained, the infantrymen stabbed them, these stuffed dummy suspects. Eradicating any suspicion of hesitation, Joe rammed his bayonet blade hard and swift, then moved on to the next stuffed figure. Thrusting, he jabbed another dummy figure with deadly precision and orgiastic release. Joe moved down the line, overtaken with murderous incentive to pierce another scarecrow-like figure, his blade puncturing through to hard earth beyond. Stabbing, stabbing, fake killing in a vividly real frenzy.

'Drop the blade!' The corporal's sudden bark broke through the red mist of Joe's rage. Voiceless amid the violence, he heard again, 'Drop the fucking bayonet, McCleary.'

Joe relented and released the bayonet blade but was adrift to a moment of searing madness, had no control over his body. The adrenaline-testosterone cocktail intoxicated. He shook, growled a breath, saliva leapt off his lips. In that moment, the masquerading sacks covered with clothes were skins covering people. If real, he could have pierced them just the same, shed the memory and moved on. A good warrior, the army got inside his head, and bayonet held ferociously, made Joe more of a soldier, less of a person.

Chapter 11

Second Arrest

Six months on from his first arrest and questioning, Joe is sitting in his room in Wellington Barracks pounding with angry ferocity, his Sony PlayStation controller in hand. At the intense depression of his thumbs, animated avatars zing colour back and forth like a firestorm, an idle distraction from the anxiety of the lingering investigation. While Joe has been here at the London Barracks, he hears that the RMP are continuing their work throughout the summer of 2004.

McGing is arrested and interviewed in mid-May, then Selman, and over the following months more statements are gathered from other members of No. 1 Company. In June, at Wellington Barracks, Joe and the other men parade, not in military formation but in front of a two-way mirror for identification by the Iraqi witness, Ayad. Joe is feeling the swelling strain at the repeated reminder of the events in Iraq. With it there's a sense of dread that Joe is battling. In his room is his bed, a wardrobe and a TV. It's early in the morning and he's hanging out with his Platoon Sergeant, Ferguson, or Fergie, and they have been idly talking about TV licences and how they don't think they have one on an army base. It's idle conversation, the type that whiles away the downtime between guarding duties at the barracks, while the digital world entrances Joe. Disturbing his game is a firm pounding and the door of the real world opens as two men dressed in familiar formal dark suits stride in. Joe notices, but tries to ignore them, keeping his attention on the screen.

'Joseph McCleary?' asks one of the men. Joe keeps pounding the buttons of the handset.

'Are you Guardsman Joseph McCleary?' repeats the man, his words filled with impatience and forcefulness like a battering ram.

Joe finally relents and shoots a glance upwards as if to say, 'what's it to you?'

'Oh no, mate, maybe you got the wrong person,' he says evasively, starting to turn back to the computer fantasy.

'I'm gonna ask you again …' The tall blocky-built figure with the black trimmed crew cut gives no ground, and to Joe, he is starting to sound bolshy.

Although trying to ignore the visitors, the interruption makes Joe think of the exchange with Fergie: maybe these two are TV licence inspectors hunting down their errant prey. He's half right; they are inspectors but of another kind. Here again.

'I'm Staff Sergeant Jay with the Royal Military Police, SIB, Special Investigation Branch.'

'All right. So what d'yer want?' Joe allows, hardly looking up, with undisguised contempt.

'Are you guardsman …?'

'Yes, I am.'

'I'm here investigating the civilian drowning in Iraq last year and I'm arresting you on suspicion of manslaughter and assault in connection with the incident at Bridge Four in Basra on Thursday 8th May 2003 and for since conspiring to pervert the course of justice,' Jay says.

'What the fuck?' Joe tosses aside the computer controller as though it's the rein of an out of control beast, stands.

Joe doesn't want to go through this again. Six months ago, he'd told an officer everything. Rage pipes quick breaths through Joe's nostrils, his adrenaline on the march and temples pounding, dizzy. One of the RMP stands straight, toe-to-toe with Joe and his arm reaches to grasp a set of polished metal handcuffs that cling to his waist. He directs a look at Joe, indicating his wrists. At the sight of the cuffs, Joe mutters something incomprehensible, guttural. From behind, Fergie leaps up from his side of the room and he addresses the RMP officer.

'You do not have to say anything but …' begins Jay.

'You fucking put those cuffs away!' fumes Fergie. 'That guy's going nowhere.'

Fergie stands-off towards military policemen. This is a chain of command violation; SIB shouldn't walk in without coming and speaking with Ferguson first.

'This is an SIB case, sergeant,' responds the RMP firmly, making towards his prey.

'You piece of shit,' amped up Ferguson. 'Stay away from him.'

'Let's take this outside.'

Joe is raging inside. *This guy is fucking gunning for me*, he thinks to himself, *he's treating me like shit. I hate the man's attitude.* Joe sits back down, disorientated and angry that this is happening again. The still open door between the room and the corridor only muffles their voices, it doesn't silence them.

'Listen, you can't come and cross these lines. There's a fucking military code,' Joe hears Fergie bark to the RMP. 'You don't come in to these lads! You come and see me first!' As Fergie's fury rises, his volley of words spits out faster and faster.

Joe overhears the RMP men argue back but the words are lost to the distance. Through the door he sees the second RMP man try and push Ferguson out of the way.

'This is a police matter,' says the second man. 'Back off.'

Outside in the corridor the commotion brings big bulky lads out of their rooms; they stare at the gathering storm.

'If you put the cuffs on him there'll be fucking trouble,' Fergie says squarely at Staff Sergeant Jay. These are some of Joe's brothers, formed in the womb of war. Fergie and the investigator are face to face and the platoon sergeant fears the RMP are a flame around the corridor full of still-trained oil. Fergie needs to defuse.

'Let me speak to him,' Fergie says calmly. 'And let me get him out away from his mates. If you don't put those cuffs on him, he's going to cooperate. Let him walk out.'

A moment passes; the RMP officer considers.

'Alright.'

Fergie backs up and looks at Joe, giving his head a sharp tilt towards the RMP men.

'Go 'wiv 'em, Joey. We'll work it all out. I'll speak to MacMullen.'

Joe takes an uneasy step forward, almost stumbling. Fergie turns and looks directly into his face. 'And don't you say nothing to them.'

Staff Sergeant Jay and his associate take Joe out and down the stairs from the officers' quarters towards the open rectangle and road that leads out of Wellington Barracks. The other RMP officer opens the back door of a military police vehicle and gestures for Joe to get in. From inside looking beyond, the tint of the windows gives the world outside a bruised appearance. Joe stares, feeling the hum of the car ignite to life. The vehicle slowly rolls into motion moving only a few feet until there's a pounding on the front window. The interruption brings Joe from a daze. In the front, Staff Sergeant Jay lowers the rear window to reveal the company commander, Major Peter MacMullen. He leans in and glares at Joe, concerned, slightly breathless from striding at top speed across the barracks. He looks at Joe.

'Don't worry Joe. I don't know what's going on,' he calls. 'Stay calm.' MacMullen is angry; he's already made a complaint to Jay's senior officer. The major leans away as the rising window wipes him from view. The military police vehicle rolls away. Joe hoped it was over, that due process had played its course. The accusation rolls in his mind: *manslaughter?* The car pulls out of the Wellington Barracks kicking up loose gravel as it speeds out on to Petty France, SW1, and west.

After a couple of miles, the RMP vehicle turns swiftly into Hyde Park Barracks. It leaves the road and passes through an archway into an enclosed courtyard. In the back Joe turns, glances out of the rear window to see the closing of the big wooden doors that remind him of an old church, cutting off the secular world. The car comes to a halt and someone opens the door.

'Get out!' the RMP officer orders.

Joe climbs from the car and steps on to the hard gravel of the courtyard. He catches a glimpse of the low descending canopy of late September grey clouds. Above him he sees the towering thirty-three storeys of Basil Spence's tower, the modernist monstrosity that had recently been voted one of the top ten eyesores of Britain. Dwarfed by architecture and events beyond his control, Joe feels alone and adrift amid the shame of another arrest.

Jay says something that Joe interprets as the accusation: 'You killed that 15-year-old boy, didn't you? You murdered a 15-year-old boy. You murdered him, didn't you?'

Joe thinks that Jay seems still angry and agitated.

'No. No! I never,' Joe protests. The cold of the autumn day causes him to shiver.

'He was a 15-year-old boy!'

Joe's mind tries to barricade itself against the intensity of the inquisition. He feels the tightening of his chest and is on the verge of gasping for air.

'Fifteen,' hears Joe, then repeated: '15 years old.'

His age – why is he fixating on the kid's age? Joe thinks. *I never asked him for a fucking birth certificate.*

Jay has recently made a breakthrough in investigating Ahmed's case. Two days earlier, 28 September 2004, Jay had interviewed Martin McGing for the third time, but the young soldier frustrated the investigator, answering 'no comment' throughout. The next day, however, the arrest of Sergeant Selman and his questioning yielded answers. He claimed that he reported his plans to the watchkeeper at their Basra HQ before leaving with the looters, something the radio operator denied. Selman said that the radio operators must be closing ranks, maintaining that they replied and said 'Yes, move to Bridge Four'. He also told the investigators that he took the four looters to the bridge after hearing that Major MacMullen had caught looters and taken them there before because it was somewhere that everyone knew. When they got to the bridge, Selman said the looters got out of the Warrior and he saw two soldiers as they made the Iraqis get into the water. Selman had thought it was 'another fucked up scenario' and he saw the soldiers at the water's edge laughing. He maintained that the soldiers were Wayne Sampat and Joe McCleary.

Joe hears what he feels is an RMP officer goading him.

'Listen, leave him,' the other officer says to Jay but looking at Joe. 'He's a fucking idiot. He killed a rag-head. It doesn't matter, does it?'

'What are you doing?' Joe pleads.

'Just tell us, mate, what happened.' The second RMP officer, acting the Good Cop says directly to Joe. 'It'll be all over.'

No way are you my fucking mate, thinks Joe.

'I told ya, I didn't fucking kill that lad.' *This guy loathes me,* Joe muses, *it's like he's got it in for me. He shouldn't be investigating me.* 'I haven't done anything.' Joe is convinced the RMP is going to make sure he goes down for what happened in Iraq.

Jay had been at the autopsy and witnessed the decomposing body barely wrapped in plastic, which had a name: Ahmed Jabbar Kareem Ali. He knew how awful the situation had been.

The RMP officers lead Joe across the courtyard, up three concrete steps and into the building. They take Joe down a corridor to a small windowless cell with a heavy metal door.

'Get in there.' Joe steps in and sits on the bench; an RMP officer remains in the doorway.

'Here,' he says, holding out a cigarette like an olive branch.

'Ta,' says Joe. The officer pulls out a lighter and offers a flame.

'Listen, mate,' he almost whispers. 'I know you killed that lad in Iraq, didn't you? You drowned him. You forced him in the water, didn't ya?'

'No, I didn't,' Joe shoots back.

'You know you'll be sound if you tell me. I'm just doing my job, mate.'

The battering of accusation and temptation lures at Joe, like a temptress calling a sailor.

'If you tell me now, you'll get yourself out of here.'

Something in Joe's gut suddenly screams that this seems all wrong. *Why is this guy talking to me like this?*

'I didn't do it. I. Did. Not. Do. It.' Joe says forcefully. 'I want my solicitor here. He needs to be here.'

'Wait in that cell!' The RMP is defeated. He grabs the cigarette from Joe's mouth and tosses it to the ground. His outburst done, the officer slams shut the door. Joe is left alone.

After his first arrest six months previously, Joe's mum made a call to Merseyside's go-to solicitor. His name is Rex Makin but to many in Liverpool the flamboyant character is known as 'Sexy Rexy'. He's famed throughout the city and travels around in a chauffeur-driven Bentley, but still buys his veg from a local store not far from Joe's house. For anyone accused of a criminal offence or injured in an accident, the immediate thought was to 'get Rex'. Rex's connections are celebrities and his court cases charted the modern history of Liverpool. He was friends with Beatles' manager Brian Epstein and was the first to popularise the word 'Beatlemania' when representing some of the band members in court. He represented the underdog dockers, militant in their strike against the city. He served the hopeless victims and families of the Hillsborough football stadium and the heartbroken parents of tragic Jamie Bulger. Rex was honoured as the first Liverpool solicitor in 100 years to be given the freedom of the city. Rex and his team of lawyers are known for mounting an aggressive defence and finding the best QCs.

Receiving news of Joe's latest arrest, they despatch one of their top lawyers to London. John Joseph Ignatius O'Leary is well renowned and one of Liverpool's sharpest solicitors. A veteran of hundreds of cases, O'Leary has little time for army procedures or prevarications. He arrives and demands to meet with Joe immediately. An RMP officer brings Joe from his cell and O'Leary makes his introductions and explanations. He's representing Joe from now on or until this case goes to court. During the first interview, the army's appointed solicitor made Joe think that he was heading to jail for the rest of his life but he feels better now, surrounded by the familiar tones of a Liverpudlian lawyer.

'What do you need?' O'Leary says with the formalities over.

'Well, a cigarette I suppose,' says Joe. He seldom smoked, until deployment where everyone smoked or when he is drunk and craving a casual nicotine hit.

'Right,' said O'Leary, abruptly. 'Sergeant?' The distracted RMP sergeant cocks his head and listens.

'I'm taking my client to that shop over there and I'm buying him a sandwich and a drink and some cigarettes.'

'He's not allowed to leave,' the officer states firmly.

'I'm telling you now, this boy is going with me to that shop down the road. He's not a threat, he's not going anywhere,' says O'Leary forcefully. 'I'll take full responsibility.' O'Leary turns to Joe and says, 'you're not gonna run are you Joe?'

'Run where? Where am I gonna go?' Joe says. The military police officer relents and permits O'Leary to escort his client.

Outside the afternoon is cold and wet, and heavy London clouds grey. Rain soon soaks Joe's short brown crew cut as he darts down the street with his solicitor. Joe feels the prying eyes of the military policeman watching from the small side door of the RMP building.

'Don't look at him Joe,' says O'Leary. 'Let's just go drink some tea and smoke a smoke.'

Joe's hands shake as he updates O'Leary, burning through one cigarette one after another.

Staff Sergeant Daren Jay has been following this case through since he was in Iraq where the grim stories and massacres continue. In May, there had been an ambush close by a checkpoint named Danny Boy, just 3 miles outside of Majar al-Kabir, site of the last stand for the six RMP officers.

At the checkpoint, a dozen insurgent Iraqis with guns opened fire on nine British members of the Argyll and Sutherland Highlanders regiment. The soldiers were making their way down the long highway to Amara, two hours north of Basra. The attackers were fighters from cleric Muqtada al-Sadr's Mahdi army and they were on the offensive against the Coalition after the breakdown of peace negotiations. The soldiers' vehicles were repeatedly bombarded by small-arms fire and RPGs launched by Al-Hutamah-bent fighters. Seeking an urgent escape, the British soldiers stamped down accelerators, Land Rovers growling. The Argyll and Sutherland Highlanders churned dusty asphalt away from the ambush, but ran into two dozen more insurgents, waiting with improvised roadside bombs. The enemy congregated like a small army of ants, spread out and waiting near an abandoned industrial factory. Festered in foxholes, crouched down in putrid dykes, the extremists rose up from along the desert roadside. These Shiite militiamen sprang force with a ferocious advance, giving no quarter. Reinforcements of two platoons of the Prince of Wales Royal Regiment were thrust into a classic infantry assault. They struck back using the first wartime bayonet charge since the Falklands conflict, twenty-two years earlier. Forty strong infantrymen in four Warrior armoured vehicles joined the battle against the bombers. The infantry sections were quick to dismount and take up a flanking manoeuvre as they charged carnage at the end of 5-inch fixed blades. The bayonet charge slashed bloodily at Arab bodies, rifle-butts slammed rebel rib cages, boots kicked and cracked dark olive skulls. It was three hours of aggressive, hand-to-hand, them-or-us violence. The valley eventually silenced and made red with blood.

And afterwards, a handful of British injuries but twenty-eight Iraqi corpses, or some perhaps clinging to life's embers, and more wounded. The enemy's bodies floated in the river, bayonet stab wounds seeped scarlet. Then the command came: Pick up and bring in the Iraqi dead. It was an unpopular order, telling soldiers to collect yellowing cadavers while their comrades ran top cover. The angry infantrymen recovered the bodies, Hamid Al-Sweady and the rest, to see if a suspect in the murders of the six RMP from last summer was among the dead.

The British soldiers plasticuffed the injured and the dead and saw off any remaining fighters while coming down from the intensity of conflict. A British private yelped and screamed, soaked in adrenaline still as he stamped on the head of a dead Iraqi. A spooked sergeant reacted against a gunman, spraying thirty rounds into him and a trench of twitching Iraqis bodies.

They twitched no more.

Another soldier took a young Iraqi prisoner, sandbagged his head, hit him till his face poured with blood. The boy was taken down in the ditch, up to his knees in fetid water. With the detainees' hands tied, the soldier kicked him to the floor every time he cried out, sending him splashing, almost drowning.

More brutality in the war-torn land of the liberated.

Staff Sergeant Jay's specialised training includes the Home Office Investigative Interviewing Trainer course where he gained a distinction in 1996 and time with Kent Police, where he successfully qualified in Tier 3 Achieving Best Evidence Video Interviewer of Vulnerable Persons. Joe's vulnerabilities are buried beneath deep layers of battle scars. Throughout his career, Jay has investigated deaths, fraud and fatal accidents. He follows the same meticulous process regardless of how uncooperative the subject might be. Jay is expertly familiar with a method of interrogation known as PEACE: a mnemonic standing for Planning and Preparation; Engage & Explain; Account, Clarify and Challenge; Closure; and Evaluation. The PEACE model has been used since the string of miscarriages of justice that blighted the British legal system throughout the 1980s. In response, a Royal Commission on criminal justice report in 1993 examined the series of wrongful convictions, including the Guildford Four and the Birmingham Six. The inquiry found many police investigators were operating under their own rules. They gained confessions using illegal tricks and techniques and placed pressure on young suspects to admit to things they hadn't done. With so many convictions deemed unsafe and suspects having their sentences overturned in the court of appeal, a new model of interviewing was needed. The British Home Office set up a group to investigate interviewing techniques and developed the PEACE method. PEACE would try to obtain comprehensive witness accounts and defensible evidence in a more ethical and professional manner than the confession-focused interviews used around the world. PEACE is now investigating war.

Peace isn't what Joe feels, still carrying the calluses of conflict. He is now assembled with his lawyer John O'Leary and sitting facing-off against a determined interrogator. Staff Sergeant Jay, who has been joined by a second service policeman, Staff Sergeant Davidson, has planned and prepared extensively for this interview, the first step in the PEACE process. He's lived this case for over a year and feels he knows the soldiers involved. He studies them. In preparation he considers his interview quarries' mental state, how fatigued or hungry they may be. Jay formulates his interview scheme in advance; he is strategic. There are certain things that he is holding back until later during the interview, specific allegations he is aware of, and he is looking to establish a breach in his opponent's story. Jay reviews photos, notes, and witness reports. To hand, neatly compiled in a two-ring binder, are the statements, interview transcripts and photos. Jay works hard to avoid confirmation bias, trying not to have his interviewee affirm what he already believes true. Sometimes, according to PEACE training, it can be a good thing to know little or nothing about the case. But Jay carries within him the burning imprint of Iraq and the pallor-ridden body of a 15-year-old that cries for some kind of justice.

Jay's informality is part of the Engage and Explain step of his process, trying to create a rapport with his subject. He gives the obligatory caution and lets Joe know what to expect.

'During this interview what I'd like to do is ask you about what happened back in May 2003,' says Jay calmly.

Jay begins to lead his suspect through the events of more than sixteen months before, knowing how he does so is critical. The RMP officer prepares his third approach. Account, Clarify and Challenge, by pulling an exhibit from his folder. It is a photograph which he shows to Joe.

'Can you have a look at that photograph and tell me if you recognise that male person?' says Jay.

'Yeah,' the young guardsman returns.

'Who is he?'

'Ahmed Jabar Kareem, whatever,' Joe says, unable to stop the tired anger and impertinence seeping through his words.

'Sorry?' Jay says.

'The boy who's on the picture, what it says there.'

'Okay. How do you recognise him?' Jay prods.

'He was in the back of the wagon.'

Jay continues his questioning, asking who had the highest rank at the canal bank, he interrogates the guardsman's responsibility to the looters in his care and brings up Ayad's accusation that Joe punched and kicked him. Jay challenges Joe over James Cooke's claim that the lads had their wrists tied, something Joe has denied, and picks at this discrepancy.

'I can't remember if they were tied or not,' says Joe. 'Come to think about it, there's a possibility they were tied.'

'So I'm suggesting to you,' says Jay, 'that they can't have run straight off if they were tied up when they got out of the vehicle.' He sits opposite his suspect perhaps with growing impatience at the seeming lack of consistency between the accounts. 'Which presents the fact that maybe you're lying.'

'Or maybe I just, do you know what I mean, that it was a year and a half ago, and that me mind's not as good as Guardsman Cooke's or Guardsman McGing's or Sergeant Selman's,' Joe retorts, with growing agitation at the implication that he's not being honest.

'Did you see Guardsman Cooke push any detainees into the water?'

'No.'

'Cos he's told us that he pushed two in.'

'Mm.'

'And that you pushed one in and Guardsman McGing pushed one in.'

'No. Can't remember that,' Joe says.

'Okay. Did you throw any stones or other objects at the ...'

'No.' says Joe forcefully, interrupting the investigator.

'... detainees whilst they were in the water?' The voices layer over one another, struggling for dominance.

'No.'

'Did you cock your weapon, Guardsman McCleary, on the canal bank?'

'No. Weapons were already made ready,' answers Joe.

'Okay. When you were on the canal bank were you laughing at the detainees in the water?'

'No,' snaps Joe.

'Sergeant Selman says that you were,' Jay returns rapidly.

'No.' The repeated battering of questions frustrates Joe. All he can hear is seeming accusations by the investigator and he feels a sense of betrayal from his fellow soldiers.

'Do you know that Sergeant Selman seems to be placing the blame for the drowning on the dismounts?' Jay puts to Joe.

'Well Sergeant Selman's bound to say something like that, isn't he?' Joe seethes. 'You know, full sergeant, or whatever he is, and he's going to lose all his career. He's going to say anything isn't he, so, you know what I mean?'

'Okay. He even said actually "I thought to myself, I'm not getting the fucking blame for that, because of that, because of them dismounts." Are you protecting him?'

'Fucking no,' Joe replies angrily. 'Wouldn't protect him. Not at all. I didn't know we were going to the river, he took us to the river not me. He's the commander.'

Jay continues, bringing up Joe's attempts to calm Ahmed in the back of the Warrior, insinuating that the guardsman pushed the boy. *Is he fucking joking me?* Joe thinks. *This guy is painting me out to be some like torturous monster. The more he goes on, the more it feels the SIB man is trying to break me.* Joe tries to escape within himself, but there is nowhere he can go. He denies Jay's interpretation, getting frustrated with the line of questioning and describing what he saw Iraqi kids doing for fun.

'I see them swimming all the time.'

'All right.' Jay listens.

'You know what I mean, they're always in there. So, to me I just thought, well, you know, he's probably swum round the back of the post, do you know what I mean?'

'Yeah.'

Time seems to slow down in the purgatory of this interview room as the questioning continues.

'Did you mention to somebody that somebody had drowned at that time?' Jay asks.

'No.'

'Guardsman Fleming says you did.'

'I know, I didn't,' Joe denies flatly.

Jay moves to wrap up his interview, the Closure and Evaluation phase of the technique.

'How do you feel now?' he asks.

'No comment.' Joe is seething at Jay, with anger thick, yet he doesn't want to admit his hot rage.

'How do you feel now, bearing in mind that you told us at the start of the interview about the duty of care side of it. Personally?'

'Don't really know, because of course I'm upset and depressed, you know what I mean? You don't have to go over it. I have to live with this every day. You know what I mean? That you're all on my case.' Joe allows.

'Yeah, do you feel, is that because you feel responsible for what occurred?'

'No. I'm not responsible no.' Joe assures.

'You don't?'

'I don't feel responsible at all.'

Joe swears he sees Jay turn off the tape machine that's recording proceedings.

He's only trying to rattle you, Joe thinks, but he has no idea what it was like. *He doesn't have a clue.*

Images Joe has been trying to suppress since Iraq boil to the surface: the fight and fallen bloody comrades; the exhaustion of almost falling asleep on his feet; furious crowds in Basra braying for blood. 'He was 15! You killed a kid. You fucking killed him,' thunders in Joe's ears. 'He was a 15-year-old boy, a 15-year-old boy!'

They're trying to pin this on me, Joe thinks. *Or maybe he's trained to say these things.* Adrenal glands pour adrenaline and cortisol chemicals into Joe's bloodstream. Muscles tighten with the agitation. He feels his heart in the tenseness of his chest. He gives his fists a taut pump.

'I didn't do anything.' Joe says a little too aggressively. 'How many times do I have to keep telling ya!'

'Joe, calm down,' O'Leary interrupts forcefully. 'You're getting upset.'

'I'm bound to be, if I'm having to repeat meself all the fucking time,' Joe answers, the agitation and dizziness of rage flowing through, the Liverpool accent getting thicker.

'I fucking … Could you please stop! Could you stop saying. I didn't kill a fucking kid.'

'I think that we'll adjourn there,' says Staff Sergeant Jay finally, rationally, cautioning Joe again and serving him with a note explaining his rights.

He can return to serving his accusers. Jay adds that he's not to leave the country and must surrender his passport. Jay and his fellow RMP officers leave the room.

Joe has parting words with John O'Leary before they step back out into some freedom. Above in the damp London grey, birds fly overhead, circling Hyde Park. A black crow screeches, beating its wings unsteadily.

Chapter 12

A Soldier at Peace

Joe was a crow. That was what they derisively called the soldiers newly arrived from boot camp: CROWS or Combat Recruits of War. When he came in through the gates of the British army's Oxford Barracks, on the outskirts of the German town of Müenster, the more senior soldiers stood, seeing the blue sash on the young soldiers arms that marked them out as new recruits, and they squawked, mocking with bird calls as they passed. A CROW could do nothing right. In the early days the CROWs were tasked with grunt work like Outside Areas: collecting rubbish along the base's grounds and stag duty guarding at the barracks' gates. Yet all the same this was a step up from the harsh times of infantry training.

As a soldier, Joe had survived boot camp and beasting to finally join his regiment as part of No. 1 Company Irish Guards. He would be part of the tip of the spear, the army's first line of defence. It was 1998, a time of calm in Northern Ireland and when plots against the westward hegemony were still embryonic. In the Middle East, Saddam was still emboldened by his sustained grasp of power and he resisted the mandate of UN Resolution 687, the 'destruction, removal and rendering harmless' of his biological, chemical and nuclear arsenal. The dictator had beckoned Armageddon as he denied UN inspectors' access to suspected weapons' sites across his arid land until, after obfuscation and evasion, the UN WMD detectives all withdrew. In response, Saddam was put in his place by America's president, whose Desert Fox air strikes proved a convenient distraction for his sexual dalliances and impending impeachment; dead Iraqis blown up to cover an Oval Office blow job. In a speech months later, Tony Blair reminded American economists of the rising threat of Iraq, its leader one of 'two dangerous and ruthless men, Saddam Hussein and Slobodan Milosevic. Both have been prepared to wage vicious campaigns against sections of their own community.' As Hussein had done to more than 8,000 Kurds in the city of Halabja with Sarin, Tabun and VX on Bloody Friday in 1988, so Milosevic did to more than 8,000 Bosnians in Srebrenica with guns, rape and burial alive during a grim July in 1995. The link between the two dictators went further than a speechwriter's parallel:

MI6 had intelligence connecting Belgrade and Baghdad, two pariah states that hated the West. Saddam saw in Serbia a key ally, the reports said, eager to help him rebuild his country's military from the damage of Desert Fox and in exchange the Serbs toured Iraq to learn how to hide their anti-aircraft missiles, amour and aircraft.

Around the time that Joe arrived at his regiment in Germany, 1,600 Irish Guards had just been sent into the Balkans, deployed to training at Petrovec Camp in Macedonia and then onwards as peacekeepers in war-ravaged Kosovo. The regiment was the first British unit to enter the liberated Kosovan capital of Pristina as retreating Serbs fled, and north-west of the city, the Irish Guards' Warriors, each vehicle named after Irish towns, lined the long and bleak highway to Belgrade. At the blood soaked Vranjevac Hill, site of the white cross monument to the thousands fallen to German forces in October 1915, Kosovar Albanians now welcomed the Irish Guards with chants and bouquets of roses. The troops were there in support of NATO to call a halt to the scourge of ethnic cleansing, but even without a UN mandate their presence was justified under the notion of Responsibility to Protect, the moral imperative. Most of the UK supported the NATO intervention, at least two-thirds were behind Blair and the same number backed British troops patrolling the Balkans peacekeeping agreement. This was still the era of outward interventionism, spreading liberal democracy and policing, of post-Communist realignment of the eastern-bloc. Summed up by Blair, answering his critics who had exhorted him not to act and to seek a political solution, who said that involvement in the Balkans was 'simply the right thing to do'.

With Joe's regiment returned, he met his company commander, Captain Peter MacMullen, a tall and confident officer with a mane of blond-brown hair, narrow-set eyes and an affable smile. MacMullen was educated on the Isle of Man at King William's private school, among its greenery and sea view surroundings, before he was accepted at Sandhurst's Royal Military Academy. After his training he served as an officer since 1990 and in Germany had his own regiment.

For the first time in years Joe was back to sharing a room with his brother, David, who was stationed at the German barracks for the early part of Joe's time there. He'd been there a couple of years and was crafty. David often swapped names and army numbers around on the stag duty list. It took Joe asking how come he was doing so many of the night guard duties before he realised what his brother was up to. A few months in, David felt he wanted to be closer to his girlfriend so left the Irish Guards and returned home to

Liverpool. In his place, Joe shared a room with Guardsman Mawhinney, who became a good mate. Joe and the rest of the regiment would spend their days training, exercising and taking care of equipment. The Warrior troop carriers were back from deployment in the Balkans and needed stripping down and servicing. They'd get them fixed up and do regular infantry training drills in the nearby Westphalia countryside, practising with the GPMGs, General Purpose Machine Guns (known as GIMPYs for short). They stayed sharp at CQB, Close Quarter Combat, on the firing range. Physical training was a given, and Joe was 18 and at his peak, always the first one into the gym and last one out. When it came to the long runs, Joe was one of the fastest and felt like one of the fittest in the battalion. There were marches and inspections and Joe was often commended for his fitness.

There were drunken scrapes too, it was how the soldiers let off steam in a place known for its Pilsner. Joe received a separate conviction and caution for being drunk and disorderly. He was once so worse for wear on German beer after a night out that he got into a drunken fight and woke the next morning with his face beaten to a pulp. Although bust-ups between the German populace or local Polizi and soldiers were minimal, fights were inevitable when there were several thousand British soldiers bottled up in the more than a dozen barracks that made up Osnabruck Garrison. Many different regiments were stationed there, helping to make the garrison the largest British army base outside the UK. The oldest parts of Osnabruck had been built as a German military base in 1899 but Oxford Barracks dated from 1936. The place Joe called home was built for the Luftwaffe and named for a Nazi leader, 'The Herman Goering Kaserne', until it was occupied by the victorious forces of the 4th Armoured Battalion, Coldstream Guards on 3 April 1945. From then on, succeeding British army regiments made their home around the dull white clock tower and in the light beige buildings with one-, two- and three-storeys topped off with tall triangular roofs.

Most soldiers lived in barracks, as Joe did, but some of the married officers had army residences, especially those with families. Sergeant Major Pat Geraghty was one of those lucky ones, housed with his wife and three young children, in the military accommodation block. There was a primary school on base and Pat, who'd been stationed in Berlin before Müenster, thought this base was great for families. Geraghty was a formidable and thick-set soldier, whom Joe always admired. He was smart, knew his military history inside out and Joe respected his dedicated religious faith. Geraghty was the Company Sergeant Major for No. 1 Company Irish Guards, a role he held with distinction. Pat and Joe shared a lot of banter; he liked the young

Liverpudlian lad's happy-go-lucky attitude. Both Pat and MacMullen, saw the makings of a good soldier.

Pat would wait and watch at the entrance to the barracks just before 10.00 pm on Friday nights when the lads left for the town pubs. He'd say that it was like watching the London Marathon as the herd of lads were picked up by rows of German taxis as the bugle was blowing Last Post and the gates were being closed. The war-ready soldiers spent the nights out in the town of Müenster, nestled in the North Rhine-Westphalia, which in 1998 had been the heart of celebrations making '350 Years of the Peace of Westphalia'. Worst was the last Friday of the month, known as Millionaires Weekend because that was when the lads got their pay. They brought lively revelry to the sleepy corner of Germany and the barracks' The Naafi bar was filled to the rafters.

Joe and three other lads had got into a big fight in the town, a stupid drunken bust up with a couple of other army lads from the base. Word had got back to their commanding officer, Captain MacMullen, and in the morning there were consequences. The four lads, still feeling sick from the night before, were called in to see their CO. They all sat impatiently in the waiting room for their names to be yelled. The first lad was beckoned and was inside a short while before he came out and uttered angrily his punishment.

'Fuck! – Four days restriction of privileges!' In the army one of the worst punishments was restriction of privileges, which meant being confined to barracks. The soldier would be treated like a CROW all over again, up at 6.00 am sharp, marched around the base like being back in training.

The next lad was called and moments later came out with the same sentence, four days restriction of privileges. Facing the loss of privileges was a serious deal and fierce discipline.

When the third lad came out, he too announced four days restriction of privileges and Joe knew with a grimace what to expect. *I'd rather they take my wages from me; take the fucking money but not my privileges!* Joe thought. He was called to enter and when he marched into his office, MacMullen awaited and by his side was Sergeant Major Pat Geraghty.

'A'right, sir?' Joe said cockily.

'Oh, Joe ...' said Geraghty, casting a glance at the company commander.

'Oh Pat. What are we gonna do with him?' said MacMullen with a sardonic yet severe look of disapproval.

'Sir ...? I swear to you, it wasn't my fault,' Joe said.

'I'm disappointed, Joe. I'm giving you ten days restriction of privileges for fighting ...' said MacMullen sternly.

Joe fumed inside; the other lads only had four days so he couldn't believe the heavy penalty: ten fucking days just for getting in a fight?

'That's a fucking joke,' Joe said finally, 'Come on, sir. Ten days?'

'You've been here over a year now, Joe,' said Pat 'You should know better.'

'Oh, and Joe' started MacMullen. 'Can you babysit for Pat for a few hours tonight?'

'Me and me wife are going out so you can drop us off down the road and then you can come back and sort the kids out.'

'Alright, sir, yeah,' said Joe. 'I'll see you at seven.'

After they'd finished making arrangements, Joe left the office to where the other lads were waiting and walked past them.

'Alright boys,' Joe smirked as he walked cockily by. 'So sorry, but I have to babysit the sergeant major's kids!' Child-minding the CSM's kids was an occasional task for a young trusted Guardsman and for Joe it meant something more. He'd worked hard, become a well-liked soldier and forged with Pat Geraghty a close allegiance, developed through the mostly untroubled times in the Rhineland.

Chapter 13

The Palace

The troubling RMP interrogation takes its toll on Joe, leaving him distraught and emotional when he goes to find Pat Geraghty a few days later. Pat is no longer Joe's company sergeant major, having been the regimental quartermaster sergeant looking after stores at Wellington Barracks since mid-2003. This posting is coming to an end and Pat is being sent to the Royal Medical Corps in Leicester. He's heard about Joe's arrest and when the young guardsman appears, Pat invites him to his office in the Regimental HQ.

'Alright Joe?'

'Can I have a talk, Pat,' says Joe wearily.

'You know you can, Joe,' asks Pat softly, reaching for two tea mugs. 'I'll make us a brew.'

Joe tells him about the questioning over the events at Bridge Four back in Basra, the allegations that he killed a teenager and that the Iraqi is saying Joe threw rocks at him from the canalside.

'They charged me with manslaughter, sir,' Joe says to him mournfully. One thing he trusts about Pat is that he's smart and a solidly religious, honest guy.

'It never happened like they're painting it out to be. It never happened … I don't know how …' Joe says, his voice trembling. 'But I swear to you now, Pat, I'm not lying to you. I just don't know what to do.'

Joe knows that Pat would always keep his word and give sound advice.

'I strongly advise you, Joe, not to talk with anyone in authority,' Pat reassures seriously. 'Not unless you have legal representation with you.'

'Sir, I just wanna …' Joe starts to say with tears filling in his eyes. He feels a deep weight bearing on his chest and the pressure of the arrest and investigation crashing upon him.

'C'mon, shake out of it,' Pat says to him. 'Let's drink our tea.' The hot cuppa takes the edge off the threatening charges that hang over Joe.

'If I go down for this, for manslaughter, I'll be in there for twelve years. That's what they say,' Joe vents. 'I can't cope with that. The RMP guy was going to see me go down for it.'

Awakening the next day, Joe's sense of grim orientation comes only stubbornly, as he wrestles himself from another night terror. The dreams make constricted breaths hard, a struggle to inhale as his galloping heartbeat calms. It takes a moment for Joe to realise he's in his room at Wellington Barracks, his head sore and body tired from restless sleep. The vestiges of night terrors linger through the day. Joe groans inwardly when he remembers he's on the much-despised palace guard duty today. As part of the Household Division, four Foot Guards are on daily sentry duty on the forecourts of Buckingham Palace. This has been the permanent London home of the Crown since the 1837 accession of 'Mrs Brown', the Empress of Britain's violent boot print on the world before she became Britain's widow in residence. Long before that, in the Middle Ages, the site of the future palace was once marshy swamp grounds watered by the Tyburn River, which still flows below the courtyard and south wing of Buckingham Palace. A Sir William Blake first built a house on this site in the early 1600s, not long before the then British monarch fled in fear of the uprising Parliamentarians. It was in the aftermath of the Civil War and the Restoration of Charles II's throne that the Horse Guards and Foot Guards regiments of the British army were first given responsibility for guarding the sovereign's palaces. In 2004, more than 2,000 troops from the five regiments of Foot Guards in the Household Division and the regular infantry were employed on public duties, responsible for guarding Buckingham Palace, St James's Palace, the Tower of London, Horse Guards Parade, and Windsor Castle.

Many of the guardsmen hate this task of patrolling the residence of their monarch. Their task is as sentries on duty at their post for a precise two-hour period. Every ten minutes, coming to attention and 'slope arms', the name for lifting and lowering the leg and raising the SA-80 weapon on their left shoulder with the sharp-bladed muzzle pointed skyward. They then conduct a march of fifteen paces across the area of the post. Each sentry does this four times before halting. He'll shoulder arms and stand at ease. The sentry soldiers' orders are read out before each two-hour 'tour of duty', reminding them that they: 'may not eat, sleep, smoke, stand easy, sit or lie down during your tour of duty'. They are to stand, stoic, stern, briefed to avoid and disregard distractions. Foot Guards can eliminate persistent public irritants with a bark of 'Stand back from the Queen's Guard' or with an aggressive stomp, coming sharply to attention. It is hardly warfare for the well-oiled, war-scarred warriors. Joe is an infantry soldier crafted for violence and battle, not for parade as objects of spectators and photo-hungry tourists. This role demands little athleticism, zeal, initiative or strength, beyond the strength of discipline of mind against the monotony. The dreaded ceremonial duty in front of the home of Her Majesty is indignity and honour, respected and reviled.

Joe transforms himself for the task of being assigned to guard the palace. He prepares for sentry duty by dressing in his 'Home Service dress tunic', the scarlet uniform worn during these autumn months. Unique to his Irish Guards attire are buttons arranged in sets of fours. On Joe's collar badge is a Shamrock, and a St Patrick Star adorns his shoulder badge. Joe pulls on his long black trousers and tightens his tunic over the top with a white belt and brass buckle bearing the regimental cipher. Finally, Joe places on his head his black bearskin cap that's 18 inches tall, a pound-and-a-half of fur skinned from a Canadian black bear hunted by Inuits. The bearskin marks him out as Irish Guards with its blue plume on the right of the cap.

Soon Joe heads the short distance from Wellington Barracks across to the guard house at the ostentatious palace. He takes his place, a lad from poverty-blighted Bootle, guarding the decadent 775 rooms of his queen. This palace, of which another William Blake, this time the poet, unrelated to the honorific first builder on the site, once wrote 'the hapless Soldier's sigh runs in blood down Palace walls'. Blake poured his vitriol and contempt on the power of the kings and the colonial British atrocities. 'To drown the throat of war!' Blake pronounced. 'When the senses are shaken, and the soul is driven to madness. Who can stand?'

Joe stands, tourists snapping eager pictures from beyond the fence. As the autumn of 2004 draws on, the mongrel days of insurgency and hostages in Iraq loom, while England is grim after its wettest summer in fifty years. The familiar noise of drizzle cascading through nearby drainage, like the sound of ill-tempoed drumming, is Joe's only distraction from the recently unearthed memories that the RMP's investigations have dug up. Anger, stress, anxiety have a pathology.

Motionless, Joe stands and stares out beyond the thick metal bars, the railings that separate the Queen's Guards from nuisance members of the public. He feels caged, not just like a zoological specimen to be captured in every tourist's tattered photo album, but trapped. Joe cannot move on from Iraq and the events of May 2003. The memories stalk him and he sees a twisted tapestry in his nightmares. The forceful encounter with the RMP officer Jay feels as though it has a toxic effect, emerging into waking life. In the mandated silence beside the palace, the poisons of anxiety, stress, rage metastasise. Joe is watchful for trouble outside the palace, but thoughts attack him from the inside.

Joe notices the swarm of tourists taking aim, their lenses oblivious to the trauma. His height means he barely fits inside the sentry guard box. Alone, he can concentrate on nothing but his tormenting thoughts. The SA-80 rests on his shoulder, its bayonet inches from his head. Despair floods and Joe actually thinks about using it to knife into his head. To end it all. A memorable photo for the assembled spectators.

After ten minutes, Joe strides, lock step in time, the rhythm for the sake of royalty. Disquiet marches along too, gnawing unease erodes in his gut, anxiety taking form. Raw flashes of being on stag in Iraq intrude, then the exhaustion, the flies over dead Arab bodies, the dread, panic and certainty of Jay's words as he remembers them. 'You killed that lad in Iraq, didn't you?!' Undigested chunks clot in Joe's oesophagus, the roof of his mouth dry. He can't blot out memory.

What's next is inevitable. The guardsman quickens his pace. He reaches the palace sentry box and leans over to his side and vomits. Then Joe buckles and collapses to the floor.

Part II

Battle

Chapter 14

Chemicals

The buildings buckled, then collapsed, erupting a plume of ash a little over an hour after being hit at high speed by human and jet-fuel-filled missiles. Everyone remembers where they were when the world changed. Joe was in Portugal on leave when on distant shores the two pillars were struck. His mum, Portuguese stepdad, Carlos, and he, didn't think much about how the targeting of deadly planes that day would alter the trajectory of his life.

While he was on holiday, several platoons from his Irish Guards regiment were on their way to the Middle East for a massive military war game. When the fundamentalists enacted their airborne attack, Company Sergeant Major Pat Geraghty was in an airport, waiting to fly with a contingent of troops to Oman. The military exercise, named Saif Sareea II, had long been planned but in the shadow of terror's dawning new age it took on extra meaning. The mock battle was the largest single deployment of British forces since they were in Iraq in 1991, a decade before. Now, 22,500 troops, with 13,000 Omanis, were to undertake major mock assaults with 42 RAF fixed-wing aircraft, 44 helicopters and 6,500 vehicles. In October 2001, the warfare exercise revealed early weaknesses: British combat boots that literally melted in the harsh desert heat; the unreliability of the Challenger II tanks when, to cut costs, they were not properly desert-ised and the SA-80s rifles that suffered stoppages due to sand and dust. But Saif Sareea, Arabic for 'flashing blade', also showed the world that the Americans were not the only force capable of swiftly projecting strategic strength in the Gulf region. It reminded America too that they would still need allies because while its special forces raided Afghanistan's rocky mountains, Bush junior had a score to settle with Iraq, something inherited from his father. The beast of war was brought to life from slumber for a battle that was inevitable long before the towers fell.

In February 2001, the month after the fight over hanging chads, the American president had his first meeting with Prime Minister Blair. It was at this discussion where 'IRAQ' was inked in bold on the agenda and Bush made clear to Blair that Saddam should not 'cross any line or test our will'. A few weeks later, a group of American administration officials met with plans for peacekeeping troops and war crime tribunals in Iraq, which resulted in a Pentagon document being produced entitled 'Foreign Suitors for Iraqi Oilfield contracts'. They were maps for black gold exploration.

Saddam spent the summer before the world changed pushing boundaries, and on the day that defined the next century, over live pictures of the smoking north tower and in those moments of innocence and speculation, when naïve commentators pondered about an accidental crash caused by the blinding light of the morning sun or some suicidal pilot, there was Iraq. Almost unnoticed in text on the scrolling morning TV news ticker was the story of Iraq saying it had shot down a US spy plane. Ten days later, after Bush's Deputy Director of Defense claimed he had a 'gut feeling' Saddam was involved in the attacks, the American president name-checked Iraq in his belligerent speech. It was a reminder of an unfinished war in his promise to Congress that 'we will not tire, we will not falter, and we will not fail' in their new fight against their old enemies.

Joe returned from leave back to Germany and it wasn't long before he began to get tired of the army life. He'd trained and then been stationed in Müenster for the full two years of his contract. Joe spoke to a company sergeant major about leaving and was convinced to serve for another year. His commanding officer could offer a £2,000 bonus for staying on; Joe felt a bit conned into another twelve months. (And the army, he thought, knew that all they had to do was to give a soldier money and he'd happily go out and get pissed for a week, which Joe did.)

From the start of 2002, while the US search for al-Qaeda was still underway, there were rumours circulating in the army about a second phase in the war on terror, something echoed by political posturing on all sides. In Iraq, a robust Saddam used 17 January, eleven years to the day since the start of the first Gulf War, to patriotically remind his people that 'today is a day in the Grand Battle, the immortal Mother of All Battles. It is a glorious and a splendid day on the part of the self-respecting people of Iraq … the first day of that battle, since Allah decreed that the Mother of All Battles continue till this day.' Bush junior upped the ante in his State of the Union speech, saying that Iraq was central to 'the Axis of Evil', which threatened the peace of the world. Saddam supported terror and 'the Iraqi regime has plotted to develop anthrax, and nerve gas, and nuclear weapons for over a decade. This is a regime that has already used poison gas to murder thousands of its own citizens.' The dictator's abuse of his own people was not new. In the summer 2001, Amnesty International had sounded the reminder of the results of Saddam's reign of terror on his own people:

Torture is used systematically against political detainees in Iraqi prisons and detention centres … Torture victims in Iraq … blindfolded, stripped of their clothes and suspended from their wrists for long hours. Electric shocks … used on various parts of their bodies, including the genitals, ears, the tongue and fingers … The use of Falaqa (beating on the soles of the feet), extinguishing of cigarettes on various parts of the body, extraction of fingernails and toenails and piercing of the hands with an electric drill. Some have been sexually abused and others have had objects, including broken bottles, forced into their anus.

It was brutal, but little had really changed in Iraq's aspirations or capability since 1991, but the world around it had. With Osama hidden in caves, the terror mastermind evading his enemy between the porous borders of Afghanistan and Pakistan, America aspired to take down Saddam and his tortured state. Ground-down Gitmo detainees, hooded enemy combatants bound for Black Sites and desperate Iraqi defectors spouted spurious lies and quarter truths to their American handlers, whose ears itched to hear. These stories and Saddam's eager ambitions for a WMD arsenal melded together and metamorphosed in the minds of American and British intelligence into a certainty that he possessed them.

In response, the British army flexed its muscles and increased its soldiers' readiness. They ramped up with training exercises, refined their fitness and enhanced their infantry fighting skills. Joe was an early casualty, getting hit by the butt of a fellow soldier's rifle. A day or two later, Joe had returned home to Liverpool on a weekend of leave and, in a fog of dizziness, fallen down his mum's stairs. He found his bearings but had lost his eyesight. In the cloud of blind panic and fit of confusion, Joe called a taxi to a local optician whose examination ordered an ambulance and sent him quickly to St Paul's Eye Hospital. The blunt trauma of the rifle butt set off swelling behind his eye and he needed a course of steroids and rest to reduce its effects and return his vision and the soldier back to his battalion.

Around this time, Joe met Martin McGing, an excitable young new recruit from the Midlands with slight Brummie burr to his accent. McGing had left secondary school in Rowley Regis, west of Birmingham, even before he'd completed his GCSEs because he'd always wanted to enlist. McGing – or 'Gingy' as he was called – was a skinny young crow when he arrived in Germany, a dead-energetic lad fresh from a year at Army Foundation College in Harrogate and surviving his nine weeks at Catterick. To Joe, Gingy looked as though he was still hitting puberty, skin all raw and pimply. He was a good two years younger than Joe, but they got on well, sharing a similar humour and cracking frequent jokes.

Cruelly, tragedy visited Gingy during July 2002 when he was out training in Canada. While Joe's eyesight recovered, Martin was part of a platoon of Irish Guards taking part in a BATUS exercise on the plains of Alberta, when he got word that his dad had died. He flew home to England for the funeral and a week later he had to return back to Canada, though he had missed out on a lot of the battle training that was essential for his role as a gunner. The BATUS exercise, almost as far from Iraq as it was possible to be, took place that summer with anticipated conflict in the Middle East in the back of many men's minds. It gave some of the infantry soldiers, like Wayne Sampat, Gingy and others from No. 1 Company a chance to enhance their battle readiness.

When many of the battalion returned from Canada they were put in the forefront of a different and unexpected kind of battle. The British government was in a fight with the fire brigade over pay and the infantry troops from No. 1 Company Irish Guards went from live fire training to firefighter training because of threatened strike action. The Fire Brigades Union wanted a 40 per cent increase for the nation's 50,000 firefighters but local authorities wouldn't budge. The last time firefighters had gone on strike was twenty-five years earlier in 1977, lasting for nine long weeks. Back then 100 people died during the crisis that foreshadowed the countrywide strikes throughout the Winter of Discontent and brought about the last Labour government's demise. Then too, 10,000 servicemen from all three parts of the British military, the army, navy and air force, took over as firefighters.

What Saif Sareea told the government and Ministry of Defence in 2001 about the poor state of some of the army's kit, the fireman's strike told them about the struggle of pulling the army away into a role it was not intended for. Operation Fresco involved thousands of fiercely trained soldiers getting ready to provide emergency cover. The troops rode around in vintage Green Goddess engines while they worked with small breathing apparatus rescue teams (BART) and rescue equipment support teams (REST) headed by professional firefighters of the RAF. Even Peter MacMullen, who'd recently been promoted to major, gained his NVQ in firefighting. Army fire engine crews were again manned by more than 10,000 personnel, over 330 specialist breathing apparatus-trained teams, nearly 60 specialist rescue teams of 2,500 personnel as well as thousands of administrative and command posts, with more needed by the day. The British army was already spread thin with commitments that ranged from Sierra Leone to Afghanistan alongside a staffing shortfall of more than 7,400. The firefighters' strike was stretching matters even further. With up to 19,000 men and women – the equivalent of about seven regiments, planned to be called in, mostly from Germany, it was even a struggle to find accommodation for troops returned to England.

With nearly a third of British troop strength as stand-in firefighters, the higher-ups worried too about the impact on training, guarding of Buckingham Palace and more importantly that it might derail its planned support for American action in Iraq, which was looking ever more likely. During the summer, Bush and Blair had decided firmly upon military action, a pre-emptive war against Saddam and now all that remained was the propaganda push. A scurrilous-minded government lobbied secret services for gleanings of intelligence to compile its evidence against the regime. Late in September, Blair published his dossier and The *London Evening Standard* printed its iconic front page headline:

45 MINUTES FROM ATTACK
Dossier reveals Saddam is ready to launch chemical war strikes.

Blair and his communications man, Alastair Campbell, had cherry-picked evidence so that even its own MOD WMD intelligence analysts thought the forty-five minute point, suggesting that chemical and biological munitions could be ready to fire in 45 minutes or less, was 'so bloody silly' that it would 'destroy itself by its own lack of credibility'. It did not matter whether the message won over any of the public; the decision to invade had already been made.

Towards the end of 2002, with his extra year almost up, Joe's thoughts again drifted to leaving the army, having had enough by then. He'd given them nearly four years of his life and now prepared to give in his notice. David, his brother, had already left and Joe too missed life back home and most of all his family back in Bootle. It was autumn, the weather and colour palette of Westphalia were changing when the company sergeant major called Joe into his office.

'How's it going, Joe?' the CSM asked. 'Sit down.'

'Aye, pretty sound, like' Joe chirped. 'I'm gonna be leaving soon, sir.'

Joe knew that his years in the army had given him a lot. In his journey from Bootle to his battalion he'd trained, learned a lot of discipline and responsibility, but was now ready to go back to find a decent job and normal life. For all the army gave, Joe also felt as though he'd missed out on a lot of his youth. He'd never been on a lads' holiday during his late teens or partied in Magaluf like his mates from Merseyside; he'd spent his twentieth birthday running around the German woods in training.

'Joe …' said the CSM and Joe knew then he was after something.

'Sir. I've got three months left …'

'Son,' the CSM interrupted.

'I wanna leave …'

'We're going to war, to Iraq,' he revealed firmly. News that the invasion of Iraq was going ahead had been making its way around the CSMs.

Pat Geraghty had heard the news himself one Friday afternoon in mid-October. He'd been alone in the office, Friday was usually quiet, which Geraghty liked so he could catch up with the piles of paperwork that demanded his attention. It was part of the often-forgotten mundanity of military life. This particular Friday was different; Pat was busy with civilian tailoring contractors who were measuring up the soldiers from the Drums & Pipes (No.12 Platoon) for Home Service tunics in preparation for their imminent return to London. Pat was also occupied with nominating more soldiers for firefighter duty as part of Operation Fresco, randomly selecting soldiers to head over to Osnabruck the following day to begin training. His office phone rang with the Regimental Quarter Master Sergeant – RQMS, on the other end of the line breaking some news.

'Pat, get your guys ready. They're going out to Sennelager on Monday,' said the RQMS.

'What for?' Pat barked back down the phone.

'To conduct training.'

The order didn't make sense to Pat and it was such short notice. 'What about ammunition?'

'We're giving you the stock of ammunition from the Welsh Fusiliers.'

'Why?'

''Cos we're going to war in Iraq,' revealed the RQMS, slyly.

'I've been preparing the men to get back to public duty in London and now I'm getting the men ready to go fight fires in Birkenhead! Do I just drop everything?'

'No, no, just carry on,' said the RQMS with a chuckle, then clicked off the call.

By that point those in senior ranks weren't surprised that the situation in the Middle East was to widen into war and that military action might move to Iraq.

Joe's CSM went on to tell him that if he signed out then he would have to finish out his duty in Europe while all his mates saw action on the battlefields of Iraq.

'We're all gonna get deployed,' the CSM continued. 'And I won't be able to take you because your contract expires. Just know that you're gonna be pulled to another company and you'll mind the camp for us while we go away.'

'No way sir. No way! I've trained my life for this.'

'Well then you need to sign back up for another year,' the man told Joe. 'You'd have an open contract then yearly.' The papers were already neatly laid out on his desk. There was even a pen ready and waiting, which almost made the guardsman chuckle. He knew that he'd walked right into this one.

Joe faced a decision but not much of a choice. He was shocked to hear that they were definitely going into Iraq, despite the months of speculation. Either way he didn't want to be the one that backed out. There were some for whom the threat of war made them want to leave and others who faked injuries at the prospect of battle. Joe determined not to judge anybody, but he didn't want to be called a war dodger. He knew this was what he'd trained for and was built for. He was willing to go. He also didn't want to know that all the lads would come back with shining medals while he'd been stuck at home having missed out after four years serving and little recognition.

'It's up to you, McCleary,' the company sergeant major said, a wry look on his face as Joe picked up the pen.

With imminent war on the horizon, the Irish Guards soldiers came together for some intense training towards battle readiness. It was a mark of pride that the regiment attracted soldiers from all backgrounds and places. Joe's platoon was led by Lieutenant Dan O'Connell, the No. 1 Platoon Commander, who was descended from and named after the famed Irish Liberator and Emancipator Daniel O'Connell. Lieutenant Dan O'Connell continued a proud legacy, coming from a military family; his father was surgeon Captain Morgan O'Connell who joined the Royal Navy in 1965 and left after thirty-one years as Consultant Advisor in Psychiatry to the Medical Director General.

Others in the diverse platoon included Ian 'Molly' Malone, with whom Joe would enjoy a good natter putting the world to rights, and was from south of the border in Ballyfermot, Republic of Ireland. Molly had dreamt of joining the Irish army only to have his hopes dashed when, at 22 he was told that he was too old. Molly looked at other possibilities, even the French Foreign Legion before he crossed lines and joined the British army in Belfast in 1997. He was promoted to lance corporal in late 2000 and served on Operation Agricola in Kosovo. Molly enjoyed being in the pipes band, though his ambition went beyond his ability and Major MacMullen had gently suggested he find something more in fitting with his strengths.

Chris 'Muz' Muzvuru, meanwhile, was 20 and from Gweru, Zimbabwe, and loved his tea so much that his other nickname was 'MustHaveaBrew.' He was fresh to the army, having joined in 2001. Muz loved Chelsea FC and loved women even more, model Kelly Brook, scantily clad, adorned his barracks-room wall. Like Molly, Muz was part of the drum and pipers who played on ceremonial occasions. He'd trained as a piper in Edinburgh, where he met and became close mates with drummer Jonny Stranix, who invited Muz to spend time with his own family. Muz was also proud to be the first black piper in the regiment's 103-year history.

The wide-ranging characters and skills came together as a tightly knit group, ready to train for deployment. The army brought in some severe physical training instructors (PTI) who put the men through their paces. There were three physical training sessions a day. Joe could feel his body change, feel himself getting fitter and stronger. As part of the build-up they were sent out with the PTIs on brutal runs in the countryside of Westphalia's beckoning winter. It brought back memories of Catterick as killer routes ran the young infantrymen up wooded muddy hills. To make the trails, and them, tougher they were forced to carry a steel stretcher, something that took six men to heft. They'd be scrambling up ascents and the PTI would kick some lad in the back of the legs until they collapsed. Someone would shout 'Man down!' and they'd have to heave the immobile soldier on the metal stretcher and, three men on either side, make their way back up and down the hill. The intensity of the training told them this was real and the boys, as one company, became a solid unit ready for war. Major Peter MacMullen ran a tight ship. He told the men that if they weren't fit enough then they weren't coming to the Middle East. He told the section commanders that there were twenty newly recruited trainees coming in and they could replace any one of the men who were not fit enough. It wasn't just an idle threat: three people were replaced.

There were classroom sessions with rudimentary lessons in Arabic, teaching the mostly working-class lads the few foreign words of *Salaam, Alikam* and *Shukran* with which to greet the citizens of the country they were to invade. They received a single session of guidance on Rules of Engagement (ROE) from Captain Gary Turner. He taught the circumstances under which they could justifiably use lethal force. They presented everyone with an ALPHA Card, which listed succinctly the rules of war. Everyone was reminded of Northern Ireland and Kosovo, past conflicts that were always brought up as examples of soldiers in dilemmas or circumstances when they were threatened and permitted to open fire. In Iraq, things could be very different.

In case any of the men doubted the justification of their cause, they were vividly briefed on the brutality Saddam had inflicted on his own people. In a blacked-out closed-off room in an attic at Oxford Barracks they were shown secret films; projected flickering on the walls were images of what the dictator's chemical and biological weapons (CBWs) could do. These were video nasties, a real horror show, directed by Saddam's demented cousin Chemical Ali. The soldiers sat through the films of children's bodies bent double, spines contorted in uncontrolled spasms as they were exposed to vile chemicals, their short lives a catastrophic testing ground for lethal gas. Under the effects of virulent Sarin gas, the men saw sons and daughters vomiting and guaranteed a suffering death. Those exposed to the nerve agent Tabun, which was also dispersed as a gas and then absorbed through their skin, quickly experienced muscle twitches, spasms and painful convulsions. The toxic, synthetic chemical VX was unleashed on innocent youths who ingested that yellowish, odourless and tasteless substance and writhed in agony as the poison disrupted their bodies' nervous systems to lethal effect, causing muscles to clench, preventing the victims from breathing and killing them painfully in minutes. Joe felt bitterly sorry for these victims, seeing them have to go through this ordeal. *You know what?* He thought to himself, *I want to go to fight this motherfucker. Let's take this bastard out. It doesn't matter whether you're white, Chinese, whatever, it makes no difference what colour skin you are. Everyone is someone's son or a daughter and what Saddam was doing to them Kurdish kids in those videos, it was just awful. I'm just going to fucking go over and kill him.*

Every other soldier's brain told them the same thing when they were exposed to that footage, cured of any doubt of who this monster was.

They were going out there to disarm a maniac who had a deadly arsenal of weapons, poised to use against the British. The prospect that this was what Saddam was going to do to them scared Joe, even after they'd been shown how to use the medical needles that might keep them alive after they'd been exposed. All of them were supplied with a pen containing an antidote. An instructor showed how it worked. The device had a button and when depressed shot out a needle. Immediately after exposure, the soldiers were to slam the 6-inch point into their thigh. The medication would provide fifteen minutes to live, Joe was told. It was enough time for an air-evac mission to get them, or at least some of the men out to safety. The thought of hitting that pen, freaked Joe out. Chemical weapons were dispersed over a wide area so it meant that a whole company of men would be affected. Joe pondered the likelihood that many would suffer. If the chopper came then there would be room enough only for 10 or 20 people out of 100 or 150 to be rescued. Slim were the chances you were going to be air-evacced. It chilled Joe when he thought of the moments when those fifteen minutes were up and he died an agonising death in the desert. The only defence would be the respirators which the training led everyone to respect as being the only thing that might prevent them being exposed. The men spent a day going around wearing respirators, becoming used to the cumbersome yet life-saving devices.

Another threat some of the men feared was from *Bacillus anthracis*, if not from the weaponised pathogens spread by Saddam, then maybe from the MOD's own anthrax vaccine. There were plenty of soldiers scared about the jab, something similar to that which had been given out in 1991 to British and American servicemen who said their health had later suffered, the spectre of Gulf War syndrome. Joe hated needles and dodged the doctors giving out shots until he was overdue and he was one of the last of all the lads to be summoned for his injections. The military nurse negated any bedside manner and stabbed both arms with a series of needles, the cocktail of medicine that might cripple him but could also combat deadly pulmonary anthrax. Afterwards Joe went back to training, weak and dizzy and shivering head to toe. His drill sergeant mirrored the nurse's lack of sympathy and said with a smirk, 'It's your own fucking fault. You should have got your jabs along with the rest of us.'

Awful, shocking and terrifying was the painful prospect of Iraqis attacking the men with CBW, but there were sceptics, even in their own ranks, who doubted the dictator had the weapons. Once, Pat Geraghty was watching Sky News broadcasting a story about UN weapons inspectors. Saddam had submitted an 11,807-page dossier accompanied by CD-ROMs to the UN as part of the demands of Resolution 1441. The disclosure of details of Iraq's weapons of mass destruction programmes frustrated politicians in Britain and America, who were pushing war, because it created the illusion of Saddam's compliance. Over on East Midtown in Manhattan, the UN inspectors soon determined the documents bore little that was new or of note and were mostly old manuscripts from 1996 and 1997. Yet still the 108-strong squad of inspectors scoured Iraq for chemical and biological and nuclear material. They interrogated scientists and searched sites from Mosul in the north to Basra on the south coast. They raided paper factories and military storage facilities; liquid gas companies and technological universities. Hans Blix, head of the inspectors, told the world that the dictator lacked compliance, but so too did Blix's diligent weapons detectives lack evidence of Saddam's deadly stockpiles. Pat, like other thoughtful men, started to have doubts in his mind. He sat around with some of the men, watched and mulled the TV reports, and gave voice to his opinions.

'He doesn't have WMD.'

'You can't say that, CSM!' said a young guardsman, with barely concealed astonishment.

'Yes I can,' Pat said defiantly. He couldn't understand why, if the dictator had WMD, he didn't use them against his enemies.

'Saddam's next to Iran. The majority in the south are Shia Muslim, dominated by the Sunni. If Saddam had the weapons of mass destruction why'd he not use them? He used gas against the Kurds in the north, but that was it,' Pat explained. There was a mixture of shock and intrigue, soldiers who didn't understand the politics or religious rivalry still hung on the company sergeant major's words.

'He's just playing cat and mouse with the inspectors. He doesn't want to look weak against his Arab neighbours. There's no proof. Why the mad rush, eh?'

Still, the build-up continued apace. In January, the armour arrived for the Warrior vehicles and the soldiers quickly got them ready to be despatched on ships destined, via the Red Sea, for the Gulf; it reinforced to everyone that they'd soon be there. Once their vehicles had been fitted up and were on their way, the infantrymen were ordered to Sennelager, 80 miles east of Müenster for training exercises. The only thing this place had in common with the Middle Eastern desert was the town's name translated to 'camp on the Senne' and Senne was an old German word for sand. Otherwise, the Sennelager Training Area, in the middle of German January, was a bleak beaten down 45 square miles of open land that felt like the Arctic. In this training mission to go to Iraq, Joe and the other men were erecting tents in fields of snow. From the start though they got on with their task. The men's mindset was 'Let's do this. We're only there to do a job, no matter how tough. You just tell me what to do, how hard to hit, and I'll do it for you.' They made the most out of it. In preparation for sand dunes and dust storms they embarked on the biggest snowball fight they'd ever seen. When it was night they assembled in sleeping bags and braved the descending temperatures. To a man they were all cold, barely able to maintain a degree of body heat. Joe's platoon sergeant, Paul Ferguson, saw one of the guardsmen shivering violently in his sack and came up for some sport with Joe.

'Joe,' Sergeant Ferguson commanded. 'This lad's going down shaking! Get naked and get in his sleeping bag with him. Sharing body heat's the only way!'

'No, sergeant,' Joe declared firmly, another guardsman lying there shivering. 'Fergie, I'm not getting naked!'

'He's fucking dying. I just told you, get naked now and get in the sleeping bag with him. It's the quickest way to raise his body temperature.'

Joe contorted his face in despair.

'And then just start hugging each other,' Ferguson demanded.

'Sarge,' Joe pleaded. 'Can't he just get in my fucking sleeping bag?'

'He needs body heat. Now!' Mock urgency oozed out of the commander.

'I'll do it sir,' Joe relented. 'But I'm doing it in my fucking underpants!'

'McCleary you fucking dickhead, I'm only joking' Fergie said, laughing.

'Ha ha. You're gonna get naked with me,' the shivering lad in the sleeping bag laughed.

'I was gonna save your life you stupid bastard,' was the only embarrassed reply Joe could manage when he realised they were having banter at his expense. The banter was rife wherever they went; it was how the lads survived.

The next day, the cold conditions had wreaked more havoc with their gear. By morning, Joe's boots had frozen, rigid and icy. Rifles were not clicking right because they were jammed. All the lads were a mess, bodies still chilled to their bone marrow. A sergeant was giving a lesson and the weather unleashed near gale-force snow-sleet mix with such intensity that they couldn't even hear him and within minutes the side of his face was frozen. One lad got frostbite on his foot. *It's a fucking joke,* Joe thought as he rubbed his hands to generate heat. Someone said it was down to the budget being inadequate, that the army settled for field training in freezing Germany; no one knew for sure. When they went to try and train with the tanks they had the same kind of problems as they tried to do manoeuvres on the open plains near Paderborn Garrison. All the tanks broke down because in the cold, the mud froze hard as concrete and tore the tank tracks. The soldiers would have to spend another week back fixing the tanks that'd been damaged from the training. Joe's frustration grew: *This is ridiculous,* he thought: *we're like Dad's Army. We'll be going from one extreme to the other; from this to a desert.*

Setting up a new night's camp, Joe had to hold in place a steel bar that would support their tent. McGing held the sledgehammer and braced himself to plant it into the ground but Joe's frozen hands were shaking.

'This isn't fucking right, this. What are we doing here?' Joe shouted.

'Keep it still, Joe,' McGing yelled.

'Are you for real? It's minus 16. I've got to try and keep hold of a steel bar with bare hands,' Joe yelled through the grinding gusts. The hammer slammed down, ended up hitting the side of his hands and scraping top layers of skin. The lads' kits were a mess. Things were breaking. Tanks' tracks had to be replaced. The exercise was cut short. They were meant to be training there a week, but pulled out after three days and retreated to some warm digs. The soldiers made their way back to Müenster, Joe's hand, skin still torn and now inflamed, throbbed amid the bitter cold of winter.

Chapter 15

Insurgency

J oe is struck down by a malignant gastro-intestinal inflammation burning up in the heat of fever. His collapse while on duty outside the Royal Palace is down to the onset of violent pains in his gut. A mix of dehydration and a virulent infection causes a toxic insurgency within his body; a few thousand miles away there is a different insurgency taking hold of the body of Iraq.

Over there, bloody human capital is being taken captive tit-for-tat as a rebellion from within ravages the country. Cells of extremists target the only real victors in the military campaign, the foreign contractors. In the spring of 2004, four American Blackwater private security specialists had been ambushed, beaten and mutilated in Fallujah, near Baghdad. Their bloodied bodies publicly paraded and strung up from a bridge over the oozing Euphrates. Yankee indignation was swollen. A month of American military attacks to 'pacify' the city followed, killing hundreds of insurgents and hundreds more non-combatants. American remedial measures deployed frontline forces, meeting resistant rebels. Eventually the US command gave the order to withdraw and handed over control to the newly formed Fallujah Brigade, a CIA-backed and Sunni-led security force. The Americans supplied the brigade with a dosage of weapons, which fell into enemy hands when the Fallujah Brigade dissolved and declared allegiance to the insurgents. Fighting against the Coalition seems the only thing that unites the diverse sectarianism of Iraqi Nationalists, Shia and Sunni militia-men, al-Qaeda off-shoots and followers of clerics whose charisma gives lost youth direction amid the debris of war. From these radicals metastasised the insurgency that targets those working with the Coalition Multinational Force Iraq, or MNF-I, taking hostages of the unfortunates who venture into the ailing nation.

For Joe, the haunting trauma of Iraq, its memory freshly raked up by the investigation, metastasises into poisonous form as anxiety and stress that stimulate infection until it literally brings the man to his knees. Amid a fog, an ambulance delivers Joe to a hospital where surgeons extract his swollen appendix. Many conflict veterans of Middle East wars suffering post-stress disorder have an added risk of irritable bowel syndrome, dyspepsia and gastro-intestinal disorders and Joe joins their ranks. A jagged memory, this hospital thousands of miles from the hospital where his trauma began.

Days later, Joe is back in barracks recovering from a procedure but not from the memories which haunt him. There is night but no rest as he is lost to more overwhelming nightmares. He finds himself among the clatter and rattle of a rapid exchange of bullets. The noise seems to cocoon him. Muffled sounds of men's screams suddenly surround him, jolting with their familiarity. They are intense in volume and ferocity: the excruciating sounds of injured fellow soldiers. Even in this state of distortion, Joe is aware this is the long night of the ambush. Outside of his peripheral vision, the boys of the battalion are in near-dying agony. The world flashes again, a seizure of jarred fragments. Broken memories flash like scatterings of glass collateral. There is lightning, but instead of thunder there's an accompaniment of booms nearby – and more screams. The screams morph, becoming not the ones of Joe's night terrors but his own. They are the ones that he's making within the real-world of Wellington Barracks.

'For FUCK'S sake!' mutters an aggrieved voice. The wall is booming. A fist is slamming from a sleep-interrupted neighbouring soldier who shares the thin wall of Joe's room. He too is agitated at the disturbance.

Joe sits upright, swings both legs from his bunk and finds some faded fatigues to throw over his shorts. The imprint of the memory makes Joe's chest pump ferociously as he forces himself into disorientated consciousness. He breathes irregularly and uneasily; still sore is the recent laparoscopic incision. As he bends, he still cringes at the soreness emanating from the right side of his abdomen. This sting of a scar slows Joe's progress; before the war he felt he was strong. He winces now as he lifts his hulking figure and the movement triggers throbbing in his head from dilated blood vessels. This is the payment for the pints he drank four hours ago to seal his drowsiness. Creeping from the room, Joe merges into the cloudy London night.

Even at this fathomless time before 3.00 am the city still has its own rhythm. Night buses transport nocturnal workers; black taxis shuttle dazed drunks; the vagrant homeless litter the streets that Joe traverses. Meandering away from the barracks and along Birdcage Walk, he passes under prevalent prying eyes of close circuit cameras. They peer with intent, scrutinising every seeming detail of his steps, just as the determined RMP are searching still into those responsible for death of the boy who died thousands of miles away.

The accusations are seeping into all areas of Joe's life. Rumours of the investigation have spread round the battalion and inquisitive eyes of other soldiers peer at him. Well-meaning lads from his platoon launch a tirade of dumb questions that he's tired of answering. Over drinks other Guardsmen lark around, playing sport with the charges.

'What's going on here lads?' Joe says joining a discussion.

'Yer fucking killed someone, Joe, like? What happened?' a lad jokes with a hurrah over a pint.

'Now then, shut the fuck up, will ya?' Joe lobs back.

'Oh, c'mon Joe you fucking killed him, din' ya?' says someone else, with a laugh of macho patriotic pride and an echo of the RMP officer's probing.

'Shut up yer dickheads.' But protests are in vain as the drunken joshing morphs into song, a twisted melody.

'Oh Joe's going down in the morning; Joe's going down in the morning.' The soldier's chorus becomes a drinking chant. 'Come on. We're only messing with you,' they say, mock coddling their comrade.

But beneath the crushing weight of words hides Joe's self-contained anguish. In his mind, he rinses over and over the life of the Iraqi boy, a kid from a family and seen last by the water's edge. An unremitting worm cuts deep in his mind and whispers reminded of uncertainty, conviction of accusations, and second-guessing guilt over an Arab face he cannot forget.

Joe continues through the city night, between damp rain-coated streets and low-hanging overcast skies auguring the imminent cold of winter. His route takes him under the shadows of Westminster, passing the Gothic Abbey, in sight of the Elizabeth Tower and the Parliament that sent him to war. Sleepless seething anger fuels a search for an all-night off-licence that sells drink to help sedate the memories.

At the morning parade, Joe is dressed and weary, giving the appearance of a tough soldier. Yet shattered from the night, he stumbles as he attempts unsteadily to stand-to. Joe's head spins as he concentrates while the inspecting sergeant walks the line of soldiers. The sergeant, Docherty, pauses, regarding Joe with unnatural disdain.

'McCleary, get to my office now.'

Moments later Docherty erupts in a tirade.

'You stink of booze,' he yells. 'Who are you representing? The Irish Guards! And here you're stinking of drink in the morning?'

Somewhere in Joe's brain, a valve of pressure and anger releases. There is defiant disregard, carelessness and fatigue he can no longer fight.

'Do us a favour, fuck off!' Joe says loudly, contempt out of control, turning shoulders to walk away.

'Get back in this office,' Sergeant Docherty shouts back.

Joe looks back over his left shoulder and stares at Docherty, a soldier who didn't tour Iraq and doesn't understand. 'You have no fucking idea,' he spits through bared teeth. 'I don't even wanna to fucking live now you fucking dickhead.'

From out of nowhere, Sergeant Ferguson appears nearby. The outburst stuns the sergeant. Intervening, Fergie yells. 'Calm. Down. Now!' Fergie seethes. 'Calm the fuck down, Joe! You're in trouble.'

Joe's outburst ripples out and up through the chain of command. Senior officers consider his case, mull over the ongoing investigation about what happened in Iraq. They offer little. No solutions for the sleeplessness and the ill-tempered troublesome outbursts.

'Send him home,' they decide. 'He's not in a fit state, send him home. Let him go.'

A couple of days later Joe's called to the office of Major MacMullen. A decision has been made, he says, this blighted investigation a strain on them all.

'Look Joe, we don't know what we're going to do here,' he says paternally.

'I don't wanna stay,' Joe admits blankly. 'I'm not really sleeping, or nothing, sir. I can't keep fucking freaking out.' Joe has no understanding of how to cope with the tidal wave of depression.

'I just can't focus on anything,' his words drained of emotion, or desire and are blank as emulsion.

'Okay, let's get you home for a while,' MacMullen suggests. 'Just go home until the investigation is sorted out.'

Joe leaves for home with wounds of disgrace and scars of what he has seen and knows.

Chapter 16

Home

Joe was glad to be heading home, a soldier with some respect and a bit of admiration as a senior guardsman. It was February 2003 and over recent weeks he'd polished his skills to perfection at the barracks in Germany, the infantry making themselves mentally ready and physically strong with fitness up and training in the worst of winter. With the Irish Guards on the brink of deployment, Joe got a long weekend on leave to return to Bootle. Already on the way to Iraq was the advance Royal Naval task force who had left for the Gulf in January, headed by the HMS Ark Royal aircraft carrier with some 4,000 Marines. The UK's defence secretary had announced that more than 26,000 British soldiers had been sent to the Middle East; Joe would be joining them, part of a planned 45,000 pairs of British boots on the ground. It far exceeded the number of troops who went into the Gulf in 1991. The British would join the 120,000 American military personnel, hungry warriors ready for an action that was up in the air but never in doubt.

Joe's plane descended over England's tapestry of damp vibrant greens, yet the country was woven through with the immediacy of fear: the nation was on high alert after an alleged terror threat had targeted Heathrow Airport. Papers advertised propaganda of police trucks and army tanks around the airport's perimeter. British intelligence warned of a probable terrorist strike on civilian planes. It was said to be a threat 'on the scale of September 11'. Hundreds of troops were drafted and tanks sent to patrol against the warning of a major missile strike on an airliner. But as Joe hurtled back towards Bootle, a different warning ran through his mind. His company commander had admonished the young infantrymen about their behaviour. 'If anyone gets arrested drunk or anything else, you'll be fined.' Or worse – no one wanted to risk severe discipline and forfeit being part of the fight they had trained for: taking the terrorist battle to the enemy.

As Joe's taxi snaked its way towards familiar streets and sights a new emotion rose, the thrill of anticipation at returning home. Liverpool's St John's Beacon, the Radio City Tower, soared 452ft above the conglomerate of buildings as the city receded into the rear-view. The car carrying him home came closer to the suburbs and Joe swelled high with elation and pride. The town of Bootle had stagnated but he'd moved on. A directionless teenager once, now a 20-year-old soldier in the Irish Guards bound soon for war. Joe knew what he was doing and where he was going. He was focused and intent upon the upcoming battle to bring liberation to Iraq.

Joe's childhood home's house key was tightly clenched inside his thick fist. It was still kept as a token to return any time. The rush of excitement surged. He readied to surprise his mum whom he'd missed during his long months away. For a short while the soldier was home.

Joe crossed the pavement in quick jubilant strides and slid the key into the door of the terraced house he grew up in. He was greeted by silence of everyone apparently out.

'Hello?' He called, walking inside, peeping to the right into the living room and down the hall in the kitchen.

'Mam?'

He ran up the stairs and stopped dead. On the landing stood Lynn stark naked, her pale white middle-aged body bare and brazen.

'What the fuck?!' Joe slammed his eyes shut. *If only I could squeeze the sight from my memory*, he thought.

'Oh my God, mum, what the fuck are you doing?' Shock and embarrassment still burned his synapses.

'Son what are you doing home?' said Lynn brightly, grabbing a towel.

'I can never open my eyes again!' From beyond closed eyelids Joe heard his mum erupt into laughter. He took a blindsided step backward and lost his footing on the stairs. Legs floundered beneath him. Clumsily Joe fell down half a dozen stairs. Above, Lynn's laughter became a howl.

'Joe! You okay?' she called down.

'No, I'm not fucking okay,' He yelled. 'You can't ever take that sight away from me! I'm gonna be scarred now!' He hauled himself up from an awkward heap on the bottom step.

'What are you doing here?' Lynn asked again.

'What are you doing walking around the house with no clothes on?'

'Just open your eyes.'

'I'm never opening them again! Not until you put some clothes on!'

Joe ambled into the living room and slumped on to the sofa, rubbing his side. Lynn reappeared, now dressed in a robe.

'Well no one was in and I didn't realise you'd turn up!'

'Not even this fucking war that I'm going to will take that sight away!' Joe explained.

'Y'are? Ah, son. Come here,' said Lynn, hugging him and asking what she already knew.

'Iraq?'

'We're going. Looks like we're flying out next week. And when I get out there Mum, there's no radio contact, probably no phones. No nothing.' In saying these words, Joe prepared his mum, as if anything ever could.

A day later, in the background of the McCleary's front room, a colour television danced a flickering, half-ignored wallpaper of current affairs. The screen's glowing hue recounted the build-up and the mounting case for inevitable war – and the marching case against.

From New York and New South Wales, anti-war protestors had 'disrobed to disarm'. Women shed their clothes and lay nude upon a grassy knoll end to end, feet to head they lay, arrayed as human letters to spell out 'No War' as they were photographed from above. The war-angry women in the Australian beach town of Byron Bay said they were 'bearing witness by baring all' to protest Australian troops and RAAF fighter squadrons deployed with American forces as part of the Coalition. These Aussie girls were following American women who'd done the same and got nude and bald below to form the words 'No Bush', spelt out in pale female flesh. But it was Blair who had been caught with his pants down in making his dodgy case for war.

In late January of 2003, American President Bush confidently addressed his Congress with claims he said were from his British counterpart. 'The British government has learned that Saddam Hussein recently sought significant quantities of uranium from Africa ... He clearly has much to hide ... The dictator of Iraq is not disarming. To the contrary; he is deceiving ...'

There was deception, but it was in the administrations of America and Britain. Blair presented his latest Iraq dossier 'Its Infrastructure of Concealment, Deception and Intimidation', a Downing Street production. He declared that his government and security were not 'making it up. It is the intelligence that we are receiving and we are passing it on to people.' The new dossier was even referred to by America's Secretary of State, as he reluctantly made the case to the UN that Saddam was in breach of UN Resolution 1441 and military action was justified. Yet days later, the veil was removed and the truth revealed that this 'dodgy dossier' was plagiarised from an American student's thesis paper, facts cherry-picked by middle-grade British civil servants. A tale of an Emperor's New Clothes and Blair and Bush were the two weavers fabricating facts to create not a suit of clothes but a dossier of accusations against emperor Saddam. Iraq's tyrant emperor was televised on British screens, as he sold his own version of reality to the public:

> There is only one truth and therefore I tell you as I have said on many occasions before that Iraq has no weapons of mass destruction whatsoever. We challenge anyone who claims that we have to bring forward any evidence and present it to public opinion … These weapons do not come in small pills that you can hide in your pocket.

The UN chief weapons inspector, Hans Blix, had done the Security Council bidding but found little. There were no 'smoking guns' only a 12,000-page weapons declaration that was incomplete and the discovery of twelve empty warheads designed to carry chemical weapons. Regardless, America would not be bogged down by a quagmire of Security Council Resolutions and by the US's side would be Britain. Meanwhile, a leaked government intelligence report revealed: 'Iraq has "no current link" with al-Qaeda. There are in fact 'fundamental ideological and religious differences between al-Qaeda and Saddam Hussein's Ba'ath regime.'

A week later, the timely terror alert had tried to strike fear with rumours of a strike upon a Heathrow flight. 'The threat is real,' Prime Minister Blair reminded Britain. In days, Hans Blix's UN report of 14 February told that Iraq possessed a couple of illegal missiles: Samoud-2 rockets that exceed the maximum range of 150km set down in the 1991 Gulf war ceasefire agreement, but otherwise Iraq had complied with the team of weapons inspectors. The final report was a Valentine to Saddam and threw into disarray British and American plans to draft a new UN resolution that mandated military action.

'MAKE TEA NOT WAR' was written on a placard of an anti-war protester, one of a million whose cries mandated that their government listen. It was the biggest demonstration in British history and one of many to 'Stop the war' around the world. Up to 100 million people converged in 600 cities in 60 countries. In London, a million people on a Saturday marched through the streets of Westminster, past the Gothic Abbey, in sight of the Elizabeth Tower and the Parliament who they prayed would listen to their protest against the war in Iraq.

Blair said he did 'listen to the thousands that marched on Saturday … There is no rush to war … We waited twelve years and then went through the United Nations. It is now three months since we gave Saddam what we called a "final opportunity".' Blair urged protestors: 'Talk to those Iraqi exiles, talk to those who have seen their husbands, their fathers, their brothers tortured and killed.' Onwards the machine of war moved, a coalition of deception as

Bush and Blair pushed their country to the cusp of war as they wagered on votes from their fractured cabinets.

The McCleary family were all together, united around the Saturday afternoon Channel 4 Racing where bets were placed. Grouped around the television were Lynn and Carlos, Joe's Portuguese stepdad, and David, Joe's brother. They were joined by Nan Maria and Granddad Arthur Hartley, headed over from their home in Southport. Arthur entered the front room and clasped the back of Joe's head with his big, leather-like hands.

'Now then, Joe, lad,' said Arthur. 'You do us proud, you do.'

The 66-year-old man, still fond of stories, launched into a reassuring tale from twenty-two years in the Merchant Navy then turned back to the televised racing.

'This is the ticket that's gonna be a winner!' Arthur assured his grandson with an encouraging look and wrinkle-dappled smile. Arthur was always a betting man and had an equine vision for their winnings if the horse was first past the line. Granddad Hartley would buy his own horse and the beast would be named 'Hartley's Dream' and run in its own races. Arthur would take Joe to Aintree Racecourse and then both would watch the horse make them rich all over again.

'Hartley's Dream! He'll run for us and make us millions, Joe!' Arthur promised as partly deaf Nan Maria sat on the sofa.

Joe's grandparents were from the generation that fought and remade a new world. Arthur was from an era of polite men; Joe never heard him swear, born into a world of purpose that fought for peace. Now Arthur was in his pension years, his Ford Mondeo dented from unartful driving, his in-car cassette still played songs from old. His favourite was American Cold War hero, Johnny Cash, who'd crooned of 'the twilight colors falling, And the evening laying shadows' as the pop star reflected on his memories spent as a Morse code operator in 1950s' Germany. When Joe was younger he'd teased his granddad with the grunge of early 1990s' Britpop pumped out from the radio and received Arthur's defiant response: 'Get that stuff off.' And then Cash would croon his soulful ballad all the way from Southport back to Bootle.

The Sunday after the race was run, Arthur shook Joe's hand firmly and pressed in his palm a betting slip from the day before.

'You go and get that son before you go back.'

'Oh, all right Granddad, yeah. Thanks.' Joe replied.

'There's only a tenner on it, just you have another bet with it.'

'Oh, thanks Granddad,' the young soldier replied.

With goodbyes said, a good lad set off to war. He walked through town towards Lime Street Station and headed inside William Hill to redeem his

Granddad's betting slip. With the stash in hand, he counted the winnings then frowned as he calculated the odds on the lucky horse.

Outside in the high street he picked up a payphone and slid coins inside.

'It's Joe, Granddad.'

'Now then, son,' Arthur replied.

'I took in the bet from Saturday. There was sixty-eight quid you won on that horse, Granddad.' Joe told him.

'I know how much was on it, son.' The old man had known, worked it out. 'I want you to keep it. You're going back, now spend it. Buy yourself something at the airport.'

The corner of Joe's eyes moistened at his granddad's generosity.

'Thank you, Granddad. I'll try and write to you from over there.'

'Aye. You do. I'll write to you as well. I'm proud of you son, just be safe,' Arthur Hartley said in farewell.

Joe hung up the phone and understood why people go AWOL. He boarded the train to take him to the glories of the battlefield, heartbroken to be leaving as he clutched his winnings.

Chapter 17

The War Comes Home

The army has cut its losses with Joe. That's how he feels, looking out of the window of the slowing train carriage as it loses momentum and crawls into Lime Street Station. He slowly gets up, achingly tired as he reaches the overhead shelf for his bulging and weighty army pack to throw over his shoulder. He carries, too, the burden of both the heavy memories of Iraq nearly some eighteen months ago and the recent accusations. He steps on to the platform and walks down the concourse against the traffic of dense clusters of hustling crowds that fill him with claustrophobia. The giddiness of palpitation threatens to take hold until the mass of bodies thins out and then familiar faces help return his heart rate to normal rhythm. Beneath the wide metal arches and curved glass ceiling of Liverpool's railway station Lynn and Carlos stand waiting near an information sign.

'Joe …' his mum says, hugging him close as Carlos clasps the bag from his stepson.

Next to the information sign are three pathetic looking palm trees, looking out of place so far from the Middle East. They're reminiscent of the tree-lined streets of Basra. Joe turns away to leave, heading down the station steps.

'Tell me son, what's going on?' asks Carlos once they are home, his nervousness evident even through his Barranquenho accent. It's over thirty years since Carlos called the hill in Portugal his home; now his concern is paternal and deep for the stepson who fought for his adopted home.

On the sanctuary of the living room sofa Joe takes his mum and stepdad through everything. He's familiar now with the recounting; from the military police scratching at the wounds of memory. He tells his mum of the accusations he is facing and the interrogation by the SIB.

'Everything they were saying about me is false,' Joe says almost pleadingly. 'And they were like telling me I was gonna go to prison, d'yer know what I mean? And they fucking, they fucking said they were gonna make sure I was gonna rot and then I was telling them like, "No, no …"'

When he's done, Carlos's distress has elevated; *Zangar-se*, the Portuguese for getting angry.

'Come on. Let me get a flight for you to Portugal.' Carlos says.

'Just go.' He continues. 'Just go now. We'll leave now.'

Joe remains passive, defeat and reality trapping him, despite his stepdad's vigour.

'They're going to pin you down,' Carlos goes on, misusing the phrase. 'They're going to blame you for this and use you as a scapegoat. I'm not having it; I'm not letting them do this to you, Joe.'

'Yeah, but they took me passport off me, Carlos. The military police. I'm not going anywhere,' he replies, meek and listless.

In the terraced house of Joe's youth, Lynn and her family bear the private agony, but 2 miles away, to the east of Bootle in Walton, another mother's torment is vividly, violently public.

Bootle's neighbour Walton is a district that, like Liverpool, keeps its ties to the water. Walton is known for its 'ship roads', five streets named after Cunard ships, once headquartered in Liverpool, and its ocean liners: Mauretania, Saxonia, Ivernia, Sylvania and Lusitania. Lusitania, the passenger ship which borrowed its name from the Roman province that's now Portugal, and the boat that was torpedoed in the Atlantic, 1,198 drowning souls perishing and propelling North America into the Great War. Walton, with its road that still remembers the sunken ship, has a hospital, once a workhouse, which was the birthplace of Beatle Paul McCartney, is now a district known for death. Walton, also home to Liverpool's prison, is a place now known for a kidnapped prisoner dying in distant Iraq.

Terrorist victim Elizabeth Frances Bigley endures three weeks of hell climaxing in the devastation of her son's execution. Kenneth John Bigley, a Liverpudlian known as Ken, 62 and a civil engineer, one of the lucky contractors who saw opportunity in Iraq. It was private pain that pushed Ken Bigley to the life of a wandering expatriate, seeking contracting work overseas after making an impossible decision. Bigley's eldest son had been knocked down while cycling and the 17-year-old was left clinging to life in a coma, with a prognosis that he was never to wake up. It left his father, Ken Bigley, to make the fatal final decision. A decade spent in the Middle East left Bigley over-confident, but this contract to Gulf Services Co. was his final job, working in reconstruction to help provide for his upcoming retirement just three weeks away.

'Why are you here? It's dangerous, there are kidnappers,' asked a Baghdadi neighbour of Ken and his two American colleagues Jack Hensley and Eugene Armstrong.

'I'm not afraid,' Ken cockily replied with a wave of his arm. 'You only die once.'

Days later, Bigley, Hensley and Armstrong's local house guard fled in the face of militia threats that foreshadowed the three men's imminent abduction. Just after dawn on 16 September 2004, the electricity failed in the men's grey two-storey house. One of the three men emerged from the house to investigate what seemed like a power cut and to restart their generator, only to be ambushed. Terror descended as ten masked abductors stormed the house and dragged the Western men into a waiting van.

The three men's reappearance is two days later, lined up with eyes wrapped in tattered white blindfolds, in a video as captives of the Tawhid and Jihad group (Unity and Holy War). The first to face slaughter is Eugene Armstrong. The Jihadi group's Jordanian-born leader, Abu Musab al-Zarqawi, on whose head is a $25m bounty, clutches the American by the hair and slices his throat till all hope is severed. Jack Hensley is next, butchered on his birthday by killers who upload their brutal evidence of the decapitation to the Internet.

There is the dread. But Ken Bigley is seen again, alive on a video where he is attired in a bright orange jumpsuit, a mocking reference to Arab captives at Guantánamo Bay, Cuba. He pleads to his prime minister in vain.

'I need you to help me now, Mr Blair. You are the only person on God's earth that I can speak to … Please help me. Please help me.

'I also now realise how much the Iraqi people have suffered. The Iraqis have suffered, the Iraqi children who haven't got their mothers. It's not fair.

'A child wants his mother. It's of no use keeping a mother in prison, no use whatsoever, ever. Let the mothers go back to their children. Give these people a chance.

Please, I beg you.'

In response, a British SAS team is despatched to Baghdad, standing by for a rescue while messages fall from the heavens over the Iraqi city. Fifty thousand leaflets drift down upon the wealthy al-Mansour district of Baghdad, the British Foreign Office begging for information on Bigley's whereabouts, while the man himself is seen again begging for his life a week later.

'Tony Blair is lying,
lying when he says he's negotiating.
My life is cheap.
He doesn't care about me.'

Ken's declarations are fed through the Internet, mouthpiece of the fanatics and amplified around the world through web browsers and TV screens. The feeble man is seen hunched in a cage, beast-like placed by beasts. Bigley is exhausted, his face tattered, worn and haggard; his body pale and gaunt, his voice feeble and weak.

Down the road from the McCleary household, the trauma dragged on for Bigley's loved ones in Liverpool, the latest video withheld from Ken's 86-year-old mother by fearful family members. At Friday prayers at the Al-Rahma Mosque, The Mosque of Mercy, in Toxteth, the imam absolved his faith of atrocity and called all true adherents to compassion. Hundreds of Christians joined a candlelit vigil at St Mary's Church in Bootle, praying in vain that the Divine hand is stronger than Arab vengeance. More flakes of paper fell from above in Iraq, far away from worshippers in Liverpool, littering another 100,000 paper leaflets from the British consulate in Baghdad. They were miles from their target; the captive is kept in Latifiya, a Sunni Muslim town some 22 miles south-west of Baghdad, and a stronghold of the growing insurgency seeking to rid the world of infidels and their country of its occupiers.

Kenneth Bigley's last day is a hope ruined and a brutal display of savagery. He manages a brief escape attempt but is recaptured on barren farmland. Six men, their faces hideously hidden in black balaclavas then parade Bigley in front of their cameras, assembling in front of black and gold sunburst banner. The men wear muted black or dark green tops and grey bottoms, clutching Kalashnikovs. Below them, helpless now, sitting with knees bent on the ground is the bright splash of orange, Ken their Western hostage bound with arms behind his back. After spouting their fanatical propaganda and concluding 'the sentence of execution against this hostage', three men hold Ken down and one man attends a knife to his throat. Crouched vulnerable and foetal-like, Ken Bigley's life ends in atrocity, a bloody decapitation with his head held aloft in a blood-stain of victory.

Within the closed curtains of a Victorian terrace house that borders Bootle, an 86-year-old mother with heart trouble now dealing with heartbreak. Death in the land of the tree of life; another nightmare sent from Iraq.

Since the second arrest and his return home to Bootle, Joe's night terrors intensify. Submerged under sleep's darkness he sees repeated flashbacks of the night of the attack at the college in Basra, hears the rattle of gunfire and the grim sounds of the lads who had been shot in the ambush. Dim lights seem to strobe on and off with cracks like thunderbolts as bangs penetrate the dreamland sky. Sinking further into this estranged world, the choppy transition of one place and another. Joe is running, running, screaming for help amid dirty Middle Eastern wasteland. Then he jolts into consciousness, breathing fast, chest pumping, eyes wet and sore.

'Son, what's going on?' he hears through the dim cobwebs of waking.

'Aye, nothing Mum. Just a bad dream.'

'You were screaming, Joe. Sounds like you were thrashing about,' comes his mum's concerned reply from outside his attic bedroom.

'I was? Sorry, Mum.'

Joe wakes always disorientated but also angry, desperately clutching a pillow. On the wall next to his bed are cracks and dents, bits of plaster have crumbled from where his fists pounded. He lies for a while, his eyes stinging as if he's been crying in his sleep. Rest is elusive and he rolls around agitated on his bed. He doesn't want to shut his eyes again. *A nightmare is fuck all compared to what I'm seeing*, he thinks.

Joe can't find the words to express to his mum what he's seeing when he sleeps. Instead he drinks to take the edge off and then until he passes out. The more he drinks, the more fitful is sleep, the more vivid the memories. Lynn awakens to screams that come from up the stairs atop of which is Joe's room. She enters Joe's room and holds him while he, still in the clutches of night, tries to fight her off.

Lynn quickly becomes worried for her son. Still working at a local hospital, she calls a GP, telling him some of what her son is going through. Joe attends the appointment but it's as though the doctors can't touch it, don't seem to know what to say to him. They prescribe sleeping pills, but that feels like the last thing Joe wants. Enough cans of Stella Artois take the edge off; it's as though the anxiety is something he's feeding. It becomes hard to have a day without; hard to stop the drinking because it's like a comforting friend.

A short walk from home is The Queen's Hotel, though it's actually the local pub where Joe sees some of the friendly locals he remembers drinking with from before he left for war. The pub has been around a long time, having opened around 1886 when old William Spence was granted a licence. The public house stands at the junction of Bootle's Knowsley Road and has long endured here. When Bootle was attacked during the air raids of the Second World War this street was heavily bombed. Buildings like Scots Bakery were damaged, but its neighbour, the Queen's Pub as it was then, survived the assault.

'Alright Granddad,' Joe says, pleased to see Arthur Hartley inside.

'Joe, I've just had a pint and I was looking over my shoulder to see where you was,' his granddad says.

'I'm here now, Granddad.'

'Now look there,' the old man says pointing to a cluttered notice board. 'I put a notice up on the board when you went over there. It says, "Single lad in the army looking for a pen pal to write to him in Iraq."'

Joe grabs a pint and sits on the stool beside the bar and listens to his granddad.

'You've got three replies, Son,' says Hartley with a wry smirk. 'One was a 69-year-old woman. One was a 70-year-old. And this other one was 21, blond hair, absolutely gorgeous. Name's Harry!' he says with a cackle.

Joe laughs, thinks of the letter that Arthur had sent him when he was in Kuwait and how many times he reread that letter.

Now Joe's Granddad and his Nan Maria are close by, living in the same three-level house because his aged nan is sick. It is tight quarters, all the family living together but it is the way Joe likes it. Everyone gets on and the closeness is what he loves. When he's not at the Queen's, Joe sits at home watching old Westerns with his granddad. It passes the time, with his life in turmoil and distracts from the temptation to dwell upon having been charged and how he could soon be going to prison for something. That's a prospect that terrorises and haunts him with anxiety. When he sleeps he doesn't want to wake up even though what he sees at night always terrifies him.

Trapped, immobile, Joe's drowning in a bath and hair emerges again from the murky, tepid water. It's everywhere, dark and damp afro-like hair, at least that how it seems to Joe. And beyond he sees the face. The boy's. His eyes. Hands like tentacles yet almond-coloured and Arab-skinned, claw at Joe's face. A force starts to pull Joe below the surface. The hands are what drag him down, pulling him under. He tries frantically to pull the fingers off his face. The sensation of choking and being consumed by the agonising blanket of water. And to the sound of his own screaming, Joe snaps awake. His face stings with scratch marks where Joe's clawed his face and cut beneath his eyes with his own nails. His hands shake. From now on he will wear gloves to bed. Roused, Joe looks out of his upstairs window on to the familiar Bootle night.

Chapter 18

Arrival

Joe's first look at the Middle East was through the porthole window of a passenger plane. The army had converted a Lockheed TriStar 500 jumbo jet into a troop transporter that carried not holidaymakers or business travellers but hardy military muscle. After Joe's long weekend leave in Bootle, he'd returned to his regiment in Müenster, Germany, where they finished preparation for deployment, packed kits and flew out from Hanover. Challenger tanks, Warrior troop carriers and other heavy equipment had gone ahead, shipped on via the Suez Canal, and they'd meet up in Kuwait to get them fully ready for battle. For now, Joe and about 260 of the infantry peered out of what felt like a civilian airliner, the difference being that they were accompanied by two RAF fighter jets. After about five hours they came in on approach to Kuwait International Airport.

The region below was shrouded in night and a tension of uncertainty. Kuwait, a country smaller than Wales, was a solitary pocket of compliance as a staging point for war after Turkey's refusal to allow access to a front from the north. Instead, the once-invaded land of Kuwait would now be the base for invaders, who made use of the nation's strategic placement bordering the Persian Gulf and Iraq's south. Kuwait's sandy Arabian deserts had been settled less than 400 years earlier, the country's advancement down to the discovery of massive quantities of oil reserves in 1938. Today the civilisation of Kuwait City was marked by pinprick lines of amber and dotted white lights. That was how they appeared from above to Joe as the plane decelerated. In the cabin, 'fasten seatbelt' signs lit up as the plane banked and made its approach. Through the aisles, lads grappled with snaking belt buckles as they laughed loudly and joked crudely, though some soldiers were pensive at the approaching unknown. The long straight runway loomed ever closer until a brief scorch of rubber on concrete and force of braking against inertia told Joe they had arrived.

Kuwait heightened the senses and disorientation assaulted before Joe had even fully disembarked the plane. Along with the rest of the company, he quickly collected meagre hand luggage, filed through the fuselage to stairs that led off the plane and breathed in the dust-filled Arab air for the first time. Dizzying and terrifying sounds loudly strafed his ears.

ربكاالله,ربكاالله

Al-laa-hu Akbar, Al-laa-hu Akbar

Night chill and terror descended as noise droned around from some far distant background. Joe stood on the bottom step of the plane, awake to a fearful reality of the enveloping sound, its ghastly unfamiliar cadence. Moments before, he'd been with the lads, punching each other in the arm and enthusing, 'Go on, boys! We're gonna go out there! We're going to war.' Now he heard the foreign reality of a muezzin, appointed by a mosque to project his voice by loudspeaker. The caller to prayer chanted out, commanding to the area's many Muslims the 'Adhan', to listen. After a pause, its unsettling rhythms returned.

اللهلاالهالالانادهشا

Ash-ha-du al-laa ilaaha il-lal-laah

Joe had never before heard these Arabic alien sounds; its melody was lost on him, the calls to worship more bizarre and eerie than any Bootle church bell he knew. The evening Salat al-'isha, the صلاةالعشاء, only began after total darkness had arrived. It was sometime after 7.00 pm here, an hour ahead of Germany, and already pitch black. He descended into darkness away from the plane, across pale concrete, almost shell-shocked before a single round had been fired. Joe put his army-issue shemagh over his mouth as a cold breeze whipped desert dust, and he followed the lads in from the plane towards the airport buildings. After the strangeness of the sounds, he was confronted by signs, printed in Arabic, its ancient calligraphy indecipherable to Joe. An Arab soldier stood nearby, clutching a gun and close to a static luggage belt was a thin bearded man in a white dishdash gown. Joe looked over his shoulder and saw some of the rest of the lads following behind, taking in this unknown world.

The Americans had arrived first. Their war machine, always oiled, was well into preparations for the conflict and they had set up their State-named camps: Camp New York, Camp Pennsylvania and Camp New Jersey among them. The most northernmost of the cluster of camps was Camp Udari, an army airfield 15 miles from the Iraqi border. This desertopolis measured a mile and a half around, its fortress-like perimeter was made of ramps of sand berms and coils of barbed wire. The base had been planned since the previous summer and sandy ground broken in November 2002. Bulldozers turned over the desert earth to pave an asphalt runway, while plywood floors were installed with sandy-coloured tents hoisted and clamshell aircraft hangars erected. Now Camp Udari was home to the V Corps troops from the Germany-based 11th Aviation Regiment, the 2nd Squadron, 6th Cavalry Regiment and an apache helicopter unit. Crews of army construction and logistics teams were still building, ready for the arrival of the prestigious 101st Airborne Division. Work continued to accommodate 200 more American choppers, a fuel tank farm and a runway long enough to land their C-130 cargo planes.

Coalition presence had quickly transformed this region. Columns of American Humvees that seemed endless were arriving and so too were lines of British Land Rovers and Bedford trucks, clogging up the Kuwaiti roads and belching dust. To the western edge of camp were tent cities that were to become home to the Irish Guards and other regiments. They looked to Joe like big marquee tents, their long canvas structures, which would each sleep twenty-five, mostly men, each lying on the sand-strewn floor bedded down with their rifles. Alongside, the soldiers laid down their Bergen rucksacks containing their meagre possessions: a single uniform, a pair of shorts, beret and helmet. The most important thing the soldiers carried became their respirators. Still fresh in Joe's mind were the videos he'd seen of bodies bent double, victims of Saddam's gassing of the northern Kurdish people. These were weapons the infantry fully expected the dictator's army to deploy. The face hugging lifesaver hung on their hips constantly, an intimate bedfellow.

In Kuwait, the troops continued their training and waited for the rest of their equipment to arrive and the inevitable pronouncement of war. Early in the days after the soldiers' arrival in Kuwait, their commanders came round and confiscated mobile phones from those who still had them. Some people had kept their phones but just snapped their SIM cards in half at the airport before they left. For the infantrymen preparing to fight, this drove home the sense of isolation in this desert purgatory in which they waited; this tense holding pattern for war, already unofficially underway. During the last days of February, American pilots and their British counterparts in RAF Tornados conducted bombing runs over the border in Iraq, targeting Saddam's Soviet-designed ground-based surface-to-air missile, communications system near Basra, and three mobile air defence early-warning radars and a surface-to-air missile system near An Nasiriyah, south-west of Baghdad. It was part of the undeclared war, using the enforcement of no-fly rules to soften up the country for the anticipated invasion.

Joe's only tangible link to home was a letter he received from his granddad, telling him he'd put up a poster up in the pub looking for pen pals and reminding him to come home safely. Joe also had a small and torn paper prayer card that his Nan had given him and which he kept in his backpack; a frayed artefact that bore a Catholic blessing to keep him safe from harm.

From the government and senior army leaders it seemed as though the supplies they sent to keep the soldiers safe were sorely lacking. Within days, ships arrived into Kuwaiti City port after their month-long journey through the Suez Canal, Red Sea and into Gulf waters to reveal the inadequate state of preparation. A whole battalion's worth of armour plates, enough for over 800 soldiers, had been placed in a shipping container that had been lost en route. The soldiers were told they'd have to share out the available plates when they rolled out into Iraqi fields of fire. Warrior infantry carriers and Challenger main battle tanks each rolled off to be readied for desert action with guns mounted, but the boxes of ammunition were half the expected and needed amount. A third of the men didn't have the full NCB suits they would need if and when Saddam unleashed his arsenal. Across the board the logistics people, and company quartermaster sergeants (CQMS) especially, found the situation a 'cluster fuck'. Some of the officers were frustrated by the seeming lack of leadership by Whitehall suits sending troops out from the comfort of their cushy and expensive office seats in London. Some of the NCOs were frustrated by not even having properly fitting trousers, Joe was irritated by his backside hanging out of his desert combats and the situation becoming a running joke with another, very tall, soldier asking the CQMS almost on a daily basis, 'Have you got my trousers yet?'

The company had to get creative so Dave, one of the supply guys, had an idea. There were piles of desert combats left over from the previous autumn's BATUS exercise in Canada that were going to be burnt so they managed to 'misappropriate' the pile for use in Iraq. Tony Charles, No. 1 Company CQMS, also had some desert uniforms that he'd forgotten to send back after the training of Saif Sareea so they used those too. During Saif Sareea's training some of the troops got foot rot after their boots melted in the heat and the same looked likely to happen here, glue becoming unstuck in the temperatures. Captain Niall Brennan also lacked correctly fitting footwear so his father bought him boots with which to march into battle. Joe, being one of the tallest, had to buy his own chest rig, which clipped on to his vest instead of having one on his waist, from an Internet military shop. Logistics drove the military effort and this long-planned war felt hastily orchestrated. Amid a scrutinising public, British politicians wanted to avoid the appearance of inevitability so avoided bulk ordering quantities of supplies from Asia and didn't order the quantities of uniforms needed, since it might signal to the public the solid intention to invade. The government saved face but expected its military to make do and carry on.

The army did that and achieved incredible feats. In the Gulf War of 1991 it took twenty-two weeks to move the UK force to the Middle East; in 2003 they did it in just ten. More than 2,000 vehicles on 62 ships were transported, including 600 armoured fighting vehicles, offloaded by Port and Maritime Regiments. More than 5,000 Territorial Army and regular reservists, the largest number since the Suez Crisis in 1956, were called up for operational duties and shipped out to the Gulf. They were all fed by military ration packs or by quickly assembled kitchens run by the Royal Logistics Corps.

Joe and the other infantrymen spent time 'desertising' the newly arrived tanks and Warrior troop carriers for battle. They fitted the Challenger tanks with composite protective shielding of Chobham armour. This secret formula layering of ceramic, nylon micromesh and titanium melded together into a tough sandwich of hardened plates. It would protect the troops, but exactly what Saddam had in his weapons stockpile remained as much a mystery as the proprietary make-up of Chobham plating. All the troops could do to prepare was the relentless routine of desert training.

Out in the isolation of desert, sound carried and the thunder of artillery rounds from the Udairi firing range were heard from 8 miles away. The surrounding area of the Udairi Range Complex was largely uninhabited, except for a few nomadic tribesmen who raised camels, goats, and sheep and whose normality the soldiers shattered. Occasionally a bewildered Bedouin looked over at the mass of American tanks practising targets in the sand 'or British sharpshooting snipers refining the accuracy of their rounds. Amid the creeping heat, the infantry spent time at practice with their SA-80 5.5mm rifles and the General Purpose Machine Gun that always made Joe think of John Rambo from the 1980s' action movies. They prepared with attacks on mock bunkers and practised jumping over barbed wire in the deepening intensity of the sun, Joe's first experience of desert training. They spent hours looking for mines left over from the first Gulf War in the Kuwaiti desert, remnants of Saddam's invasion, deadly surprises still waiting to hatch. The soldiers were reminded of basic handling of prisoners, rounding up PoWs, practising the methods they'd use by placing plasticuffs on each another. Joe received rudimentary reminders of Arabic and was given a small booklet on the Geneva Convention to tell them how to deal with PoWs in battle conditions.

When night came, a cooling chill fell upon the region. In the remoteness of desert and removed from the ambience of the urban world, the stars lit up like highly defined glimmers, a sky illuminated brighter than any Joe had ever seen in Bootle. Here in Kuwait, the guardsman felt he could almost pluck a star out and hold it in his hand. Evening was quiet, vacant, a peace before battle, until early dawn and the alien eruption of distant mosque calls.

By mid-March, a desert front pushed temperatures up into the low 40s, the heat becoming intolerable for Joe and Martin McGing, sweltering as they put plates on the outside of their Warrior. The wind quickly picked up as a storm moved, punishing the men with the land. Gusts of 15-20 knots collected up sand and corrosive desert dirt, ground it to dust by powerful wind currents as sharp as if they were blender blades. The circulating mass of whitish-grey assaulted everywhere across the horizon and moved in: nature's rage. This was early for such harsh winds in Kuwait, but the war was to blame. The strong gusts, known there as *Al Sarayat*, usually occurred in April between the cool and hot seasons, but the movement of troops, tanks and other vehicles had disturbed the desert surface and thickened the sandstorm. Joe saw the swirling beast gathering and thrust a set of goggles over his eyes and the dark green shemagh down to cover his nose and mouth. The Kuwaiti sandstorm had reduced visibility to a few feet in an instant. Sand seeped in every crevice, penetrating each orifice, insidious, it played havoc with the eyes and throats of all the soldiers. But the men weren't the concern; instead it was the machines and military gear, from sensitive electronic equipment to helicopter engines and rotors. No company could operate a tank or Warrior without being able to see and navigate. While men in Washington and Whitehall could make a decision to send young lads to attack, Mother Nature's maelstrom could halt their brittle battle plans.

'What is this shit?' McGing yelled amid a cough from sand debris.

'Never seen nothing like it. Back in the Warrior till it passes,' Joe yelled and held up a hand. He could see only a foot length from his face.

'Fucking ridiculous is what it is!' Joe tried to yell to McGing, but his muffled voice was lost in the fabric of his shemagh. He turned and found himself alone and lost as the fierce blizzard of sand and grit shrouded McGing and even the nearby Warrior. Joe had to find and get inside the vehicle to hunker down until the sandstorm passed. He turned but was disorientated and stumbled around lost in the desert.

Chapter 19

Photos

Joe stumbles his way, dizzy and lost through the Mersey's early rising mist. He's woken up in the cells of Bootle's Marsh Lane Police Station and now ambles home. Officers last night put him in here for the second night in a row. He has scrapes on his knuckles and bruises between his ribs from a fight with three nutters he met after the pub shuts for the night. Joe's clothes are creased and his head is thick and aches as though he has the flu, as he walks home with fragments of memories. Joe had taken cocaine and felt like the Hulk; not angry but unstoppable and confident as he wrestled some townies to the ground. He remembers the uniformed boys arriving, bathed in a sea of blue flashes, to separate the scrap. Joe had struggled, thrown fearless threats at the PCs and then after a ride faced the duty sergeant, all pissed off at seeing his face in a cell yet again.

'Walk out here and nothing gets said. Go home. Get yourself some help,' the officer said sourly, followed by a threat to set him up with something worse than drunk and disorderly. 'Or else we'll plant a screwdriver on you.'

After sleeping the morning off at home, Joe emerges in the late afternoon to walk towards Bootle. It's cold and the trees are stark as he heads to the Strand Shopping Centre. With some time back home he'd sifted through his army kit bag and discovered a disposable camera that had sat untouched and undeveloped since his return. He'd taken it in a few days before and now Joe enters Max Spielmann, with its bright blue banner and white letter declaration as 'The Photo Expert.' An adolescent girl with long auburn hair, soft skin and a bright button-up pink shirt takes Joe's return slip then looks for his pictures.

The girl returns, ghost-like pale as she hands the packet of prints over the counter.

'Are you … are you okay, pet?' she asks nervously.

'Yeah,' *What the fuck?* Joe thinks. 'Why?'

The girl looks worried and scared.

'Errr … that's £6.99 please,' she finally says.

Joe hands her the money and heads back into the cold, walking from town with a glance at the plastic wallet of images of Iraq. They give him a weird twisted laugh as he remembers the scenes they show of liberated Iraq and its conquerors.

Joe's mum is home by the time he returns and she's eager to look at the photos. Joe hands them over to her and she flips through the images, one by one, each more quickly than the last. She glares in shock at her son.

'Oh my God son, oh my God,' she says. 'What is this?'

'Oh, they're bodies, them, they're all just dead on top of each other.'

'Fuck, Joe,' says Lynn, incredulous, his mum's jaw almost hitting the ground. 'No.'

'No, they are, Mum.'

'Why, why did you take pictures like this?' she demands. 'Why are you behind them? Like you're posing with an Everton trophy?'

'I don't know. It's what it was like,' Joe says. 'I never shot them all.' Joe's not sure if she thinks he meant the photos or the Iraqis who were all dead.

One photo shows a dead Iraqi man. His eyes have gone and there is barely any skin on his face and there are flies all over him. A second shows Joe lying next to him in a pose straight for the camera. Another shiny image has the dead Iraqi staged with a cigarette in his hand – it had probably been Joe who'd put it in his hands so it looked as though he was having a 'bifter', the Liverpudlian slang for a joint.

Joe's mum goes through a few more and from her reaction he realises that taking the photos is probably not the most professional thing he's done as a soldier.

'Joe, what the fuck?! We can't have these.'

'Why're you … Why're you … I don't know what you see wrong,' says Joe, his mind and sensitivity tainted by his experiences.

Joe hadn't been alone in taking those kinds of photos on tour in Iraq. Four British lads in Osnabruck, Germany, were under investigation for photographing far worse brutalities in Basra. The twisted events took place at a humanitarian aid distribution centre, known to the locals as 'Camp Bread Basket'. Looting was rife at the camp so a regiment of Royal Fusiliers instigated a crackdown with an action nicknamed 'Operation Ali Baba'. The operation took place a week after Joe and the Irish Guards left in May 2003; the British forces rounding up the Iraqis with orders to be tough and 'beast them good'. They did that and more, some soldiers amusing themselves with a bunch of Iraqis. These soldiers photographed each other driving a forklift with a bound and terrified Iraqi suspended from the prongs. Another image portrayed a soldier simulating a punch on a net-covered prisoner. Yet another showed a soldier in his underwear standing on an Iraqi man in a feeble foetal position. And another showed two humiliated Arab men forced naked and simulating sexual acts.

'I won't have those pictures in this house,' says Lynn of Joe's images. The photos of her son and dead Iraqis are a reminder of war she won't have. 'We need to burn them Joe,' she says sternly. She acts immediately. Outside is an old metal bin and she tosses the photos in and uses a lighter to ignite the corner of the packet of pictures. The rectangular images catch fire, smoulder as an orange wave crests across the glossy paper. The photos are another reminder of Iraq, like the flashbacks, that feel almost as bad as the war. Glancing down at the peeling pictures, Joe watches the smoke drift into the cold evening air. *Fucking hell, maybe this was a bit wrong,* Joe thinks.

Joe's the last to leave The Queen's pub that night, wasted and dizzy as he turns down the road to head for home. He makes his way, weaving down the street, pints of Stella and snorts of cocaine seeing off the memories of war that he's fighting. Joe pauses, grabs a cold, rusty drainpipe for support as he arches over and feels the sick rising from his stomach up into his throat as lumpy bile and beer spew out of his mouth to decorate a red brick wall. He spits out the unvomitted chunks and ambles onwards. Finally at the front door, he wavers in uncontrolled circles with the key in his hand struggling to hit his target. He finally plunges it into the lock to let himself in. Pitching left and right he makes his way down the hall to the kitchen, the world careening on its axis. He opens the side cupboard, turns the tap on and holds out a clear pint glass, haphazardly catching some of the plume of cold water. Climbing both flights of stairs to his room in the attic feels a long way. The hyper-energy and confidence he's clung to all night is starting to recede, the nebula of narcotics beginning to fade. Slain by the amount of beer he's consumed, he collapses to his bed sloshing spillage of water, sliding into sleep.

Joe awakes, head throbbing, eyes shedding more tears at all he's seen beneath the surface of night. The accusations, the face of the boy by the canal, the dead and the desperation he saw bleeding on the streets of Basra. He's bitter, raging and weeping. In a convulsion of fury Joe clenches the toppled glass from the carpeted floor. With a hard slam he smashes the glass to his head. It erupts to a shower of glass fragments, jagged shards cutting his skin. The side of his face seeps with blood. Beads of broken glass lodge in his forehead. A crimson stream stains the pillow. The whole of Joe's T-shirt becomes soaked through with blood. At the pressure of the pints, he lets his bladder give way and pisses in the bed. Cut, crying and leaking, Joe clenches his elbows into his chest and rocks himself on his bed, weeping until unconsciousness overtakes again.

Joe comes to with his mum leaning over, soothing a damp cloth on his cuts. She carefully pulls chunks of shattered glass from his scalp.

'Oh, Joe,' she says tenderly.

He's awake, head sore, stomach cramping; all he wants is something to wash away the guilt and the grief, another drink to put him to sleep.

Chapter 20

Big Speeches

The men dreamed of a cold pint amid the climbing heat of Kuwait in mid-March. It was a Monday, St Patrick's Day, and foremost on many of the minds of the infantry was a glass of Guinness to quench their thirsts. Instead the Irish Guards paraded on the dry desert ground of Camp Coyote to celebrate the patron saint, assembled before a US top brass in whose veins flowed Irish-American blood. Lieutenant General James T. Conway was commander of the mighty 1st Marine Expeditionary Force and he watched the Shamrock Parade, the ceremony usually presided over by a member of the British Royal Family but in whose absence the American stood. Before him Joe and the other guards stood to attention with a general salute while the piper unit played their flutes. Lieutenant General Conway returned their salute and prepared to hand out freshly cut shamrocks, previously green and leafy but now wilting in the sun. The shamrocks had been especially flown to the desert by the RAF two days earlier and kept in iced tubs all weekend to maintain their freshness. The army could not get its lads all suited up and armed for war but shamrocks could be sent in from afar.

The American general had taken a break from bolstering his military forces and preparing for the long march up from Kuwait to Baghdad, to instead hand out clumps of limp leafy greens along a long line of Irish Guards. A press photographer captured the tall general smile as he said 'good luck' to the young troops who attached the shamrocks to their berets. The guardsmen and women marched, sweating in their desert uniforms of yellow combats or green camouflages. The precise formation of feet back and forth kicked up dust from below, while intermittent gusts of sand engulfed them from above. Bladed US war helicopters descended, their roar threatening to drown out the sound of bagpipes proudly blown. With their display done the men prepared to pray and took their right knee to the ground, head bowed, caps in hand, SA-80s slung across their chests with muzzles rested on their left shoulders. The padre led a prayer of reverence to their saint who in myth brought the light of the Gospel to backward Ireland, words spoken to half-attentive soldiers who were here to bring the dimming lamp of democracy to ensnared Iraq.

The shamrock ceremony was a long-standing Irish Guards' tradition. When not on operational build-up, a member of the royal family, regularly the Queen Mum herself before her death the previous year, would present the regiment with their shamrocks. The symbol marked the patron saint's day but also reminded men of the birth of the regiment. In 1899, Britain's widowed monarch, the bitter Queen Victoria took the country to war against the Boers. Like Iraq, resources were also an incentive when South Africa's Dutch-descended settlers discovered gold in the Transvaal. The mighty British Empire expected the Boers to be quickly beaten, but the settlers knew their lands, and defiant guerrilla warfare ensured. In the three-year campaign the British soldiers carved up the land, led assault after assault and introduced the world to concentration camps. Essential to the war's effort were the Irish volunteers killing for empire amid their own mounting casualties. In an act of shrewd recognition, the queen formed a new unit, the Irish Guards, in March 1899. Her benevolence extended a year later to allowing the Irish Guards soldiers to adorn themselves with a sprig of shamrock. It was a step deemed unusual in an era when the wearing of green symbolised Irish dissidence against the Crown. The queen's gesture of forming the Irish Guards was a compromise to entice more new recruits into the regiment and maintain Irish support for the bloody South African war.

Support for the bloody invasion of Iraq evaded leaders Blair and Bush. On the day Joe prayed for St Patrick's blessing, the United Kingdom and the United States had abandoned any chance of gaining United Nations support when France, a favoured Iraq trading partner, promised to veto any UN resolution authorising military action. China, Germany and Russia joined in opposition to the threat of war and even members of Blair's own party turned against him. The leader of the House of Commons, Robin Cook, resigned in protest at the government's decision to back a war without 'international authority nor domestic support'. In his defiant final speech, Cook warned how 'history will be astonished at the diplomatic miscalculations that led so quickly to the disintegration of that powerful coalition', the European neighbours forsaken in favour of being a superpower's sidekick. Having spent the previous day on the Portuguese island of Azores discussing battle plans with Blair, President Bush delivered Saddam with a final ultimatum.

'Intelligence gathered by this and other governments leaves no doubt that the Iraq regime continues to possess and conceal some of the most lethal weapons ever devised,' goaded Bush. 'All the decades of deceit and cruelty have now reached an end. Saddam Hussein and his sons must leave Iraq within forty-eight hours. Their refusal to do so will result in military conflict commenced at a time of our choosing.'

The only ones who left Iraq were most of the UN weapons inspectors, who took five helicopters from the country after the US advised them to pull out of Baghdad and after their insurers pulled their coverage. Saddam remained, emboldened by the division among some of the once united nations.

The following day, 18 March 2003, Joe and others in his platoon sat around radios in sand-swept Kuwait, and listened for intelligence on the war. Blair delivered his speech and reminded his Parliament of Saddam's pernicious acts of defiance and the illusionary WMD.

'This is a tough choice,' he said. 'But it is also a stark one: to stand British troops down and turn back; or to hold firm to the course we have set. I believe we must hold firm.' While protestors piled up outside the hallowed Westminster halls, Blair spoke of choices; choices and consequences as he held young men's lives on a string. 'This house wanted this decision. Well it has it. Those are the choices. And in this dilemma, no choice is perfect, no cause ideal. But on this decision hangs the fate of many things.' That night, after ten hours of duelling debates and a total of nine resignations in protest, 217 doves were defeated by 396 hawks and the prime minister's prerogative was endorsed by a second vote: 412 to 149. With military action authorised, British Chief of Defence Staff Michael Boyce received the Commons call: 'The vote has gone through in support of the government.' As the head of the British army, Boyce first informed his American counterparts and then issued the directive to his military generals that parliament had favoured war and their forces should be ready to engage.

The battalion of Irish Guards waited in readiness and anticipation among more than 45,000 British service personnel, poised in Kuwait just miles from the Iraqi border. There was a general feeling of hurry up and wait. As Wednesday, 19 March wore on, Guardsman Wayne Sampat of No. 1 Company wanted to try and make a quick call home to his family. The Americans owned the bank of payphones and Wayne was in the queue to phone his mum and let her know that he was safe when a US soldier rushed out of a tent and shouted that they'd cut off the phones. Wayne knew that something was going to happen, but he was still in the queue and he'd not even made his call. Thankfully Sampat knew the other best way to phone home was to chat up a female reporter and try and use her satellite phone.

Out on the edge of camp, Chris Muzvuru stood with his Scottish bagpipes, preparing with a solitary moment of practice.

Pat Geraghty wandered over and looked to Muz.

'How on earth did you end up in the Irish Guards, Muz?' the CSM asked.

'I like Guinness,' Zimbabwean Muzvuru said plainly with a smile.

It made sense to Pat, who nodded and listened.

Amid the swirling sands and distant hums of army machines moving, Muz played. His tune was the century-old Scottish lament *Hector the Hero'*. The music had been written as a tribute to Sir Hector Macdonald at his death in 1903, 'Fighting Mac' having held the rare distinction of rising from a private to an esteemed major general. Muzvuru's elegant piping was defiant against the noise of imminent war.

As Saddam's deadline counted down, the military leaders were in no doubt of the prospect of their forces' action. The commanders used the time to give final speeches and bolster the steels of their soldiers. Across at Fort Blair Mayne desert camp, Lieutenant Colonel Tim Collins delivered his aspirational words to his 800-strong battle group of the 1st Battalion of the Royal Irish, part of the 16 Air Assault Brigade.

> 'We are entering Iraq to free a people and the only flag which will be flown in that ancient land is their own. Show respect for them.'

Collins exhorted his troops with the hopes that the most worthy commissioned officers had for their advancement.

> 'If you are ferocious in battle remember to be magnanimous in victory. Iraq is steeped in history. It is the site of the Garden of Eden, of the Great Flood and the birthplace of Abraham. Tread lightly there. You will see things that no man could pay to see and you will have to go a long way to find a more decent, generous and upright people than the Iraqis.'

He reminded his men that the enemy should not question their resolve and cautioned his troops to use their force wisely.

> 'It is a big step to take another human life. It is not to be done lightly. I know of men who have taken life needlessly in other conflicts, I can assure you they live with the Mark of Cain upon them. If someone surrenders to you then remember they have that right in international law and ensure that one day they go home to their family.'

In the early hours of 20 March in Iraq, ninety minutes after Saddam's forty-eight hour deadline expired, the Coalition, including RAF planes, warships and two Royal Navy submarines, launched their first assault. A strike of 2,000lb bombs and nearly forty Tomahawk cruise missiles, each loaded with 1,000lbs of explosives were aimed at the outskirts of Baghdad, location of some high value targets, before full hostilities began. It was called a 'decapitation attempt', based on recent intelligence to attempt an assassination of the Iraqi president, his family and senior leaders.

President Bush took to television to inform his country that 'at this hour, American and Coalition forces are in the early stages of military operations to disarm Iraq, to free its people and to defend the world.'

For the Americans this was 'Operation Iraqi Freedom', a name chosen with purpose and determination to propel the myth of their national exceptionalism. The British military codename was 'Operation Telic' (Op TELIC), supposedly selected at random by a computer, but there were meanings aplenty to be found. Telic came from the Ancient Greek to mean 'final' and 'end'. A verb, an action, used to indicate that an action or event had a clear and defined end; its opposite was something with no natural endpoint. For the wry military humour, TELIC also became an acronym for the British troops: Tell Everyone Leave Is Cancelled.

After the pre-dawn raids attempting to strike against the high-level Iraqi leadership, the dictator appeared defiant on nation's state television. The Coalition staging post in Kuwait was also targeted in retaliatory strikes by Saddam. At around 10.30 am, the first two missiles fell, their payload crashed into the northern Mutlaa desert in the vicinity of where the US Camp Commando was set up. After this first strike there was fear. Joe clutched his respirator and checked he knew how to quickly reach his Atropine nerve agent.

About two hours after the first attack, air raid sirens sounded again in Kuwait City. No. 1 Company's second-in-command, Captain Niall Brennan, and an infantryman were walking back from the officers' mess tent when the alarm cried out.

'Oh shit, what is that?' Brennan said. 'Fuck. It's a gas attack.'

Brennan and the other soldier ran, bolting the 500 metres back to their bunker for safety. They reached it quickly, and breathlessly put on their respirators. The mad-bollock-scramble caught the laughing eye of MacMullen's radio operator, Eugene McGillycuddy, who stood wearing only his pants, a cowboy hat and gas mask.

Some soldiers, like Joe, spent the rest of the day wearing their masks. In the afternoon three American Patriot missiles intercepted and knocked a pair of Iraqi scud missiles, which were aimed at the Coalition tents, out of the sky.

Captain Brennan was with Danny Burton, a Brummie, and Tommy Major, a Scouser, checking the vehicles in advance of their departure, when the alarm went off yet again. They waited in their masks for some time, listening for the all-clear. The men would risk a two man sniff test when they felt all was clear. Niall told Major to go first.

'With the greatest respect sir, no fucking way!' Major replied.

'Why not?' Niall demanded.

'Boss, it's not going to happen.'

'Christ, why not?' Niall shot back.

Sighing, Niall gingerly peeled off his mask thinking, *I hope I don't die.*

Burton and Major sat watching, anticipating: Would Niall's pupils dilate? *Here we are, Britain's finest,* Niall thought, *reduced to being like a canary in a cage.* It was, to his relief, another false alarm.

The constant scrum for respirators continued to be a frustration.

'Oh, Jesus, if someone says gas, gas, fucking gas, again …' one guardsman said exasperated – and at the overheard use of the word 'gas' he triggered 10,000 soldiers to don their masks. For company commanders like Peter MacMullen it was better to demonstrate an abundance of caution than not. Some of the 101st Aviation Brigade on the American base had begun to ignore the alarms, but there was still the terror that the next attack could be when Saddam decided to unleash his chemical and biological weapons.

By 4.00 pm there had been a half dozen alerts, a threatening alarm going off each time, thankfully all false alarms. It mattered less and less to the soldiers who had already stripped down their tents and bases to leave. One of the first units across the borders were the Corps of the Royal Electrical and Mechanical Engineers (REME) with their massive armoured bulldozers. REME, which prides itself on 'keeping the punch in the army's fist', used its heavy machinery to breach the Kuwaiti/Iraqi border berms. The man-made defensive mounds were quickly cleared so that the vast column of the US 3rd Infantry Division could begin its rapid march north towards Baghdad. Meanwhile, 16 Air Assault Brigade and the British 1st Armoured Division had already headed over the border alongside the US 15th Marine Expeditionary Unit moving to try and secure the Rumalia oilfields on the Al Faw peninsula. In the sky, an unmanned Phoenix drone deployed by the 32nd Regiment Royal Artillery was sending back early intelligence on enemy positions.

Joe's regiment would deploy north towards Basra the following day as part of the 7th Armoured Brigade Battle Group, also known as the Desert Rats, commanded by Brigadier Graham Binns.

The brigade was made up of 112 Challenger II tanks, 150 Warriors, 32 AS-90 155mm self-propelled howitzers and around 3,400 combat troops. The 7th Armoured consisted of two armoured regiments and two infantry battalions, the latter of which included the Royal Scots Dragoon Guards Battle Group, which had two companies of the Irish Guards attached. Of the two Irish Guards units, No. 1 Company was led by Major MacMullen and No. 2 Company was led by Major Ben Farrell.

Before the departure, Joe and the rest of No. 1 Company were given a last rousing speech by a tall American general. Joe noticed the many stars that decorated his military collar as he stood up to speak. He exhorted them to bravery in the upcoming battle. All the lads stood straight, listening respectfully, especially the young soldiers, some of whom had only just turned 18, the legal age for war-fighting, while in Kuwait. The American soldier was almost preaching now, throwing Biblical verses into his speech.

'As you walk through the valley of death you shall fear no evil,' the general told them piously. 'God will lead you. And may God carry you through that battlefield.'

Joe chanced a quick look at some of the lads who viewed each other with bemused expressions as if to say: *What the fuck's going on here? We're not used to all this God talk.*

Finally, the American confidently reminded everyone what they were there for, the hunt for Saddam's deadly cache of weapons of mass destruction, they wouldn't give up until they had found them.

Chapter 21

Pills in Winter

I t's January 2005 and the Americans give up their two-year search for weapons of mass destruction, the motive for their fight. They have been searching for stockpiles of nuclear, chemical and biological weapons since the first days of the attack on Iraq. American troops are hopeful of evidence early on, but their finds are discovered to be false alarms. The post-war search unit, the Iraq Survey Group, appoints a weapons expert as its leader, who gives up at the start of 2004, defeated and declaring that pressure from UN inspectors and Iraqi action led to the ridding of weapons before the war; there are no WMD to be found. 'It turns out that we were all wrong,' he says. His replacement and 1,200 experts continue the hunt until again it is announced that there is nothing to be found and, in 2003, two years before, there never had been. The American administration defends the war with an appeal to past atrocities.

'We had a regime that had a history of using weapons of mass destruction and had a history of defying the international community,' an official speaking for the president declares.

'We had the attacks on September 11 that taught us we must confront threats before it's too late.' This war, its narrative being rewritten, is now 'about making America more secure'.

It is security at a cost. Almost 1,500 Americans, including both contractors and soldiers, have been killed in Iraq since 2003. The violence is steadily growing in Iraq as the country lurches towards its first elections. They will be the first multiparty elections for the country since 1954, in the years before King Faisal II was killed in the coup that led to the rise of the Ba'ath Party and Saddam Hussein.

It is democracy at a price. Gangs of terrorists are seeking to destabilise the political progress. Dozens of lives are lost every day. A curfew is instated. The state of emergency, imposed the previous November during the siege on Fallujah, is extended. The bodies of eighteen Iraqi men, recruited to work for the Americans on one of their bases, are found in a field, murdered for their crime of collaboration. The nation is enjoying the freedom the Coalition fought for. There are also more and more cases coming forward of abuse and death, some part of a familiar pattern.

At Fort Hood, Texas, at the start of 2005, four US soldiers are investigated and tried for forcing two Iraqi men into the Tigris River at gunpoint, one of whom subsequently drowns. The Iraqi civilians, Zaidoun Hassoun and his cousin Marwan, were transporting plumbing supplies from Baghdad north to Samarra in January 2004, when their truck broke down before the 11.00 pm curfew. American soldiers stopped the two men and took them to a 10ft-high bridge over the Tigris and the army staff sergeant ordered the platoon to force the Iraqis to jump. Earlier that evening, two of the soldiers had joked to one another that 'someone was going to get wet tonight' and 'someone is going for a swim'. When the four military men left, Marwan climbed out of the river but claimed that the current swept his 19-year-old cousin, Zaidoun, away.

At the military trial in the USA, the court is shown a post-mortem photo of Zaidoun and told that three weeks before his death he had proposed to his fiancée and planned to start a family when he graduated from school. The picture of the corpse, which the Iraqi family say is the dead man pulled from the river before burial, is dismissed by the defence who say the body belongs to another man and that both Hassoun cousins made it to shore alive. The soldiers stand accused of involuntary manslaughter, aggravated assault and assault consummated by battery and obstruction of justice. They face up to a decade in jail. The trial says the men's actions jeopardise US operations by stirring up anti-American sentiment and providing insurgents with vital propaganda. The jury finds the staff sergeant innocent of manslaughter but convicts him of obstruction and assault, sentencing him to six months at a military prison. At the verdict, the soldier breaks down in tears, claiming if he could go back, he would definitely do something different on those days.

Joe McCleary's case, the first recorded drowning of an Iraqi civilian after the invasion, is still being investigated and the Army Prosecuting Authority is yet to decide upon its course of action.

Joe waits at home in Bootle, battling the prospect of a trial and years in prison that he thinks loom over him. The thoughts, the possibilities, threaten to bury him with dread. In South-east Asia, the tsunami, a result of an Indian Ocean earthquake the day after Christmas, has recently killed over 225,000, so many people overwhelmed as the almighty wave swept over them. Inside that's something of what Joe feels, post-conflict but still fighting, unable to hold back the tidal wave of panic and stress that the investigation brings. Bitterness and rage seep in, enveloping Joe.

He's alone, his mum is out but there are cans of Stella stashed in the kitchen. He grabs one, flips down the push tab and swigs. Joe stumbles up the stairs with desperation and half-decided intent. He reaches the bathroom and avoids the reflection in the cabinet mirror as he opens the cupboard. Inside are the painkillers, fast-acting tablets of 50mg of Tramadol. The drug mimics endorphins, binding to receptors in the brain and blocking the pain messages the body sends to it, fooling it into thinking a person is experiencing less than they are. Joe holds the small box in the palm of his hand, opening and closing his fist, wavering. He decides. Opening the small box, he pushes each pill out of its foil blister. He places one after another into his mouth, swallowing them with swigs of Stella as though they're Smarties. Joe just wants this to end. He can't carry this weight of anxiety and uncertainty. He wants to sleep and not face the night terrors. To rest and not hear the repeat of accusations he's heard from the angry RMP investigators that echo in his head. The strong painkiller is prescribed to treat moderate to severe pain. It blocks pain and that's what Joe wants. No more than 400mg Tramadol should be taken in a day and Joe takes three times that amount. He doesn't want his mum to come home and find him, guilty for the stress he feels he's already bringing on her so Joe stumbles out of the house. Outside, the January night is freezing and a veneer of snow covers the ground. The drug and drink combination are already going to work on his system. Joe staggers out towards the main road, the nearby dual carriageway out in front of him. Joe takes uncoordinated steps left along the footpath, past a bus stop, towards a big tree where the twin toxic poisoning of painkiller and alcohol causes him to capsize; his body slumps on the cold pavement.

Time blurs past and it must be the smudges of Joe's footsteps in fresh snow which lead David, his brother, to where he's lying. The heap on the pavement is semi-conscious and indifferent to the cold and dark of night; none of the occasional cars along the A565 bothers to stop. Maybe seeing the blister packets, spent of their contents, tells David that something is seriously wrong, or he comes home to see his younger brother stumbling away from their front door. David calls the ambulance and soon the blur of flashing blue bathes the main road behind their estate. Joe is taken the 3 miles south to The Royal, Liverpool's University Hospital and where his mum, Lynn works. The urgency of a gastric lavage pumps the pills out of Joe's stomach, sluicing his gut of the deadly medicine while activated charcoal is given to absorb the poisoning.

Joe's lucky, they tell him when he comes to. They found him quickly. But the young veteran didn't want to wake up. He recognises that he's in hospital, but doesn't want to be here; just wants to be allowed to die. It feels as though he doesn't see colour any more; he just sees grey. Living with the scrutiny and memory and prospect of military prison is horrible and painful.

Seated next to Joe is his mum, called down from her ward, now with eyes swollen, and nearby are Carlos and David.

'Thank fuck,' says David at noticing Joe awake. Then his demeanour changes, like the passing of clouds over the sun. 'You selfish bastard!' he says. 'You were going to leave me on me own.' Tears stream down his face and he's battering Joe as he lies in the hospital bed.

'You're going to leave me on me own without a brother,' he cries.

'David, I don't want to be here no more,' Joe replies hoarsely. 'I don't want to be in this place with everything that's happening. I don't want to do it. I just wanna close my eyes.'

'Well you fuckin' think about us when you do that next time,' David replies. 'You want to take your life away from your brother. I won't carry your coffin. I won't be there,' his anger almost spent. 'You're selfish. What about me, your brother?'

At the calm after his outburst all Joe hears is the familiar sobbing of his mum.

The curtains around them are pulled back and a doctor emerges.

'I think we should let the lad get some rest,' he says in thick local Scouse. Joe's mum gives him a gentle hug and Carlos squeezes his hand as the family all leave.

'You brother's really upset; your mum too,' says the doctor. Joe doesn't want to look at him. 'I work with your mum here, y'know. And she's scared,' he says, continuing. Beneath the short sleeves of his dark blue surgical scrubs, Joe notices his thick-set arms covered in tattoos.

'Look son, I know you've been through a tough time but this is not the right way,' the doctor says softly. The doctor who worked on Joe to save his life doesn't want his efforts to be in vain. Joe respects him for doing what he does, but the stomach pump hasn't rid his body of the anger and the despair.

'I know I can't understand what you've seen or done,' the doctor says.

He's right, of course. The mental trauma of war, a struggle that many medics can't grasp and the military has long dismissed. Young men, returning from The Great War almost a century before, were the first who started to fill hospital beds with odd symptoms. They were unable to walk; they shook and had night terrors. A quarter of a million sufferers soon with this strange and unknown psychosis. Even the strongest of men returned from seeing the smashing of human beings on the frontline were somehow breaking down.

What an earlier conflict had once called 'war neurosis' was termed 'shell shock' by psychologist Dr Meyers' Lancet paper in February 1915. At first it was believed that the ailment's cause was a soldier's proximity to the percussive effect of munitions' mighty blasts. Yet this 'derangement of the nervous system' affected sufferers who were nowhere near the shock of exploding shells. As treatment, some soldiers were told there was nothing wrong and ordered to take a few days rest while others faced the frightening sting of faradism, the use of painful electrical current for 'suggestion, re-education and discipline.' In this era, when psychiatry was in its infancy, combat stress was in the mind and meant the men were weak or cowards or both. The military needed men quickly back on the front so their treatment was to ban 'shell shock' as a diagnosis and hundreds who struggled with symptoms were courtmartialed for desertion and shot.

The Second World War sent more young men again for a sustained and traumatic fight on foreign fields. An estimated one in ten war-weary soldiers suffered battle fatigue or combat stress reaction, as symptoms were then called. British doctors prescribed barbiturate for fast relief of extreme anxiety and hysteria to beaten down soldiers who'd witnessed friends blown to pieces. 'Every man has a breaking point,' doctors realised but still the military could not accept it and stigmatised the sufferers 'lack of moral fibre.'

Soldiers in the US, out of the nightmare of Vietnam, were battling with flashbacks and nightmares from their experiences. Post-Traumatic Stress Disorder (PTSD) was first coined in 1980. A realisation slowly dawning that the human brain cannot comprehend the horrors of war. More war followed, the Falklands conflict with a single psychiatrist for a task force of 30,000, where struggling veterans were prescribed to go home and get hammered. They'd wrestle not just with alcoholism but anxiety and deep depression. Not till the *Diagnostic and Statistical Manual of Mental Disorders* was published in 1986 was PTSD fully recognised, yet still its stigma was scorned and considered bad for the British army's regimental system. Lessons still not learned, long after the trauma of the First World War and its secret shame.

Chapter 22

Shaibah Blues

No. 1 Company Irish Guards were deep within Iraq, 26 miles north of the Kuwaiti border, and had arrived at an abandoned Iraqi airbase called Shaibah, a place founded by the British in the days after the First World War. In 1918, when the war was won, the old Ottoman order had fallen and two years later the British received the mandate to control Iraq. However, after the yoke of the Ottoman dynasty had been broken, Iraq had gained a taste for independence; it did not want to be ruled over by another empire, this time the British one. This cause was enough to unite even divided Muslim brothers. Sunni and Shia came together, declared a holy Jihad against the British and revolted against their new colonial administrators. In response, the RAF bombed the revolution into submission and the No. 84 Squadron set up Shaibah Airbase in 1920, as their foothold in the south. Little trace of the RAF remained eighty-three years later. Instead the Irish Guards were greeted at the gates of Shaibah's deserted airbase by a grounded Iraqi army Mig fighter jet. The rusting showpiece was a relic, on display as a reminder of the former glory days when this was the regional headquarters of the Iraqi military, long before its wings were clipped amid the UN sanctions and mid-1990s no-fly zones. From the moment they arrived, Joe McCleary saw the scars of the first Iraq War at Shaibah, with aircraft hangars still pierced with JDAM bombs and left unrepaired since 1991. The company took over the deserted base and leaguered up, making camp by lining up their Warriors along the runway.

While a mostly American military movement powered its way north towards Baghdad, the mainly British-led forces quickly faced challenging progress as they sought to secure the country in the south. Coalition fighter planes began to soften up Basra from the air on 21 March, with bombing raids that destroyed high-tension cables and cut off the city's power. Precise aerial attacks also struck Basra's Wafa al-Qaed water treatment plant, knocking out the major sewage pumping and treatment facilities which supplied more than 60 per cent of the desert city's clean water.

On the same day, the Battle of Umm Qasr was the first major military confrontation of the war as the Coalition forces sought to secure the strategically important harbour and haul in desperately needed supplies. The resistance took military planners by surprise as Iraqi soldiers defended their docks against the US 15th Marine Expeditionary Unit and the British 26th Armoured Engineer Squadron's initial assault. Iraqi forces scored a US fatality and attacked the American hubris, after the Coalition had already publicly declared that the city was secure. Small-arms fire from Iraqi snipers and some with machine guns and RPGs attacked and put up a good fight against the might of two Abram tanks, a pair of RAF Harrier jets and a squad of Navy SEALs. Resistance in the town of Umm Qasr cut off the Coalition access to Iraq's only deep-water port which denied them access to the 3,500 tonnes of supplies and aid that sat aboard ships waiting in the Persian Gulf.

To the east of the port of Umm Qasr by 30 miles was the Al Faw peninsula, where most of Iraq's oil was exported to offshore oil platforms. During the first Gulf War, the oil and gas facilities here had been a weapon for ecological catastrophe when 11 million barrels-worth of crude oil were unleashed into the Arabian Gulf, contaminating more than 800 miles of Kuwaiti and Saudi Arabian coastline. The Coalition needed to quickly control the Gas and Oil Platforms (GOPLATs) to avoid a repeat disaster. A contingent of 800 Marines from 40 and 42 Commando sought to secure Al Faw with an assault that dropped Marines into the area using helicopters. Their progress was halted by ferocious desert storms and dust clouds which impaired the accuracy of their targeting. Mines and anti-ship missiles along the coast forced an aerial insertion of more Special Forces, but a planned British helicopter assault was aborted when a US CH-46 Sea Knight chopper crashed, killing all twelve on board including the headquarters of the Brigade Reconnaissance Force. It took American Navy SEAL teams engaged in furious fire-fights with Iraqi forces to secure Al Faw's oil terminals and pipelines. This action didn't stop the fiery sabotage of several oil wells at Rumaila, the third largest oilfield in the world, by retreating Iraqis.

In the north-west, the Americans led the charge up towards Baghdad, but were halted still 100 miles from Iraq's capital. As they headed up the country's main artery of Highway 1 they too encountered heavy resistance as they tried to take the city of Nasiriyah. Five US soldiers were captured and set upon by Iraqi forces, who later broadcast the broken American bodies on Al-Jazeera TV. They were just some of the more than thirty Americans killed and more than fifty wounded at the Battle of Nasiriyah as the Iraqi resistance hit back.

On the day before the Irish Guards rolled into Shaibah Airbase, the first British 'friendly fire' fatality of the war occurred not far away. Killed in action

(KIA) was Steven Mark Roberts or 'T.C.' to his mates, who was 33, married and a father. T.C. was a sergeant in the 2nd Royal Tank Regiment and had been trying to sort out an angry Iraqi mob at a checkpoint in Az Zubayar, the town named after an early convert to Islam who was martyred in battle in AD 656. In March 2003, the place, located 7 miles from Shaibah, was a ferocious stronghold of Iraqi Fedayeen forces. But T.C. was killed not by his enemy but by one of his own men and would have survived if supply problems hadn't deprived him of armour to save his life. One of the town's protestors, his face daubed in white paint, which marked him as a possible martyr, had started to pelt T.C. with rocks. T.C. tried to use his Browning pistol but found it had jammed in the desert dust. The Challenger tank's machine gun failed too, so Trooper Gary Thornton leapt to the rescue and got behind the secondary armaments of the tank's 7.62mm co-axial chain gun, a weapon he'd not been trained on. The young trooper failed to realise that the co-axial was a long-range weapon and had an undisciplined trajectory when fired from close range. The 7.62×51mm NATO rounds sliced through nearby T.C. Roberts. He was wearing only standard body armour when he was shot, having handed over his full protection only days before because of the army's shortage of supplies. Nearly a third of T.C.'s squadron had had to surrender their enhanced body armour with ceramic plates for infantry soldiers, considered more at risk, to use. Instead T.C. became one of the first who wore a Union Jack, draped over his wooden box. Blue on blue they call it, when the biggest risk is not one's foe but the inadvertent firing by one's own side.

From the first couple of days of the conflict, the Coalition was becoming its own worst enemy. A RAF Tornado was shot down by a US Patriot missile, killing its two crewmen as they returned from a bombing raid and approached Ali Al Salem Airbase in Kuwait. An American Air Force major was murdered by one of his own men, the first case of fragging since the Vietnam War, when a former sergeant who'd converted to Islam threw four grenades into tents at an army base in Kuwait. Two British Sea King helicopters collided with one another and killed all seven souls aboard in a deadly accident over the North Arabian Gulf.

From the Gulf coast at Al Faw, water flowed the 30 miles down canals to Basra where British Forces had to make a tactical retreat on their first attempts to conquer Iraq's second city. Challenger tanks belonging to the Scots Dragoon Guards had encircled the city until they faced up against the Iraqi 6th Armoured Division bolstered by armed militia who forced them to re-cross the Shatt al-Basra river. The British heard intelligence that with

60 per cent of Basra without running water, Ba'ath party activists were using the state of siege in the city to galvanise locals. They were even offering a bounty on killing Coalition soldiers: financial rewards for attacking the British.

As the few quick-burning Rumaila oil wells fuelled huge plumes of smoke, so too did the quick deterioration of conditions inside the city fuel attacks. Strong militia resistance defended their city with RPGs, snipers and machine guns. Unrelenting mortar fire forced the retreat of the 7th Armoured Brigade, the Desert Rats, leaving behind their dreams of an easy victory. Basra was contained but the commanders were desperate that the city not sink into Stalingrad or Grozny. Breaking the Ba'ath party was key.

Joe had been at Shaibah airbase for less than a day when word came that the Special Air Service (SAS) had captured some senior Ba'ath party members on a recent raid into Basra. Information was needed on the movements of Ba'ath leadership and the infantrymen were sent out an operation to assist, the tracks of Call Sign One Two's Warrior rolling into action. The beast of a vehicle ground to a halt near a collection of concrete buildings on the outskirts of Basra. The lads strapped helmets on, got SA-80s ready and surged with adrenaline. The doors gave birth to a new reality: the surround-sound of nearby sniper fire that alerted Joe that he was in one of his first real battlefields. He jumped quickly out of the Warrior and ran behind a wall where a team of three SAS soldiers were standing, weapons ready in their bulky arms. Seated captive on the ground were four thin and straggly Iraqi men, each with a Saddam-like moustache and ragged-looking fatigues. The prisoner's hands were bound up with plasticuff ties and they seemed almost shrunken in comparison to the great towering statues of the SAS men. Joe had never seen fierce determination as that which he saw projected on those Special's faces. They were likely part of D Squadron that had been inside Iraq for over a month before the invasion as part of the secret Operation Row, launched well before Blair's vote. They had been there to conduct reconnaissance operations and gather tactical information from inside Basra. Now Joe was among this crack team of the army that had started as a Commando unit in 1941. From beyond the wall came a burst of sniper fire. The men didn't flinch as shattered concrete sprayed like hailstones. The lead SAS man emerged through the grey dust and shouted to the assembled Irish Guards infantry section.

'Listen, we have get these lot to where we can talk to them …' The SAS soldier trailed off, glancing at the crumpled Iraqi soldiers. 'These four fellas, they're Ba'ath Party …' He paused, patient, waiting out a short onslaught of misdirected sniper shots before continuing.

'Okay, we need to get into that building now.' He pointed over at a blown-out structure about 100 feet away. 'You and you, provide us cover fire against those snipers,' he said addressing Sampat and McGing before turning to Joe. 'You, come with us. Keep your fucking head down.'

The SAS men grabbed their prisoners and ran with them, half dragged them, half stumbling out from the safety of the wall that shielded them, across an exposed track. The rat-tat-tat of foreign snipers was soon drowned out by the loud assault of SA-80 rifle covering fire. Joe followed out, moving fast, avoiding the firing, and towards the entrance to the blown-out building. Its insides were bare concrete walls, cut off wires and a thick filth of dust and it looked as though it had either never been completed or long since abandoned. To the left of the entrance, against one wall, were slumped three of the four Iraqi men; to the right at the far end of the room Joe saw two SAS men drag the fourth through to an adjoining room and then the door closed. The room stank like a pub urinal and in the left corner of the room there was a dirty toilet. Joe's attention darted to a movement as something scurried into the toilet bowl. The Iraqi men squirmed and muttered to each other.

'Akhrus, kuna hadiana! Akhrus, kuna hadiana!' the third SAS operative yelled in practised Arabic with a posh British inflection. The captives became quiet.

Joe had imagined the SAS as meat-heads, built like brick shit houses and tough as nails and that was the limit. Instead their intelligence struck him. They spoke Arabic fluently, seemed to know the politics of the country intimately and radiated confidence as though they knew they were the country's new custodians. One of the SAS fellas looked as though he'd been wounded in the shoulder but carried on as if it were nothing.

'Looks like you've been shot, mate.' Joe pointed out.

'It's fine. Just a flesh wound,' he replied in disregard.

'Look, you're not to let them talk to each other. 'Akhrus, kuna hadiana' means 'shut up, be quiet' to them. If they talk to each other, you hit 'em as hard as you can. I don't care how you hit 'em,' he said. 'You just make sure that they're not speaking to each other. Understand?'

'Yeah,' Joe replied.

'If they try and speak to each other, just kick them in the forehead.' It felt to Joe as though the SAS guy was briefing someone who he didn't entirely think was up to the job.

'Walk over to 'em and give 'em a volley. Like, I'll show you how to do it,' he said and kicked one of the prisoners hard in the head. The weak man crumbled whimpering with Arabic yells.

Joe nodded and eyed the bound skinny men but hoped they didn't speak as he didn't want to have to beat them. The SAS soldier started for the door at the far end of the room then turned his head.

'Oh, yeah. Don't sit on the floor,' he said with a nod towards a large number of rats swarming around the old toilet and in pools of sewage. 'Whatever you do, don't fucking sit on the floor!' The SAS man chuckled and stormed to the shut door and closed himself within.

Joe was alone with the bedraggled former Ba'ath members, once likely high up in Saddam's regime, now feeble Coalition captives. The door behind which their Ba'ath colleague was held was closed, but they could hear the screams coming out from the room beyond. The sounds of unseen violence were agonising to endure; it was one thing Joe and the Iraqi detainees shared in common. 'Intelligence assets' they were now called. Still, Joe rationalised: *these SAS fellas are obviously highly trained in what they do.* The Iraqis started to murmur again to each other, yet their disquiet was not conspiracy or the frightened yells at the unseen interrogation.

'No speak,' Joe said, pointing his left index finger over his mouth, forgetting his quick Arabic lesson and forgetting himself. The three men kept speaking to each other, so Joe kicked one of the men in the head and emphasised his command further with a swift punch of one of the other prisoners. 'Just don't speak!' he shouted.

The three Iraqi men still muttered, their gaze away from Joe. He followed their line of sight and realised they were frantically agitated by the rats at the far side of the room. It was easy to understand why; they were huge rodents. They were the long-tailed Nesokia Bunni rats, part of the Bandicoot species, and the real desert rats. Each grows to around 33 inches, not measuring their tail, and weighs over 2lbs. They are found only in the wetlands around southern Iraq, making their home in the marshes where the Tigris meets the Euphrates. They're known for being excellent swimmers and building their nests on reed platforms above the water line. The rat was only discovered by western zoologists in the late 1970s, but locals had known about them for a long time and they too were terrified. Joe took them in with frightened awe. *If the kids back in Bootle were over there, they'd feed them thinking they were cats!* 'Mischief,' the collective name for rats, really was understating what they were. Joe watched them, some using their long whiskered noses to push rocks around. A few others came up out of a toilet bowl and scattered about on the floor with fur wet and matted, edging menacingly towards the Iraqi captives. The three prisoners, bound back to back, breathed quickly and squirmed uncomfortably. The men shifted closer to the door. Joe moved himself to block them from the exit and ushered them back towards rodents. The men's rapid breaths morphed into panicked screams and frantic Arabic spoken to one another as they peered at the rats through petrified eyes.

A few moments passed and one of the burly SAS members appeared from the doorway at the far end of the room and strode in.

'You!' he shouted angrily, selecting another Iraqi for interrogation. He grabbed one of the Ba'athists under his armpit and hauled him to his feet.

Outside, a series of crashes thundered. Mortars were falling like fists pounding the ground. Short tremors grew in intensity. Joe looked nervously through the door to where he could see a sky blotted with smoke. He instinctively gripped and tightened his helmet strap.

'Don't worry about it, mate. They're not that accurate!' The SAS soldier said as jovially as if he was off to boil the kettle for a cuppa. *Okay, mate, cheers,* Joe thought, as the next Iraqi was marched to the room beyond. Joe guarded the Ba'ath men as one by one they were led off for beating and questioning until there was one left. Joe could see him shaking, pissing himself. The rats were running all around him now. Joe never found out what intelligence the four Iraqis in that back room provided but the next day a precision 1,000lb satellite-guided JDAM bomb was dropped on a suspected Ba'ath party headquarters in central Basra.

To the north, nature prevented the Americans' pursuit of war as a 'mother of all storms', what the Arabs called a Shamal, kicked up winds of 50 knots. It halted their troops and the 11th Helicopter Attack Regiment's planned advances towards Baghdad in a maelstrom of sand.

The fog of war caused confused target identification and unnecessary loss of British life when a Challenger II Main Battle Tank took fire near the Shatt al-Basra canal on 25 March. The tank was part of Black Watch and was driven by a unit of four Queen's Royal Lancers, who were attached to the Fusiliers Battle Group. The first of two high-explosive rounds hit the Challenger and ignited HESH rounds inside the stricken tank. The explosion that resulted had such force that the turret was ripped right off and on to the back deck. Two of the men inside were killed instantly; Corporal Stephen John Allbutt, 35, from Stoke-on-Trent, a father of two, and Trooper David Jeffrey Clarke, 19, from Littleworth, Staffordshire, who had ambitions of getting engaged to his girlfriend, Rachel. Along with them, two others were seriously wounded. All four were victims of another blue on blue friendly fire.

The following day, Major MacMullen in Call Sign Zero Bravo travelled past the sad scene. He saw the burnt-out armoured vehicle looking like a shell of twisted metal, the turret torn off and exposed were the dead soldiers' Blueys, their letters home, possessions that MacMullen could identify with, blowing in the wind. *This shouldn't have happened*, he thought as his Warrior rolled past. It could so easily have been him. MacMullen's forward artillery observation officer happened to be listening to the 3rd Artillery communications net when she heard his Call Sign Zero Bravo's position being given over as a suspected target. Only her owl-like ears and quick action prevented MacMullen and his vehicle becoming another tragic blue on blue.

The tide of fortunes seemed to change with the weather. The Shamal in the north began to subside and the Americans continued their march to Baghdad, encountering resistance but coming within 50 miles of the capital. Down in the south the high pressure build-up gave way to a day of heavy rain. Reports filtered through of desperation inside Basra where the stink of undealt-with human sewage flowed with the rain. With the main water plant still out of commission, the city's population turned for water to the Shatt al-Arab, the river that was polluted with human waste. British soldiers said they saw Iraqi artillery shooting at their own people inside Basra. Reports of an uprising gave commanders hope that the Shiites might turn against their oppressors. In response, the Iraqi army unleashed an armoured column of T-55 tanks. The number was massive, British commanders were told initially. One hundred and twenty enemy tanks and armoured vehicles, potentially making this the biggest tank battle involving British forces since the Second World War. The opponent's force was, however, somewhat more feeble. On closer inspection an 'erroneous signal' was discovered from the Coalition's electronic 'moving target indicators' that suggested 120 when in fact there were 14. The tank battle just south of Basra was short. The British Challenger II, armed with a 120mm rifle-barrelled gun, could shoot while travelling at 25mph and unleash eight rounds per minute. The rusting Iraqi T-55's tanks were made by the Russians and had inferior engineering and could fire accurately only when stationary. The Iraqis followed a haphazard and suicidal strategy. Their convoy soon left the main road and headed into open countryside which had become a muddy swamp after the downpour. '14-0' to the Allies', was how one tank commander described the outcome.

On the outskirts of Basra, Major MacMullen's Warrior encountered a barricade and had contact with a new enemy. As the major stuck his head out of the turret of his call sign he saw two figures all dressed in black clothing. They matched descriptions given by intelligence that said these were members of the Fedayeen Saddam, groups of guerrilla soldiers chosen to protect the paranoid dictator. Their name had been chosen as it meant 'Saddam's Men of

Sacrifice' and they were controlled by Uday Hussein, Saddam's sadistic eldest son. The Fedayeen paramilitary group was the fierce and still loyal apparatus of Saddam's Ba'ath party, known for being utterly ruthless. On the road south of Basra, one of the Fedayeen fighters had engaged with a RPG that he launched at MacMullen's Warrior. The gunner on his vehicle quickly took the assailants out but the 30mm RPG round was lodged in the side of the Warrior. Getting out of their vehicle, MacMullen and his gunner observed the damage.

'Sir, it's struck but not fired,' said the gunner. 'At this range we should have technical people come out.'

'Thanks,' said MacMullen as he reached down, grasped the round and threw it in a nearby river.

Nine days into the war there was some initial jubilation in the south at the now secured port of Umm Qasr. The British supply ship Sir Galahad finally came in to dock at the port and brought ashore the holy grail of food, medicine and blankets. With supplies getting through to help local people, the army had high hopes that its war of attrition would soon bring Basra to its knees.

Chapter 23

Well Dressed

Joe's mum knows that the war's aftermath is bringing her son to his knees and calls up the army, hopeful they'll help. It's shortly after Joe's had his stomach pumped of his self-inflicted assault of pills and has been released from hospital. Across the phone line to military headquarters Lynn tells the army that her son, their killing machine, has tried to kill himself. Her pleas are for help more than sympathetic platitudes but it feels as though her appeals fall on deaf ears. Hopes are quickly dashed. The military seems content to know that doctors have been looking after Joe and that he's at home now. His mum can't understand the military's lack of concern, feeling their duty of care should extend much further. Joe still wakes up each day not wanting to be alive but expecting that the army, still his employer whom he served, will appear, come and fix him. Joe has yet to hear an update on the investigation and all he can do is drink to fill in the vacuum of uncertainty that lingering fears about a military trial against him bring.

Joe receives a call, not from the army, but from John O'Leary, his solicitor, asking to meet with him. He's heard little from him for several weeks, but John assures him that he's been busy at work on the case. The following day Joe heads into the city and along a dingy side street of Whitechapel, Liverpool, to enter an office for his appointment. Inside Joe sits down, John facing him from the other side of his desk. After the pleasantries O'Leary says that in all likelihood Joe will have to go through a military trial over the Iraqi boy's death and that he will need legal counsel.

'The army will be prosecuting you so we need to get you a really good QC,' O'Leary says.

'QC?' Joe asks, dazed and still trying to swallow the news of an impending trial.

'Queen's Council, Joe. It's the barrister who represents you in court,' his solicitor replies. 'We need to look at getting you someone who's a really good Queen's Council. Now, this is a list of the names of some of the best barristers in Liverpool that we'd usually recommend to represent you,' O'Leary says, flamboyantly waving a bunch of papers in line with his head.

Ahmed Jabbar Kareem Ali.
(*Photo: Mohammad Ali*)

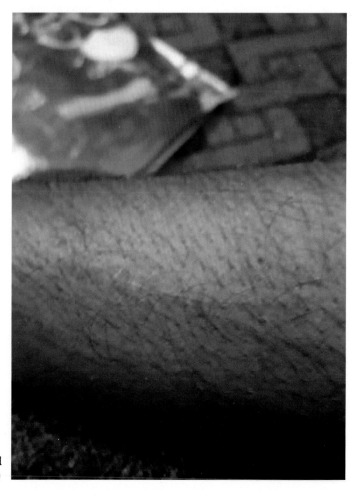

One of Ayad Hanon's alleged
wounds. (*Photo: Ayad Hanon*)

The Shatt al Basra Canal. (*Photo: IFI Evidence*)

Bridge Four where the looters entered the water. (*Photo: IFI Evidence*)

Joe McCleary out of uniform and relaxed.
(*Photo: Joe McCleary*)

Joe's pastime was always fishing. (*Photo: Joe McCleary*)

Joe and Martin as part of 1 Company in Ireland in 2004. (*Photo: Joe McCleary*)

Warriors in the desert. (*Photo: Scott Breen*)

View from back of Warrior. (*Photo: Scott Breen*)

Convoy of Warriors. (*Photo: Scott Breen*)

Challenger II Main Battle Tank in the desert. (*Photo: MoD*)

Irish Guard soldiers near the Basra Technical College. (*Photo: MoD*)

A destroyed Iraqi tank outside Basra. (*Photo: Scott Breen*)

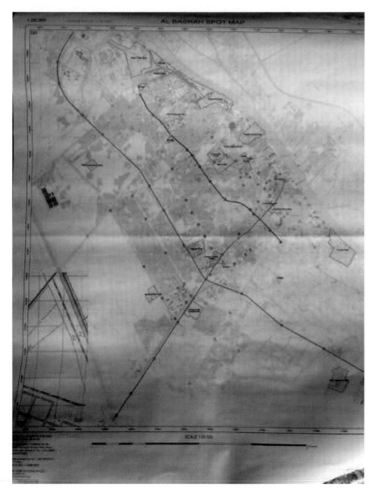

Military Map of Basra.
(*Author's Collection*)

Artist's depiction of Objective Elysium, the No. 1 Company Irish Guards' assault on the Basra Literary College, 6. April 2003. (*David Rowlands*)

Piper Christopher Muzvuru. (*Photo: Jonny Stranix*)

Lance Corporal Ian Malone. (*Photo: MoD*)

Warriors in Basra. (*Photo: Scott Breen*)

Soldier's fortification or sangar in Basra. (*Photo: Scott Breen*)

Saddam portraits were all over Basra. (*Photo: Scott Breen*)

A letter home from Joe known as a Bluey. (*C/o: Joe McCleary*)

A Basra street, Iraq, April 2003. (*David Rowlands*)

Warrior Call sign 'Zero Bravo'. (*David Rowlands*)

Basra College of Literature post-looting. (*David Rowlands*)

Bootle Beach. (*Author's Collection*)

Left to right: Selman, Cooke, McCleary and McGing. (*Photo: Alamy*)

Satellite map used in court-martial evidence. (*Photo: IFI Evidence*)

EXHIBIT CEF/1'- SATELLITE IMAGE DEPICTING
BRIDGE 4, BASRAH. 64654/03

North

To Basrah

Point of entry of looters at river bank

Site of recovery of Mstr Karheem's body

Shatt al Basrah canal

Waste ground where looters were arrested. (*Photo: IFI Evidence*)

The anguish of relief for Joe, 6 June 2006. (*Photo: Alamy*)

Joe and Martin's relief at the verdict. (*Photo: Alamy*)

Today Ahmed is remembered on his brother's wall. (*Mohammed Ali*)

Joe's Wedding in 2018 marked a new chapter, pictured with his brother, David. (*C/o: Joe McCleary*)

He then takes the papers between his two hands and rips them, tearing them straight through the middle. *What's the point in that?* Joe thinks, confused as O'Leary lets the paper sheets scatter down into a waste basket.

'Sorry to do this to you Joe; usually we pick one for you. But Mr Stephen Riordan called us. Personally! And he asked for this case himself. He wants it.'

'Okay. Erm. Who's Stephen Riordan?'

'He's the best in this business. And when Stephen Riordan calls, you take his call!' O'Leary says animatedly. 'When this fella calls you say "yes".'

'So he's who we should go with …?' Joe begins.

'I'm not going to ask you "who do you want to represent you?". I'm telling you. We're not going to argue with this one. And if you don't take him, you're a fucking fool, Joe! A fucking fool!'

'Sound, then,' Joe says to his lawyer in the affirmative. 'Let's do it.'

John O'Leary and Stephen Riordan have worked with each other on a number of previous cases over a long period. They're both based in Liverpool and while they were visiting a client for another case at Preston prison, O'Leary had mentioned Joe's case.

'I think I've got one of these Iraq cases,' O'Leary had said. 'Are you available? Do you fancy it?'

'I certainly would,' Riordan replied, jumping at the opportunity of being involved in what will be one of the first court cases related to the war in Iraq.

Joe's case hasn't gone public yet, but what happened in Iraq is already on the radar with another court martial case gaining attention. The British soldiers who'd photographed themselves abusing Iraqi civilian detainees at Camp Bread Basket in Basra were convicted and kicked out of the army in disgrace. It has been called a 'British Abu Ghraib'; Iraqi prisoners were hung from a forklift truck, tied up in foetal position and forced to simulate sex acts by liberating soldiers. The troops, all from the 1st Battalion of The Royal Regiment of Fusiliers, had their fate decided at a military tribunal in Germany by a Judge Advocate named Michael Hunter and a panel of seven senior officers. It's a process that likely awaits Joe, losing his freedom after his country sent him to fight for someone else's.

The fall-out from Iraq, a place still ravaged with instability, is radiating further and drawing radicals from beyond its borders. The much hoped-for elections at the start of 2005, the first free democratic vote in the country's history, bring little peace. In the month that follows, a Jordanian suicide bomber scores the deadliest attack since the fall of Saddam when he detonates a momentous car bomb of high explosives in Al Hillah which kills 127. Iraqis are dying daily in gun attacks and improvised explosive devices are now flooding into the country, but the weapons that drew the Americans and British there were a shimmering mirage. America's own Iraq Intelligence Commission concludes as much:

> The Intelligence Community was dead wrong in almost all of its pre-war judgments about Iraq's weapons of mass destruction. This was a major intelligence failure. Its principal causes were the Intelligence Community's inability to collect good information about Iraq's WMD programs, serious errors in analyzing what information it could gather, and a failure to make clear just how much of its analysis was based on assumptions, rather than good evidence. On a matter of this importance, we simply cannot afford failures of this magnitude. After a thorough review, the Commission found no indication that the Intelligence Community distorted the evidence regarding Iraq's weapons of mass destruction. What the intelligence professionals told you about Saddam Hussein's programs was what they believed. They were simply wrong.

Three years too late, the intelligence is being examined and now the conduct of the soldiers is coming under scrutiny.

When Joe first meets Stephen Riordan, his QC and the man who wants to defend him, he finds him to be as impressive as his solicitor suggested. Even Riordan's office chambers are as remarkable as the man's reputation. Riordan's is based in an ornate four-storey building on 25–27 Castle Street, one of the seven ancient streets of the city that date back to before the fourteenth century and just a few doors away from Liverpool Town Hall. Joe walks up to the front of a big beautiful building, towering above him, with its Victorian-era neo-classical design and pairs of Doric columns between each tall window. Outside he sees a big plaque bearing the words 'Stephen Riordan, QC'. Up some steps from the busy street and through the large oak doors he ascends to the first floor where a receptionist leads into a posh-looking room with large windows penetrated by vast light of the winter day and views of the city beyond. The room's centrepiece is a huge marble table that Joe thinks must be worth thousands by itself, on top of which is a large television and a neatly stacked folder of papers. Riordan is seated at the table and as Joe is led in, the man rises to shake his client's hand.

Riordan is tall, over 6ft so he and Joe meet each other eye to eye. *Geez, this is a giant,* Joe thinks at first, impressed from the off. The QC is thinning on top, appears distinguished, smartly dressed in suit and tie and is well-spoken as he introduces himself in a voice that Joe thinks would demand attention from anywhere in a room.

Riordan was born in St Albans, the once Roman town of Verulamium in Hertfordshire, 25 miles from London. He lived in the south of England before studying in Liverpool for his law degree. After he qualified, he went to London and did his pupillage, the year's legal training, before being called to the bar in 1972. Riordan returned to Liverpool the following year after accepting a position at a legal firm where he spent the next thirty years as a barrister on some of Merseyside's most notorious cases: from gangland shootings to violent assaults.

He has a vast amount of experience but he tells Joe that this case will be the first ever court martial that he's taken. He may not be familiar with military tribunals and nomenclature but he doesn't consider it necessary to be, because an army judiciary procedure is just the same as any other, except that there'll be a panel of army officers not a jury of civilians.

Riordan seems favourably impressed by Joe; he thinks the case is a noble cause. Many of his previous cases have involved defending or prosecuting clear cut villains, but this is a very different situation. He explains the procedure to Joe. Riordan, and likely the solicitors appointed by Selman, McGing, and Cooke, will spend time preparing the defence case but will do so separately from one another, just as the army prosecution will be preparing theirs. When the court case comes around, the prosecution will stand up and outline its case, present evidence against the soldiers and call its witnesses. As a defence team, Riordan and the other barristers will have the chance to cross-examine the witnesses and raise any legal points they want to.

Riordan's overview of how the case will proceed is interrupted by his receptionist.

'Do you want something to eat?' the woman asks Joe. He's famished yet hesitates; he's skint.

'Nah, I'm okay,' Joe says slowly, thinking of the embarrassment in front of this polished and well-schooled solicitor with needing to pay but having no money. Astutely, Riordan senses something.

'Don't worry about it, you know Joseph. It'll be taken care of,' he says reassuringly. 'And we're going to be here for a few hours going through the case.'

'Oh. Okay. I'll have a bacon sandwich and a cup of tea, please,' says Joe.

'Yeah, no problem,' says the receptionist who melts away behind the big wooden doors.

They pause their discussion of the case and the topic changes as Riordan and Joe get to know each other. The barrister says that he likes to run to unwind.

'It's a great stress-buster, running,' he says as food arrives. The stress of the morning doesn't diminish Joe's appetite as he hungrily tucks into the sandwich. Riordan says that he even once did a full marathon and in a fairly respectable time of about three and a half hours. He adds that he was going to do more, just never got around to it. The trial may be like a marathon too. It could take several gruelling weeks, he says, and at the end of it the verdict uncertain.

Riordan is intense though supportive and thorough as they get back to the business of reviewing Joe's case. Joe can feel right away when someone's trying to belittle or patronise him; it'll get him angry fast. With his barrister he feels instantly at ease, even amid the difficult questions.

Joe's sense of ease is, however, temporary. As he walks back over what's happened, the terrors can't help but return to the surface, memories with teeth like a shark. As Joe's QC, Riordan must understand every detail of all the events that led to the incident at the water's edge. Joe tries to explain things as best as he can; Riordan listens intently, taking detailed notes. Joe talks about the arrest, the fierce interrogation and how the army sent him back home to be with his family. Riordan can see the tide of heaviness, the emotion seeping in.

'Don't worry, Joe. We'll try and fix this,' Joe hears Riordan say to him confidently.

Riordan has more and more questions and has to understand the facts of what Joe went through in the days and weeks before and after the fall of Iraq. He carefully selects some papers off the desk and they talk through the statements Joe's made. Riordan has obtained a video taken of Basra that they review; the images filmed by the RMP of Bridge Four back in June 2003. The scenes bring back further vivid memories that hit Joe fast. Flickering military footage shows the familiar dust-drenched distant land. There is Bridge Four where everything happened. This is the place that would pivot the direction of his life. They are images familiar from the nightmares, distinct images of the swelling current of the canal in Basra.

Chapter 24

Mortars and Media

They were by the canal. This was the Az Zubayr Bridge or Bridge Four, one of the five crossings around the outskirts of Basra city. Joe was here, part of a Vehicle Checkpoint (VCP) that had been set up as the army tightened the net around the city.

No. 1 Company Irish Guards had advanced north-east towards their target and was now less than 8 miles from the centre of Basra. On 28 March they relocated their base from Shaibah airbase to an old bus station on the southwest side of the river. The main route from the south, Highway 8, came up and crossed the Basra Canal over Bridge Four and by now there was an exodus. People were desperate to escape the city, which the British effectively had under a state of siege. The mass of people were filing out, civilians escaping in anticipation of the battle that the Coalition was bringing to them. The innocent locals were probably fleeing for Kuwait, or anywhere else but Basra. *Stupidly enough,* Joe mused, *we're the ones trying to get into the city.* The British weren't the only ones trying to get in; they had intelligence that Iran, on the neighbouring border just to the east, was sending militants into the city so the army commanders set up VCPs on either side of the four-lane Bridge Four. A Challenger II tank and a Warrior was parked up on the bridge and their mission was to deny movement to the enemy in or out of the city. Both No. 1 and No. 2 Company Irish Guards took turns manning the checkpoints, patting people down and examining identity papers of the hordes. They were aiming for restraint at the checkpoints, unlike the Americans further to the north. They'd set up their own VCP outside Al Najaf and a confused Iraqi civilian had driven his vehicle away from the checkpoint, a fatal mistake. The US soldiers, now twitchy and trigger happy after the city's first suicide bomb, had opened fire on the errant motorist and killed seven Iraqi children.

This tension made manning the VCP a frustrating and dangerous duty. The British soldiers had to pull cars over and sight scan them first because they didn't want them to pass by and blow up before they'd searched and checked them. There were never enough translators and the few words of Arabic the soldiers had been taught barely helped against the cacophony of infuriated foreign voices. The main targets for stop and search frisks were the fighting-age males, expecting they'd be Saddam's forces, but mostly they were civilian families braving the hot zone of bombardment to make it to safety. For their searches, the soldiers had to tear men from their wives and children from parents who'd scream and beg to be kept together. There were heartbreaking scenes, like one family who were separated, the man dragged off for a search, and his presumed wife ushered through. The woman in a black abaya, only her withered face visible, looked too old to be a mother to the small child that she cradled. She held the scrawny wrapped-up newborn near her chest and turned against the tidal flow of fleeing people and reached out her hand to her husband, her dusty bronze face wailing. The soldiers searched the man as he resisted, his eyes fixed on his wife and child, crying and struggling to reach his hands to hers.

Many who were searched seemed as though they were going about their everyday business and often the angry locals yelled their frustration at the inconvenience of a western invasion. Coming up on the bridge was the slow crawl of traffic. There were truckloads of tomatoes and other goods that pissed-off Baswaris were trying to transport out of town. Intelligence from the flood of fleeing Iraqis told of the grim state of intimidation as Saddam loyalists and militias took fighters' families hostage to ensure they'd still attack the invaders. Either they face the British, or their families would die straight in front of them. The VCPs found obvious Iraqi military deserters too, such as one whose uniform was folded neatly in a plastic carrier bag among his meagre belongings. Major MacMullen needed his soldiers to stop any lunatic who wanted to target their rear and shoot them up, but it was often impossible to separate militiamen from the normal citizens.

The infantry soldiers held Bridge Four, and not far beyond it, about 800 yards, was the British forces' front line. This was the point of containment for the city. While the Irish Guards were near the bridge, they and the civilians they were searching were under almost constant indirect fire from the Iraqis. It was usually from mortars or small-arms fire. Iraqi Fedayeen irregulars would also conduct drive-by runs on the other side of the bridge in pick-up trucks with mounted machine guns which would unleash indiscriminate fire in the soldier's direction. Their militiamen would use mobile phones to call their comrades who'd fire mortar strikes and sniper attacks from the Shia flats, the nearby slum, the Basra Technical College or abandoned factory buildings that were within close range.

Civilians weren't the only hoard that the soldiers had to deal with. There was also the media. It was a dangerous place for the journalists and the threat to them was not just from the Iraqis. About a week earlier, a British ITN reporter, Terry Lloyd, had been killed, along with his Belgian cameraman and Lebanese translator, all three caught in the crossfire of Coalition weapons. Terry was a pioneering reporter, had been the first to get access inside the town of Halabja in 1988 after Saddam had unleashed the cruelty of chemical weapons on Kurds. He'd reported about the Troubles in Northern Ireland, the conflicts in Kosovo, Bosnia and Yugoslavia, yet it was American bullets that finally had his name etched on them. The luckier journalists did present some of the soldiers in a positive light. Captain James Moulton, the Platoon Leader from Call Sign Three Three, was followed by a British media embed who nicknamed him 'Captain Courageous'. A reporter from *The Sun* photographed Captain Niall Brennan and stuck his mug in the paper with a caption that he was a 'dashing soldier'.

On watch at Bridge Four, Joe was with guardsman Bojang when an American reporter walked out in full view of her cameraman, exposed on the side of the bridge checkpoint. The reporter was a blonde woman and wore a blue flak jacket and helmet. Joe overheard her saying she was from the New York-something or other and she was doing a report about the soldiers on the bridge and the stream of people coming out of Basra. Joe clutched his SA-80 across his chest with one eye on her and cast a glance back to where some of the rest of his section were searching rusty Iraqi cars heading south. Joe saw Bojang roll his eyes at the seemingly oblivious reporter.

The whistle of a High Explosive (HE) mortar in flight is a distinct sound. Even Joe was frightened of the mortars when they came down. After the high-pitched scream they boomed as they hit hard. As the woman reporter began to speak her piece to camera, shouting about constant mortar attacks, Joe heard the unmistakable whine grow in approaching volume. A HE round has a kill zone of 5 metres' circumference and an injury zone of 15 metres meaning anyone within range of the impact crater will be either dead or seriously injured with a lot of shrapnel in the legs or torso. The mortars were not accurate, but one at a time the mortars kept raining down and the guardsmen often had to get in the Warrior's protective hull quickly. Joe saw how far out the reporter was, ventured towards the centre of the bridge and saw the trajectory of a HE arcing towards her. Joe acted on instinct as he saw the fresh round of hell that was unleashed in the direction of the reporter and her cameraman. He moved quickly, ran fast and grabbed the woman in an almost rugby tackle movement.

'GET DOWN! Stay the fuck down!' Joe shouted in the reporter's pale face. Joe ducked down and moved away from the blast area, looking for cover.

The cameraman, seeing the incoming mortar, had dropped his camera and darted in the same direction.

Moments later, the HE mortar landed precisely in the place where the young woman had been standing. Its explosion was shatteringly loud. Joe could feel the soil and concrete hitting his helmet from impact, as bits of stones flicked at his face.

'What's your name? What's your name?' the reporter said, both dazed and as if seeing Joe as the best story of her almost short life.

'Just stay the FUCK down!' Joe yelled back, losing his temper.

Joe grabbed her by her vest, blazoned with the word PRESS, and dragged her towards a ditch-like embankment a little before the bridge that provided some cover.

'Stay the fuck down. Don't move. Do not move out of here until those mortars stop.' Joe shouted, his face intimately close, right up in her face. 'Do you understand me?'

Suddenly the woman broke down and with realisation dawning, she started to scream.

'Are you okay, Bo?' Joe shouted, more interested in his mates than anything. 'Are you okay? Is everyone okay?' After a few glances around he was convinced that they'd make it to the Warrior and were fine, job done; a few feet away the American girl cowered, almost foetal-like crying and screaming.

'Get in the tank,' came the order through Joe and Bojang's headsets. Leaving the woman on the bridge but out of range of the mortars, Joe and Bojang hurtled toward the Warrior.

Joe and Bojang climbed into the vehicle and to his sergeant's anger.

'You should never have fucking done that,' the sergeant yelled. 'You should have stayed with the tank.'

Joe settled into his seat and clutched at his rifle as he realised how close a call he'd had. *Fucking hell*, Joe thought, breathless from the near miss of mortars, *I don't think I did anything wrong, it was just a normal thing to do.* The Warrior pulled back, heading for a safe distance and outside the American news reporter and her TV cameraman made their retreat, running around to find their fixer and flee.

The Iraqi government had been using its own media as part of its propaganda machine and the Irish Guards had to help shut down that capability in Basra. Throughout the war, broadcasts came from Baghdad delivered by Mohammed Saeed al-Sahhaf, Saddam's Minister for Information whose exaggerated statements of Iraqi military superiority were a source of ridicule. His comments were counter to facts and reality which underscored the banality of a figure quickly nicknamed 'Baghdad Bob' and 'Comical Ali.'

'We will push those crooks, those mercenaries back into the swamp,' he promised as Coalition forces moved forward. 'The insane little dwarf Bush. The midget Bush and Rumsfeld deserve only to be beat with shoes by people everywhere,' the minister proclaimed as advanced American weapons were unleashed on Baghdad. While meagre Iraqi forces were overpowered by the Americans on their approach to Baghdad, the disinformation minister declared, 'Rumsfeld, he needs to be hit on the head. Yesterday we heard this villain called Rumsfeld. He, of course, is a war criminal.' This message was being disseminated to the people of the south via a 200ft communications mast. Commanders decided that the British forces would undertake a lightning raid to take down not only the tower but also, symbolically, a giant Saddam statue that dominated a park at a key interchange called the Gateway to Basra.

As dawn broke on 29 March, the tenth day of the conflict, a squadron of Black Watch Challenger II tanks went rolling up Red Route and over Bridge Four, accompanied by four Warriors full of Irish Guards infantry soldiers. Iraqi militia launched RPGs but none penetrated the armour of the tanks or Warriors, which each split off to their individual targets. The steel legs of the sturdy TV mast took more than a dozen direct hits from the Challenger's L30A1, 120mm rifled tank gun. Finally, the tower came crashing down away from the tank, taking Iraqi TV off the air in the region.

As the mortars fell, the Iraqis who fled through the Bridge Four checkpoints faced death from their own forces and the Fedayeen militia who cared nothing about civilians caught up in attacks between them and the British forces. During the bombardments, women and children huddled together in fear, crouching for cover as bullets and shells flew over their heads. Plumes of dirty smoke rose as the Challenger fired back towards the Iraqi fighters a half-mile away. Intelligence indicated that there were more than 1,000 Iraqi fighters, and Fedayeen hunkered down in and around Basra. To stop the assaults, the British soldiers undertook sniper missions with the intention of wearing down the resolve of the militants who remained within Basra and eliminate the Fedayeen forces. MacMullen's snipers conducted raids into Basra to known enemy locations. The snipers had trained their craft of killing for years, refined their precision skills. These were strong alpha males, mean looking and clinical, who took aim to eliminate the enemy, yet still the men were sick the first time they took a human life.

Not every sniper mission was successful. Niall Brennan spotted a sniper on the top of a water tower and local people came out to watch the infantrymen, mocking them when they couldn't shoot him down.

Major Ben Farrell, commanding No. 2 Company, had a nine-man team of snipers who could deploy quickly and would work in pairs to infiltrate Basra city and conduct harass and destroy missions against Iraqi paramilitaries. The sense that these missions gave was that the Coalition was breaching the city and getting closer and closer to being able to take Basra.

One insurgent stronghold was the Shia Flats, a poor area on the outskirts of town that resembled a large slum. The people there suffered most at the hands of Saddam's regime and the conditions of poverty were horrible. The Irish Guards entered the area with a platoon to track down some militants. For Joe and the other infantry it was a chance to get out and patrol. A lot of their days had been spent in the hot confines of their Warrior call signs, accompanying the Challengers on raiding missions ready to dismount and hold ground if enemy forces were encountered. Many of the lads were hungry for battle, those that were reserve call signs at the back sometimes whined that they were missing out, only to be assured that their time would come. Walking around the Shia Flats, the soldiers met with a hostile reception and were stoned by locals, angrily stirred up by the infiltrated militants.

The Iraqi forces fought back with what strength they had. On 2 April, Saddam's elite Republican Guard massively ambushed a patrol of Royal Scots Dragoon Guards Challenger IIs. The tanks suffered sustained attacks from RPGs and anti-tank rockets while they were 9 miles outside of Basra. The situation worsened as a missile took out one Challenger sight, leading the crew to reverse into a ditch, ripping off the tank's tracks.

The following day, the Irish Guards engaged in their first urban battle. The target was Basra Technical College, which was just a short distance from Bridge Four towards Basra and from where the militants had been launching mortars and sniper attacks on the bridge. From No. 1 Company, Major MacMullen sent his snipers to kill the fighters. Looking through the belongings of some of the dead at the south-west corner of the college, soldiers found passports that indicated foreign fighters were now in the area and had joined the battle. It was a warning that a local fight was now on the precipice of turning into an ideological one.

Attacking the college absorbed a lot of time but resulted in the soldiers securing their first target on the Basra side of the Az Zubayr canal. Establishing the presence at the Technical College was a decisive victory as it gave a beachhead in Basra for the first time. The strategy of harassment had succeeded through the determination of the Irish Guards infantry and their skilled snipers so that, by 4 April, the British finally had a foothold within the outskirts of Basra.

Chapter 25

Ties That Choke

Joe begins to place the first black cable tie around his neck with great determination, feeding the long end through the small slot of the square plastic head. He doesn't want to live any more. To be sure, he wraps a second cable tie around his jugular, the process just like the fastening of a belt around a waist. Or binding the wrists of an Iraqi detainee.

Seizing both cords firmly in his fist allows him to tighten them. There are subtle clicks as the pawl latch slowly locks into position over the small ridged cord, like a permanently sealed ratchet. Joe's mum is north up in Scotland on a trip with a friend, his grandparents are out and he's alone in the house. Lynn is hesitant to leave and before she does she pesters her son with loving concern.

'Are you going to be okay on your own, Son?'

'Mum, I'm gonna be fine. You go,' Joe placates her. It will be a nice change for her to have a break away from hearing the screaming of his night terror coming from the upstairs attic where he sleeps restlessly. Joe is replacing many of the positive memories of growing up here with the trauma that he's going through, living in the purgatory between being sent home from the army and whatever trial awaits him as the consequences of Iraq. David has his own house now with his new wife and baby. When David closes his eyes, he thinks of his child; when Joe closes his eyes, he feels as though he goes to hell, thinking of Iraq, a dead Iraqi child and hearing the accusations against him.

Joe pulls more forcefully on the cable ties, the threads tightening around his throat. The plastic starts to cut into the skin. It's painful but he doesn't care.

The day is early and Joe's still recovering from having that dream again the previous night. In it he's in the bath once more and the boy's hair is breaking the surface of the water, just dark hair everywhere. The boy's face, his eyes and then he keeps pulling Joe, dragging him down until he awakens screaming. When Joe goes to bed now it is with gloves taped on around his wrists for his own protection. His mum has made him wear them because he's been waking with blood dripping on the sheets from where he's clawed his face in his sleep.

Joe tightens the plastic ties more, pulling down harder. The notches click further and further, definitively as the cord cuts into his skin. He starts to asphyxiate, his lungs hungry to oxygenate his blood. He gags from the back of his throat.

Joe's knocked back some cans of Stella already. It steadies the anxiety that feels as though it's crawling beneath his skin and puts his nerves on edge with the lingering uncertainty. The guilt compresses him, like a collapsing ceiling that even his army training doesn't feel it can keep held above from crushing him. What Joe thinks he remembers of RMP officer Jay's words echo: 'You killed that kid; you fucking killed that boy!' That's the only voice Joe hears, blaming himself, drowning it out with another sweet bubbly swill from the green glass bottle.

Blood coughs up, leaking out over Joe's lips in small globules. He's dizzy and weak, all but given up on living. He doesn't want to wake up.

He feels he's lost the struggle against his flood of memories: the violence of the assault on the college, those that were lost, what happened in the weeks after and the young looter with the afro-looking hairstyle. Joe plays it all back in his head. If he could have turned around, acted when he saw him struggling, if they'd tried more to help. Instead …

That boy, he could have grown up to be a fucking doctor, Joe ponders. *He could have been anything if I had just fucking given him a minute. Instead it was only about time and safety and getting away so I was safe. It just became about me. I wanted to come home. I wanted to come home from that war.* Now here Joe is, at home and he can't bear living any more.

The pressure and pain in his jugular is intense. With all his remaining strength he yanks hard, forcing the cable ties to strangle himself.

Joe knows his mum's tried calling the MoD, but he feels left to rot here, the hierarchy having let him down. This is all stuff he has to deal with on his own. He knows that the majority of England are really proud of the army and what the boys do protecting the country, no doubt about that. But no one really knows. *I've lost my army career and am going to cause my family shame if this goes to a trial,* he believes.

The blood and saliva gather in Joe's oesophagus. He slumps against the wall of his childhood room. Involuntarily he coughs a hoarse, guttural noise. It's too late now.

These cable ties, which are reminiscent of the plasticuffs used by the troops in Iraq, placed abrasively around supple Iraqi skin, cut off Joe's breathing and unlike captive adolescent looters, he is free.

Chapter 26

Hades: Or What Hell Looks Like

The British soldiers had rounded up more suspected Ba'ath party suspects: often plain-clothed men whose wrists were then wrapped in plasticuffs and handed over to the military and their translators for interrogation. The captives told the British that Saddam's resistance was crumbling and revealed the whereabouts of an enemy fighters' stronghold. The soldiers had been told that there were between 80 and 100 Fedayeen fighters holed up at the Basra College of Literature, deep behind the lines within the heart of the city. No. 1 Company's infantrymen would be despatched to the college, where they would dismount from their Warriors and clear the site room by room.

The mission had been named OBJECTIVE ELYSIUM, which was not an Iraqi word as Joe first thought, but took its name from the Greek afterlife. Someone in the Scots Dragoons top brass had seen fit to take the name of a place of death, an ancient concept for the great beyond as the name of their climactic battle. Elysium Fields was the resting place for heroes of myth, the place in the Underworld where worthy slaughtered souls would go. The place was the Islands of the Blessed Dead, a realm at the end of the earth, entered only by those judged righteous and chosen by the gods as most deserving of happiness following their grim demise. Iraq was as the Odyssey described: 'a place where no snow is there, nor heavy storm, nor ever rain'; there was no cooling to men and instead 45°C of heat. Heaven this was most certainly not.

Joe felt the heat early, the sun beat strong and ceaselessly. It was Sunday, 6 April and far to the north the American forces were at last surrounding Baghdad, having entered the city for the first time and bombarded the capital with artillery. Perhaps the Yanks were hoping to repeat the victory of 141 years earlier at the Battle of Shiloh of 6 April 1862, when Confederates met the Union on the bloody battlefield. That collision of flintlock rifles, smoothbore muskets and men fighting left 23,000 dead and wounded, but was a turning point in the uncivil war and brought Ulysses Grant's forces victory. The British commanders, however, were following the lessons of Viscount Montgomery, veteran of desert campaigns eighty years later, whose edict was to outnumber the enemy 3-1.

The British 7th Armoured Brigade charged into Basra in overwhelming force. The two Irish Guard companies, which had 150 men apiece, were to head up the main route into the city and storm the College of Literature to meet the Fedayeen enemy. They called it a 'Lightning Strike'. Before 8.00 am, the forces rolled out from their bus station base just to the south-west of Bridge Four. It was about a 4-mile advance from Bridge Four to a roundabout that was known as the Gates of Basra and near it was the college. The Irish Guards were the first British troops to enter central Basra, their Warriors charging up the main highway that military maps had called 'Red Route'. Pinned to the front of Niall's Warrior was a warning to the enemy: 'If you can read this you are closer to Allah than you think. Have a nice day.' Fourteen Warriors, with support from Royal Scots Dragoons Guards' Challenger artillery tanks, stormed towards their target.

Inside Warrior Call Sign One Two, Joe could hear and feel the aggressive roar of the powerful Perkins-Rolls-Royce V8 Condor engine. The sea of sound failed to drown the distant guns going off. It sounded as if they were getting closer to weapons fire and he could hear the noise of someone firing back. There were nine in Joe's Warrior personnel carrier, which was commanded by Sergeant Carle Selman; there were five Warriors in their platoon, commanded by Daniel O'Connell in Call Sign One Three. As the tanks rolled down that highway, Joe could sense the fear, almost smell it. He could see it in the faces of the other men in the vehicle, tightly packed together, almost on top of each other. In every man's face was apprehension. There was also determination, not a flinch in their muscles. They were eager for the mission and also bolshy, confident that enemy RPG couldn't hurt them in their Warrior. Joe was in the back with the rest of his section: Hollander, Sampat, Wheeler, Fleming and Bojang. Cooke was in the driver's seat and McGing was up top in the gunner's hatch. Gingy's spot gave him the best view of their approach into Basra. What he saw was a line of civilians fleeing in the opposite direction. Mini-buses, old cars, pick-up trucks that sped from the town. Like the infantrymen, the civilians didn't know what was coming, but they expected the worst. Still, the locals seemed to support the soldiers, at least initially, honking horns and waving at the column as it passed by.

Attacking a college in an urban area meant that there were limits to the help the soldiers could expect from air support. Before the infantry set out for the college, planes from B Squadron and No. 2 Company of B Squadron destroyed some enemy defensive positions. It did not go without a hitch since there was initial confusion to straighten out as the soldiers' timing was off-synch. The soldiers were still operating on GMT; the RAF pilots conducted their bombing runs using an artillery time zone. After being softened up by aerial bombardment, Ben Farrell's No. 2 Company then had to deal with Iraqi tanks left blocking the perimeter of the college. The Irish Guards called up a bladed REME unit from the rear with a Challenger Armoured Repair and Recovery Vehicle (CRARRV). The CRARRV was a regular Challenger II tank fitted at the front with a massive mustard-coloured plough blade. The Challenger and its big chassis pushed aside the two abandoned Iraqi T-50 and T-80 tanks with ease. Another Challenger II, commanded by Major Chris Brannigan, then smashed through the perimeter fence and drove into the grounds and encircled the college. Then hell broke loose.

The Basra College of Literature was a collection of three-storey white and washed-out yellow buildings. Several 'H'-shaped block buildings made up the large campus and the windows had metal grates over grey shadowy rectangles. These windows made perfect sniper positions and almost instantly Fedayeen fighters emerged and unleashed a volley of RPGs towards the arriving infantry. When the Warriors ground to a halt, they didn't just stop suddenly but rocked like a boat, ceasing momentum on its tracks. Inside, men's shoulders hit metal and it told them that it was just a moment until the rear door opened. Joe's heart was in his mouth, not knowing what he was stepping into. Suddenly the back door of Call Sign One Two went bump and started opening. Joe heard the bang, bang percussion of bullets. A second later was the chaos of men screaming, 'Move!' The air was a haze of the morning, white dust kicked up from the vehicles and exploding weapons fire.

The call sign let loose its infantry. Dismounts sprayed the building's windows with chain-gun fire. A rapid hail of 7.62 ammo erupted. Fire and movement. The lad next to Joe grabbed his Light Anti-armour Weapon (LAW). It was a two-piece launch tube with a ready-to-fire rocket within. He flipped up the sight, took aim at the main entrance and shot the weapon. A half second later the powerful round tore out of the tube. It decimated the door, the blast igniting an instant cloud of splinters, shrapnel and smoke. The lads from Call Sign One Three stormed the building first, led by Commander Dan O'Connell. He was standing, arm raised in the air pointing forward. It looked as though he was leading his men onwards in a cavalry charge reminiscent of the Battle of Waterloo. Muzvuru, Malone and Holland and others followed, their boots thundering a powerful mass of leather soles up the stairs. With the door blown open and the entrance cleared, the men started to search each room. Joe grabbed an H-L109 grenade, pulled the pin from this bronze ball of death and threw it in. Then a second for the smoke to clear. He peered in clutching his SA-80, scanning to see if it was empty of insurgents. They were young infantry soldiers, lads trained for one round, one kill.

Joe made his way with his section, flushing room to room. The soldiers took care not to blow down doors and fire indiscriminately; this was still an educational compound, which complicated their Rules of Engagement. In some rooms and down corridors, some Iraqi civilians inside the building seemed to be standing about. The Iraqis became frantic and tried to dodge the soldiers in the chaos. Some lads were ordered to pull these apparent Baswaris out and search them to find out if they really were civilians. Unlike the Geneva-bound British soldiers, the Fedayeen played by their own undisciplined rules, dressing as civilians and hiding among local people. Some of them emerged from sandbagged defensive positions, well-armed and fired small arms and RPGs, trying to aim in the guardsmen's direction as they moved from one building to another.

The men fought hard. Room after room, following the same routine. Soft posture clearing each, one by one. Door opened, grenade in the room, survey eyes-on and spilling rounds to make sure everyone suspected of being a combatant was dead. The hot late morning drew on and sweat coated Joe. His helmet strap was tight, rubbing uncomfortably around his chin. The pack on his back was weighty. He had sacks of ammunition on his shoulders and they cut the side of his neck under the weight of the belt of ammo. In every room he saw there was a portrait of Saddam adorning a wall. A flamboyant gold bust of the dictator decorated a foyer in the college. Joe was like a silhouette that passed through lingering grenade smoke and drifts of light into the college's library. Once beautifully ornate, now the place had become a battleground. Long-studied books and a coat of fresh dust littered the ground; exercise books once marked with fine Arabic calligraphy now stained with soldiers' boot prints and splatters of red, dripped haphazardly like a Pollock painting. Sand and shattered glass fragments covered an open book that was spread-eagled with recognisable words of English that Joe would still struggle to read. He moved on. Through the library, left. A stairway, up, and into a windowed room. He burst the doors open. A sudden eruption. Non-uniformed Arab men inside, glimpsed as shadows but actually figures adorned in black. They retaliated against the Irish Guards infantrymen and pounded them with gunfire. The Fedayeen militia let loose a torrent of rounds. Foreign shrieked words hoarsely shouted at the British soldiers. A surge of bullets sent them scattering again. The Section battled to stay in formation. It was crazed intensity.

'Head down! Head down!' screamed a couple of lads.

'I want to fucking get out of here,' came a Brummie-accented yell from the commotion.

'Grenades!'

Joe pitched another grenade amid the popping cracks and they filtered through, SA-80s vibrating death. He took aim at any movement, anyone not killed instantly by the grenade's explosion. If they were injured, they'd be shot dead. These fighters had guns themselves, they were fighting to kill and the infantrymen returned the favour. A beat passed and the soldiers re-entered. Paused at the room's threshold, Joe took a knee to survey the clearing smoke down the sights of his rifle. A couple of Arab bodies twitched; then limp, bloodied.

'Clear?' came shouted questions seeking affirmation.

'Clear! Room's clear.'

Joe moved on. His battered muscles tingled with the pounding sting of adrenaline. Spent assault rifle rounds rolled beneath his boots. He forced himself to take a breath as he backed into the stairway.

A lot of the Iraqis were giving up by now, a good couple of hours into the assault. Some were running through the corridor clutching anything white, waving their desperation. They'd dropped their weapons and were filing downstairs like an evacuation.

'Oh my friend, my friend …' cried a middle-aged Iraqi man as he came down the stairs. He pushed up against Joe, shoving as a small crowd of descending Iraqis and ascending infantry soldiers jammed the stairway.

'My friend. My friend …' the man muttered aggressively. Joe butted him straight in the forehead and he just hit the floor. Iraqis were getting dropped, knocked out left and right.

A handful of Iraqi prisoners, three or four of them, were pulled stumbling down the stairs, arms forced behind their backs. The infantrymen put sacks over their heads, tied them up and then took them out of the building and threw them into the back of a Warrior. *We're not giving them a fucking table for two,* Joe thought. *They'll get a good hiding along the way.*

Captives had to be detained, processed, interrogated, but the soldiers didn't have time to deal with them when there were still people actively shooting, so they just got dragged downstairs. The process was like a chain. There were infantrymen behind Joe and he'd pass the captive suspects through down the line.

'Clear. Clear.' It was like an echo shouted, penetrated from the shattered shell of the college.

'Clear! Clear!' The shooting started to subside; sporadic now, the occasional pop. It was towards the end. Dust was settling.

'Is that the end of the shooting?' someone shouted.

It had taken more than five hours of the fiercest fighting that most of the men had known. Joe was exhausted. There were plenty of enemy bodies but no Coalition casualties. They had all survived. The place was theirs.

Once they had cleared the rooms, they wrapped up the bodies and began to bring down the dead fighters. Joe carried down one of the corpses and dumped it in the college grounds. It was the first time he'd seen the sunlight for hours and its power stretched his irises painfully.

Joe saw Niall Brennan, back out at his Warrior where he had a map. It illustrated the buildings and hostile blocks around the college. His 'Kill Box', he called it. He'd marked it up in a heavy black wax pencil; the few areas still waiting to be secured were hatched out with their codenames. Pat Geraghty, with the remainder of his packet, had stayed back at the base, having been held there by the Company Second in Command in case there'd been casualties or a need for more ammunition.

The company's vehicles had a secure circle around the college's perimeter. It created an all-round defence. After they'd searched the area, they examined a few prisoners. Whoever survived and was hurt got taken to the medics; rules of the Geneva Convention meant that they had to be provided with care. Rifling through the dead, the infantrymen found some foreign passports; it was the same story with the prisoners, one of whom was a Frenchman or Algerian. In Call Sign Zero Bravo, MacMullen's Warrior, there was a French-speaker who interrogated the man. The fight here had attracted the fanatical hordes from across the Islamic world.

As if from nowhere emerged Red Crescent volunteers, working hard and fast to get their dead collected, true to their Muslim beliefs, before sunset.

It was getting dark and everything was done. Basra city was almost theirs.

'This is gonna be the first night in,' Joe said to McGing.

'It's not bad, is it? I'm fucking knackered out, though,' he replied in his Brummie accent.

'I dunno what tomorrow's gonna bring, mate,' Joe said.

Everyone was shattered. Some of the men stayed inside their Warriors, cooking up their Meals Ready to Eat (MRE) rations or resting. Joe and some of his section found a concrete building alongside their Warrior with some space in which to camp out. Inside was a glassless window so the men could look out and there were ledges where they could place their rifles. *This is cushty*, Joe thought. Then it hit him: *My God, I'm so tired.*

Every bone seemed to throb.

It was finally calm.

They rested there.

Darkness fell.

The two Fedayeen in civilian clothes must have been hiding in wait. Four of the main college buildings had been fully cleared and the Irish Guards had set up a perimeter around them using their Warriors to create a defensive formation in a semicircle. The soldiers thought they had secured the area around the college. Then the two men struck.

Call Sign One Three was around the eastern side of the perimeter. Inside the Warrior, Daniel O'Connell's section, Ian 'Molly' Malone was heating up some rations, the day's fighting had made them all hungry. Chris 'Muz' Muzvuru was inside too along with Richie Martin and Rod Holland. Someone inside opened the door at the back of the Warrior that caused a red light to come on. All had been dark but the blood red glow of illumination must have drawn attention. It provided a patient hidden insurgent with a target. There was shooting all the time at all hours in Iraq, often for celebrations, but this was different. Joe heard the night air as it splintered with a loud bang, bang, crack of automatic weapons fire. Someone had broken cover and sprayed gunfire towards the Warriors. It was followed instantly by screaming of young familiar voices. This was a sound of terror such as Joe had never heard.

By the rapid pounding of rounds Joe could tell that there were at least two enemy combatants taking shots at them. In the back of Daniel O'Connell's Warrior, Malone had turned from heating his rations at the opening of the door, when a bullet struck him in the head. Muzvuru was also standing near the door when the assailant opened fire and he was shot. Richie Martin, a Scots Dragoons soldier, took rounds in the chest. The pounding of weapons rounds continued. Lance Sergeant Rod Holland took a bullet in the shoulder. Holland struggled quickly to his feet, bleeding profusely but returning fire. He bravely went to give chase after the insurgents, but then went to help his injured fellow soldiers. Daniel O'Connell leapt up quickly and let off some retaliatory rounds.

Wayne Sampat, from Joe's section, was on stag doing sentry duty in a small concrete pill-box-like structure just away from the main building. He'd heard the shooting and his section second-in-command, Jay, rushed in.

'There's a gunmen; there's a gunman!' Jay blurted needlessly.

Sampat was wearing night vision goggles and peered out of a slit in his out building. The night was transformed into a world of speckled green and black. A figure moved into view and Sampat trained his SA-80 on the target. He steadied his weapon, zeroed-in through his sight. Quickly moving, he closed his finger around the trigger.

'Wait. Don't. Fuck!' said Jay rapidly.

'I think that's Holland out chasing insurgents!'

Someone from the driver's seat of Joe's Warrior jumped up into the turret and tried to aim the 7.62mm machine gun but was unable to safely make out a target.

Joe was inside the small building next to his Warrior where he scoured the darkness for the origin of the shots – and the identity of whoever had been hit. The shots seemed to come from the area around which all the vehicles were encircled. If the soldiers started shooting they were likely going to hit whoever was opposite and start killing each other in the crossfire. This could be a blue on blue situation waiting to happen. There was shouting amid the wailing from the injured. There were shapes moving fast in the darkness, maybe infantry lads running or maybe the enemy. No one knew whether to shoot or not.

'Where is he? Where is he?' lads yelled out. People wanted to return fire but didn't know what to do.

'Do we open fire on them or not?' echoed frantic screams.

'Get in the tanks now. Get in the tanks now,' someone yelled. 'Everyone mount up. Mount up.'

'No fucking way,' someone countered. 'It's not secure out there!'

Intermittent rifle pops cracked, but the infantrymen quickly realised they were like a circular firing squad. It was a mess. No one knew for sure what was going on.

'Someone's died. There's some people that are dead from our company,' someone called. Joe didn't know for sure what had happened and his mind started running.

The screams from those Joe knew churned his guts, made him feel sick. He was still inside the out-building but knew that some of his section were out near their Warrior. Joe thought of the lads he knew who were out there; some of his best mates including Craig 'Marshy' Marshall who was as close a brother. Was he among the dead who had been picked off by the sniper? Joe didn't know.

Company Commander Major MacMullen was the first on the scene. It was around 8.00 pm and a streetlight had just flickered on. Darkness was their enemies' friend as they probably knew the college compound better than the soldiers from No. 1 Company, but the lack of light didn't hinder the infantry men; they had advanced night vision equipment. MacMullen wanted to even things out so he shot out the light with his pistol. He'd left his Warrior and, using the vehicles as cover, made his way to Call Sign One

Three which had been targeted. The men had gone to ground, hiding around the Warriors and near the Challengers; frightened, his soldiers in tatters huddled around their vehicles.

'Hold fire.' MacMullen yelled.

'Hold fire, hold fire.' came a chorus of echoes as the guns stopped.

MacMullen found Platoon Commander O'Connell, whose men had been hit.

'Daniel, give me a sit-rep,' MacMullen called firmly.

'Corporal Muzvuru's dead, sir,' O'Connell said with incredible effort.

'Malone and Martin injured. Pretty bad.'

MacMullen swung around bravely to the rear of the Warrior. What he saw was a mess. Muzvuru was splattered in the vehicle. Malone was still alive, barely clinging on to life. He'd taken two bullets, one through the wrist, one through the head and his brains were seeping out. MacMullen leaned down and stabbed Richie Martin with a shot of morphine. MacMullen was terrified of the pen's auto-inject function and having it upside down and injecting himself. The area wasn't secure, meaning MacMullen had to reorganise the perimeter. He approached Platoon Sergeant Fergus.

'Right, Fergie, we're getting hit. I need you to get a sniper position from out there. See what we're dealing with. Happy?'

'Not happy, sir. But I understand.' Fergus replied.

Several miles away, at the Technical College, Pat Geraghty heard over the radio that an ambush had happened and people were hurt. This was the last phase of the fighting and everyone was feeling pretty untouchable, he thought. Pat waited back at the other end of Red Route until a call came out to bring forward the field ambulance.

MacMullen got on the radio; it was abuzz with chaotic chatter. Fergus had a vantage point and radioed in that he could see two men but not identify them. Were they the Fedayeen gunmen or Irish Guardsmen? MacMullen radioed Captain Mick Garraway, an Australian who was on secondment with No. 2 Company Irish Guards, and he confirmed that all members of his company were accounted for. MacMullen had 173 people under his command in No. 1 Company and had discovered one soldier, Paul Caughers, unaccounted for. After a call around, Sniper Ally reported that he had Caughers with him; all of No. 1 Company was confirmed accounted for. MacMullen got on the net with Ben Farrell and had him close the perimeter. They weren't quick enough. The Fedayeen gunmen could have hidden under rubble or metal sheets, waiting for hours, perhaps feigning death before rising up to attack. Now in the commotion they'd escaped.

Still waiting at the Technical College, Pat Geraghty heard the radio operator confirm news of two deaths. It was heartbreaking. Shortly afterwards, Pat was told that a vehicle containing both bodies was moving down Red Route to his location and he slowly made his way to the entry point to meet them. After a few heartrending moments, two Warriors rolled up; one commanded by Captain O'Connell containing the bodies, the other, commanded by Captain Brennan, acting as escort.

When the Warriors' movement ceased, Geraghty surveyed the scene and saw the two bodies covered with military medic sheets. The dark-skinned arm immediately told Pat that the first body was Muzvuru; he had difficulty identifying the second man. The CSM saw that the feet protruded out, longer than the sheet would cover. The two tallest men in the company were Ian 'Molly' Malone and Williams 'Speedy'; Geraghty didn't know who the body was. Colour Sergeant Frankie Howell then told Pat with sadness that the second man lost was Ian Malone. Both remains were placed in body bags and a solemn prayer for the dead was said over the corpses before they were moved to a temporary morgue overseen by soldiers from the First Aid Post.

Field surgeons were doing their incredible work stabilising Rich Martin and Rod Holland. The Warrior Call Sign One Three was similarly shot up badly. To Brennan, peering through the back door, it looked to be almost a foot deep in the blood from his fellow soldiers. Geraghty turned on his torch light and surveyed the devastation inside the Warrior in which the men had died. The inside of the vehicle was in a mess, with blood splattered across the ceiling, internal walls and gathered as a pool on the floor. It was essential that the vehicle be returned to an operational state as soon as possible.

'What do you need me to do?' asked Captain Ed Megan.

'I need you to get this Warrior back and ready again for service,' Pat replied.

It was a grim and unenviable ask, but Captain Megan, along with Colour Sergeant Crawley, began the task of cleaning its interior. To the men's credit, the job was completed and the vehicle back in service within a couple of hours.

The aftermath of everything was surreal. A Para regiment was brought in for relief and kept watch while the Irish Guards rested. Major MacMullen brought a lot of the men into a cleared and secured building to confirm what only a few of them knew at that point.

This was their first night inside Basra and it was a terrible introduction to the city. Joe held tightly on to his rifle, cradling it, as MacMullen, the gentle soul, broke the news.

'Molly's died and Muz has died,' he related, his voice struggling to form composure.

'There's two others, Holland and Martin, who were injured and they're in a critical condition. Holland's stable. We don't know if Martin's going to make it.'

Everyone was spent from the day's fighting and finished off by this news. The room seemed to become even darker.

'Rest up 'cause we're going in the morning again.' MacMullen concluded.

The weary infantrymen unrolled sleeping bags and bedded down. Joe lay in the room and the only sound he could hear was everyone crying. He felt almost as if the floor was shivering as grown soldiers wept.

Fucking hell, this is one night, Joe mused to himself. He got deeper into his sleeping bag and curled into a ball. Exhausted, yet he never slept that night. He just cried. So, he imagined, did those around him. No one spoke. The noise sounded only of tears and softly mumbled prayers. Joe's only overriding certainty in those moments was that he wasn't going home; his mind flooded with the notion that he'd not make it back from this. *This is the enemy's backyard we're in and this is the first night. There's no way I'm going home.* He remembered his mum. And Carlos. David. Even his Helen, the sister he sparred with and took the mickey out of still. Joe thought about everyone back at The Queens Pub. And he felt so selfish because all he could think of was himself and yet two lads had just lost their lives. Ian Keith Malone, 28, and Christopher Muzvuru, only 20, both gone. *God, there's no way I'm going home.*

Joe could tell that others around him felt the same. Craig Marshall, lying next to him, was crying. Lads were saying prayers even if they'd never said a prayer before in their lives. These lads, who if they stepped into a church would probably cause the roof to fall in. On a Sunday, when these lads were supposed to go to service, many avoided it. There wasn't much holiness in that black room, and yet in the darkness they were all saying prayers, desperately sought the sanctuary of the Divine. They were holding on to any memory, fearful of their advance and begging a God they barely believed in that he needed to protect them.

It had been nearly twenty-four hours since they arrived at OBJECTIVE ELYSIUM. This day and night had felt like a taste of what hell was like.

Chapter 27

Sectioned

The wound on the back of Joe's neck hurts like hell. It's where David sliced into his skin with scissors to cut the cable ties that had been choking him to death.

'He's not coming back,' the social worker says stiffly. 'We can't sign him back over to you, Lynn, I'm sorry.' Joe's mum listens with sad concern. 'We really believe that he's going to try and take his own life again, you know. We think he's definitely going to kill himself,' the man explains to Lynn, who views him with scepticism.

'You can't,' Lynn begins.

'I'm so sorry,' the social worker continues. 'We're going to section him under the Mental Health Act.'

'No, you can't.'

'Unfortunately, we're going to have to take your son over to Stoddart House.'

Joe hears his mum burst into tears and plead in reply, 'you'll make him worse if you take him there. Please don't take him,' she begs the doctor.

'He's asking for help. Obviously, he's asking for help. He's in that frame of mind, where this kid's gonna die,' the social worker says in thick Scouse.

'Go on then, take him,' Joe's mum reluctantly agrees, a tide of tears ebbing, torn about what is the right thing to do. She goes over to her son and tries to explain to him what's about to happen before he leaves, but Joe doesn't want to hear that it's for his own good. He doesn't want to be locked away. He doesn't want to be here.

'Don't do it mum. Don't let them take me away,' is all Joe can manage to say.

Soon two orderlies come to move him from the hospital to Stoddart House, the mental health facility that's located behind the hospital and in the same grounds. Joe's still exhausted, recovering from trying to hang himself with plastic cable ties, as they push him in a wheelchair along corridors with muted coloured walls. Joe's mum walks with him nervously until they reach a set of double swing-doors for a brief exposure to the outside world as he's helped into the short white in-patient ambulance that will shuttle him to the psychiatric ward. It takes two security guards to drag him into the patient transport vehicle, although Joe barely puts up a fight because he's little awareness of what's going on, apathetic to his surroundings, groaning still groggy from sedatives.

'Joe!' he hears his mum scream, and catches sight of her clutching the outside of the ambulance van. David is there at her shoulder as she tries to climb inside until she is told by the orderlies that she has to make her way around to Stoddart House on foot. The doors close with a crunch, Lynn clammering at the windows. She pounds as the diesel engine drowns out what else she's saying. During the short journey across the hospital grounds, Joe rouses himself and as the ambulance pulls up he's ready to fight to stay out of the secure ward. The orderlies open the van's rear doors and Joe rushes them to make a bolt for it, unsteadily, until two sets of firm hands clasp his weakened forearms. He glimpses his mum having made it around and sees her as they drag him through two sets of main doors, one to a reception area and the second heavier, of reinforced glass and key fob access controlled. The latter set lock securely. The two men who have hauled him in slacken their grip and he takes the opportunity to try and prise open the doors to get back to his mum. The two orderlies again move in to grab Joe, but he loses control, gunning for them.

'Come on you fuckers!' he screams, droplets of spit cascading from his mouth. 'You don't stand a chance, I'm telling you now.'

As he struggles, Joe observes a young nurse pull his mum from the glass door, which is inches away from his face. He sees the woman's mouth make the words: 'You're making it worse.'

Joe can see his mum is screaming outside, a frantic messy family scene as she's joined by his brother, the stability of support. Joe struggles hard, rowing his thick set shoulders back and forth.

'You're gonna kill him. You can't leave him like this,' Lynn is shouting. 'I just need to get him home. You got to let him go. You got to let him go!'

'Don't take me away. Mum! Tell them not to take me away,' Joe is screaming now. 'Don't, don't, just let me go back. I'm sorry, I won't do it again.'

'We need to get him calmed down,' Joe hears a nurse yell. The two orderlies are joined by a third and they pull him away. His family becomes a diminishing sight as he's dragged to a room in isolation, locked inside. His throat is still wound-raw from the self-inflicted strangulation as he screams. Joe punches and punches and punches, fists pulverise a hole through the plaster wall. The wall echoes with his screaming.

Everyone in Liverpool knows about Stoddart House, Mersey Care NHS Trust's acute mental health unit. It has been around for thirty years, a bruised red, almost purple, brick building; part of Aintree's Fazakerley Hospital, and the Broadoak Unit, in the Broadgreen area of town. Locals know that Stoddart is a rough psychiatric treatment centre, teeming with drugs and alcohol. Some of the youths are there to escape drugs and yet they're surrounded by them at the place where they try to get clean. The staff try to do their best, but it's an under-resourced mental health ward and morale is low. Three years prior, in 2002, a depressed factory worker slashed his own wrists there, having taken a razor blade and some cannabis into the mental health facility. He was found dead in a bath, despite being under close observation for trying to throw himself off a ferry bound for Ireland. This place is for healing but its reputation is anything but.

After Joe's calmed down, the Stoddart House staff take him from isolation to one of the dormitory-style wards where the patients, like inmates, have to stay. Only a thin fabric curtain separates one from another.

Joe awakens with rage during the night, unsettled by distant moaning and disturbed by his disturbed neighbour. The man makes guttural, throaty sounds clearing phlegm and then spits loudly on the floor. Again, croaky coughing, a wheeze and spit. Globules of spittle coagulating as frothy slime on the linoleum floor. Spit after spit from the man lying in the bed closest to Joe's.

'Shut the fuck up, will ya,' Joe mumbles.

Again, a throaty grunt, then ejection of spit. He keeps doing it. Grunt, spit. Grunt, spit. Grunt, spit. *The man must be some addict or something,* Joe thinks, trying to bend a thin pillow around his head.

Cough. GRUNT. Hacking SPIT.

Enough!

Joe leaps to his feet, yanks the curtain aside. He's alongside the spitting man and pummels his fist into the man's face.

'You bastard,' Joe yells as he makes to batter him again.

Like a switch flipped, alarms go off. It's as though Joe's robbed a bank. Lights blink on. Two nurses rush in. They try to tackle Joe. He catches one in a firm headlock. He's still physically fit; has easily shaken off the sedatives from earlier. The second nurse tries to wrestle with Joe and he catches their faces using a free arm. Joe is gone, lost in a rage.

'Come on!' he yells. In his anger he makes towards the door and freedom. More orderlies flood in from other wards. He wrestles with the pile of men, throwing some aside, struggling against the tangle of restraining limbs and hands. Eleven people surround Joe, some on top of him. One forces his pants down. He's naked from the waist down as they force injections into his arse. The more the sting of needles injecting, the more he rages. He clenches his fists, strains his muscles. The first nurse in the headlock in the crook of Joe's arm starts to choke. He won't release them; deaf to agonising gagging and screams. Another needle jabs Joe, a sedative. Hands bash. Fingers coil and clamp Joe's leg, pull it down from under him. He stumbles, knee on the floor. A surge and he comes back up. Another needle. Streaming serum flows in his veins. Strength ebbs, suddenly. All is dark.

Joe comes around, groggy in a fog like a dull hangover. It's been a day and a half, they tell him. There are blood pressure monitors alongside his bed and he's in a different ward. Alone.

A nurse walks in, checks his pulse, blood pressure and other vitals. They see he's conscious.

'Mr McCleary. Are you feeling a little calmer today?'

'Yeah. I'm sorry,' Joe says, contritely, partly slurring. 'I sorry about fucking earlier. This isn't really who I am. I'm in a bit of a bad place.'

The woman nods curtly as she places a clipboard at the end of Joe's hospital bed.

Joe's first week in Stoddart House is horrible. He feels as though it's his worst point. When he gets up and explores the mental asylum he's been committed to he finds it a place of people drugged up; deals being done in the smoking room where the vulnerable inmates on Ebony Ward are largely left to their own devices. They put Joe on a diet of tablets that he can barely stomach, little paper cups containing different types of meds. He struggles each time to take them, every swallow regurgitates emotion and the memory of his overdose taken a few weeks back on a winter night.

This hospital is just as bad as the war, he feels. There are counselling sessions with doctors who he doesn't let inside his shield. Joe keeps silent, to himself. All he wants to do is hurt himself. He's on a destruct mission, just to die. Nobody knows what to say, the staff psychologists not knowing how to deal with someone who's not fighting drugs but battling memories. They don't see what he's going through.

The only time Joe speaks is when his mum visits. She attends her son's mandatory psychiatrist visits, trying to get Joe to talk while he stares at the floor.

'You've got post-traumatic stress related to your time in Iraq,' they diagnose. 'But the longer you don't speak to me, the longer you'll be in here,' says the doctor. He pauses, giving Joe the opportunity to reply in the silence, before he continues.

'You're a serious risk to yourself.' After another pause Joe responds.

'Can I go home now? Get out?' is all he says.

Joe spends days staring at walls. He gazes blankly as the television flashes numbingly. During one weekend of the time that mushes into inconsequence, John, Joe's dad, looks for his son in the visitors' centre. Accompanying him is Joe's uncle, John's brother.

'Aye, son?' John asks unsteadily, several beers already past his tongue.

Joe says nothing while his dad stands, drunk, awkward.

'Heard you're in a bit of a bad way, son.'

'Get him out now!' Joe snaps finally, 'Get out now!' He's almost growling. There's a nearby table that Joe grasps and throws across the room.

'I said get him out now!' Without even looking at his dad, Joe adds. 'Get him out!'

Nurses hurry over. They utter something and rush John out.

'I don't want to fucking see his face again,' Joe seethes, panting. His uncle steps forward, putting a calming hand on his nephew's shoulder.

'Joe,' his uncle says. 'Your dad doesn't know how to deal with stuff like this.' No one does.

The MOD don't know how, or seem to care, when their help is sought. Joe's mum has called them six, seven times. They fob her off with: 'Yeah, I'm sure he'll be fine.' Or, on hearing he's locked away: 'He's better where he is.' She pleads for help, leaves more messages for someone to call. Someone will come, Joe hopes. If Major MacMullen knew or Pat Geraghty get wind that he's here, locked away, they'll be here. Joe feels he's been left here to rot. *If he can get hold of them they'll be here. They'll be by my side till I'm better and out of this hell.* He believes that firmly, holds on to it. *They will protect me,* he thinks.

Lynn keeps calling, but is defeated by the Ministry of Defence. No one returns her calls. For all the military might, Joe battles this alone. He must climb out of this himself. Three weeks in and the doctors speak to Joe's mum and tell her to encourage her son to share if he wants to get better.

'They said you've got to open up, you've got to speak to them,' his mum pleads softly, words she prays will filter through. 'They're not going to let you go.' Lynn cries but it's Joe who breaks inside.

'You want to do this?' Joe finally relents during his next session. 'Let's go, let's do it.'

He opens up the sluice of his experiences and the advancing trauma spills out. The listening doctor sits in shock. Joe tells them about the nightmares, what he's seen in Iraq during just three shocking months of war, a society breaking down, his arrest and the trial that looms over him. The psychiatrist listens, stunned, uncomprehending.

Chapter 28

The Voice

Joe awoke, still exhausted, uncomprehending, still stunned at the loss of two of the platoon. It was cold in the blown-out building that was part of the college they'd fought and died for, then bedded down in. The night was interrupted by rage, distant gunfire and grief that yielded barely any sleep. Hardened tears glued his eyes shut and in the confines of his mind he thought for an instant how lucky he was to see a new day. And then he blamed himself for feeling lucky to be alive.

Molly and Muz were gone. *It could have been me,* Joe thinks. *It could have been any of us. It just so happened that their tank door was open and they were easy targets.* Malone and Muzvuru were in a different section to Joe, but they'd always speak and sit next to each other. Joe remembered Molly's stories about his family in Ballyfermot, near Dublin and Muz talking about his homeland of Zimbabwe. Their loss made Joe frightened and enraged. Nothing softened the anger, not even hearing that a Coalition strike may have managed to kill Chemical Ali, a claim that Iraq strongly denied; nor hearing rumours that the Americans had found the first evidence of WMD in Hindiyah, a town on the Euphrates, south of Baghdad, despite claims that the discovery was just agricultural pesticides.

With daylight, 7 April, No. 1 Company was told that most of them were needed to push on into Basra's centre. Several platoons went into the city and started to establish a base and hand out bottles of water to try and win the hearts and minds of the local populace. It was needed. After two weeks of holding back and engaging in a war of attrition, Basra was now in the hands of the British. It was a generally bloodless takeover. With their oppressors largely overthrown in the city, the restraints were off, human nature seeped out and lawless looting began. Angry scores were being settled as several Shia lynch mobs took revenge and began to kill Ba'ath party militiamen.

Joe's own section was left to fully clear the College of Literature grounds and keep an eye out for the militants who had made their sneak attack the previous night. Joe and the others moved out, wearing backpacks, water, radios, mouthpieces for their radios, with headsets hanging down from helmets, and carrying SA-80s. One section moved through the college again; they would radio in each room until they had confirmed all were now vacant. Joe's section searched the perimeter of the college grounds. He surveyed the remnants of yesterday's devastation; twisted metal of mown-down fencing, RPG casings, blood stains where enemy bodies had laid slain. Joe heard a short bolt of static announce a radio transmission, probably another room cleared. Then a ghostly foreign voice interrupted; invaded his ears.

'YOU BASTARDS! YOU BASTARDS! YOU'RE ALL GONNA DIE!' It was broken English, the voice heavily accented Middle-Eastern. Its tone was vindictive, murderous, local. The sound haunted Joe, spoke down into his bone marrow.

Joe's sergeant, Carle Selman, kicked him swiftly in the sides.

'Who's that? That's not funny,' said Selman annoyed.

'Sarge, it's not us,' Joe pleaded.

'Where the fuck's it coming from?'

No one could identify the voice on their frequency or how it was there; this was a network used by their platoon alone. The men made a fast accounting of all the radio units and quickly discovered one was missing. They reasoned that a headset must have been lost during the darkness and chaos of the firefight the previous night. Maybe it could have been Muz or Molly's headset, lost amid the carnage. What chilled Joe was the knowledge that the range of their radios was only about a hundred metres. Whoever was taunting them on their comms frequency had to be close by. They were likely watching the soldiers' every move, probably through the sights of an assault rifle. The guardsmen were within range of some three- and four-storey neighbouring buildings so the enemy could be above, looking down on them, tracking them, picking them out as a target.

'Everyone take cover; search those buildings,' the men were told.

They had to get the headset back. It's either them or us was Joe's attitude. So much anger and hurt rippled through him. Hours earlier they'd just lost people, and he felt a determination to find whoever it was out there. The owner of that disembodied voice was probably responsible, at least in Joe's mind, and probably those of the rest of the platoon, for the death of Molly and Muz, and the injuries of the others.

To the east of the College of Literature were houses and the few men fanned out quickly into the fringes of this urban centre of Basra. Testosterone- and adrenaline-flooded intensity shoved them through the nearby narrow alleyways, staying close to walls for cover, looking ahead and always above. Confused Basra residents, those who hadn't fled, were going about their daily routine. They looked confused as the infantrymen pounded the streets in their armour, pushing those in their way roughly aside. Joe felt single-minded, determined to find the voice on their radio, it compelled him. He had tears in his eyes as he moved onwards. He dragged a nearby Iraqi man, middle-aged, white-robed, thin, all withered skin and stubble, pulling him close and yelling to him.

'Where is he? Where is he? Man with radio! Get me him.' These common Iraqis, victim of an oppressive regime, persecuted Shias with a broken education system probably spoke not a word of English. The storming of soldiers further into this suburb sent many of these people hustling, desperate; just getting out of the way. They probably had nothing to do with the situation, Joe realised. For the young infantryman, adrenaline took over as he was desperately trying to find a person he believed had killed two of his mates. There was little holding him back.

Joe went through what seemed like an old cinema, dingy, with ragged seats. Back out on the street, there were seven of the infantrymen and they raided every room of the nearby houses. Some of the Iraqis they came across got battered. Joe looked down and saw there was blood on his fists. In the back of his mind he knew innocent people got hurt, but he couldn't get to grips with what he was doing or even where he was. He felt as though someone had ripped his heart from his chest. Some of the others lost it, too; everyone was upset. They were lads who had just been through a day and a night of hell. Joe was utterly convinced that the enemy taunting them over the radio and responsible for the attack was nearby. Around him, the olive-skinned, tired-looking people all looked the same, blurred indistinguishable features. Joe entered into another room, another Arab man. He was desperate to interrogate people to get the answers that he wanted.

'Where is he? Where is he? Now!' Joe yelled. The man, wearing a long white caftan robe, flushed with terror.

'No Mister, Mister, not me,' the man cried in barely passable English.

Maybe he knew something; he knew words of English. Joe smacked him in the face. Blood was on the Arab's gown. Glancing around the room, Joe hoped to find their missing headset. All that was there were meagre belongings, bedding, a dark Quran, and shadows.

'Get out of my way!' Joe was on a mission to kill someone that day. There were so many raw nerves. People were frightened and frayed.

Selman appeared in the doorway.

'Get back out here now,' he roared.

Joe's hands were washed in blood; his army shirt stained with it. He was shaking violently, his chest thundering.

'Come here quick,' Bojang yelled.

He had been out searching with Wayne Sampat and they'd found an insurgent who they suspected was one of the shooters from the previous night. The men gathered round a shaken, pale-looking man who wore combat trousers. He had been hiding out in one of the houses, clutching tightly to an AK-47 and bore a recent wound to the chest. The guys had already searched the suspect and he was in possession of an Algerian passport.

All in all, the men detained seven or eight people that morning and searched them. Some of them were from the Ba'ath party, although in Iraq anyone in any kind of senior position usually was. Then the soldiers moved out and left the college behind. Joe never heard that voice from the radio net again, nor found the radio headset. Whether it had been dropped by the assailant, Joe didn't know. He did know that the eight awful words he'd heard over the comm system that morning would stay with him for as long as he lived.

Malone and Muzvuru were memorialised with a service once the men had made their base inside Basra. The padre led them in a church service; both men were Catholic. Major MacMullen had had to take a moment with Pat, to decompress after everything that had happened to his company, then he had to pull the group together. At the service MacMullen gave a reading from a quote he'd found while flipping through the back pages of Molly's notebook. It had been taken from a book by American historian Steven Pressfield, *Gates of Fire*, the story of the 300 Spartans and the battle of Thermopylae, 480 BCE, which was required reading for warriors in training at America's West Point and Annapolis and for all officers in the US Marine Corps. MacMullen addressed some of its words to the company.

> But for the warrior, the seasons are marked not by these sweet measures nor by the calendared years themselves, but by battles. Campaigns fought and comrades lost; trials of death survived. Clashes and conflicts from which time effaces all superficial recall, leaving only the fields themselves and their names, which achieve in the warrior's memory a stature ennobled beyond all other modes of commemoration, purchased with the holy coin of blood and paid for with the lives of beloved brothers-in-arms. As the priest with his graphis and tablet of wax, the infantryman, too, has his scription. His history is carved upon his person with the stylus of steel, his alphabet engraved with spear and sword indelibly upon the flesh.

Part III

Trial

Chapter 29

Alternative

In the beginning the terror is unseen, exploding at first below the ground, then above, as the self-proclaimed martyrs send their message inscribed with a homemade IED to leave its indelible mark upon London. Joe doesn't remember much about where he is when the first suicide attacks on British soil occur; he's still drowning out much of that summer with Stella and a growing dependence on drugs. Lost to him are the shaky mobile phone images and shaken voice accounts which emerge from that day of loud bangs and faces hidden by blood-soaked bandages; derailments and smoke in the darkness. At first thought, in naive moments of innocence and speculation, it is put down to a simple power surge. That morning when the nation wakes with jubilation and justified pride at being chosen to host the 2012 Olympic Games, when dancing turns soon to mourning as twisted Islamic terrorists strike.

It happens a few months after Joe returns from the gruelling stay in Stoddart House mental health hospital, behaving and holding himself together during his prescribed month of day release. Joe is still self-medicating so doesn't dwell much on the reasons behind the targeting of the transport network, near Aldgate, Russell Square, at Edgware Road and Tavistock Square at the tail-end of rush hour. He thinks not about how the attacks, masterminded by an Iraqi former major in Saddam's army and associate of Osama Bin Laden, might have been a consequence of the invasion. Or how one of the home-grown perpetrators of the coordinated series of bombings on the country's capital recalls military intervention in the Middle East in his taped message describing his motives. The decisions of British parliamentarians that led soldiers to invade Iraq lead also to 52 fallen British civilians slain, with over 700 injured as victims of extremists.

Less than two weeks after the attacks, discussions in British Parliament put Joe's name into the public domain in relation to the death of the young Iraqi civilian and he seriously starts to worry if he'll be an extremist's next victim. In late July 2005, the government's highest legal authority, the Attorney General Lord Goldsmith, announces to the world that the Army Prosecuting Authority has made its decision concerning Joe's future:

Four individuals should stand trial by court martial for the offence of the manslaughter of Ahmed Kareem, an Iraqi civilian.

The cases against all four servicemen were reviewed by prosecutors of the independent Army Prosecuting Authority who applied the evidential and public interest criteria set out in the code for crown prosecutors. The Army Prosecuting Authority, following advice from highly experienced counsel, is satisfied that there is a realistic prospect of convicting all defendants and that the prosecutions are in the public interest.

The servicemen who have been directed by the Army Prosecuting Authority to stand trial before a court martial have already been informed of the charges by the Army are:

Sergeant Carle Nicholas Selman, (38) currently serving with the Scots Guards, currently in Germany.

Guardsman Martin McGing, (21) with the Irish Guards, currently based in London.

Guardsman Joseph McCleary, (23) with the Irish Guards, based in London.

One serviceman, a Lance Corporal (21), with the Irish Guards, has yet to be informed of the charge against him.

No date has yet been set for the trial or preliminary hearings in this matter.

The case, surrounding the death of young Ahmed, has also been highlighted by a British-based civil rights group, the Iraqi League. Its chairman, Mazin Younis, has interviewed Ahmed's family and aided them in bringing a High Court civil case on behalf of Public Interest Lawyers, a Birmingham law firm run by solicitor Phil Shiner who has long protested against the war. The announcement of Joe's pending court martial is coupled with the announcement of another incident: that of seven soldiers accused over the alleged mistreatment of Baha Mousa, the Iraqi who died in British custody in Basra in September 2003. The stories that hit the headlines almost seem to presume the men's guilt:

First British Soldiers Face Charges for War Crimes
and
UK Soldiers Face War Crimes Trial

The case relates to the death of Iraqi civilian Ahmed Jabber Kareem Ali, who was detained in Basra as part of a group of four suspected looters on 8 May 2003. The men were allegedly punched and kicked before being forced into a canal, where Mr Ali drowned. Four British soldiers are facing courts martial accused of his manslaughter.

Any counselling at Stoddart House about this ordeal is surely undone, piling on top of the anxiety of uncertainty at the trial hanging over Joe with the public revelation of his identity. With his name out there he can't sleep at night. He keeps a knife underneath the side of the bed. His fear is that someone will target him as a way to atone for everything that's happened and is happening in the Middle East. Joe becomes convinced that there are vengeful Muslim lads who are going to come after him, knowing his name and finding his mum's address. It terrifies and angers him that the disclosure puts her in danger, too. His mind loses itself in the almost unthinkable scenario that some extremist armed with a cleaver, knife or gun might target a British soldier or his family on UK soil. Joe is so convinced that he spends nights peeking through the blinds of his mum's windows, watching who's outside past dark. He peers constantly, nervous, drinking and breathless at the occasional shadowy passers-by striding through pools of amber streetlight.

'Joe, this has got to stop,' his mum begs, barely understanding the paranoia. 'You have to get back to your old ways, son.'

It doesn't stop and it takes more and more to survive. Joe drinks more and takes cocaine, picked up from the Queens. It gives him a euphoric boost, but he soon needs more and more to take the edge off life. A massive side effect of the drug is that it heightens Joe's anxiety, but at least it keeps him awake. Whenever he collapses, exhausted, he wakes up with his mum cradling him as he cries on the sofa. A grown man, 6ft 4in, a former soldier, sitting with his head on his mum's knee as she strokes it.

'Son, I wish I could take it away from you. I wanna take this pain away from you,' she tells him, her words comforting tones.

'I didn't do it. I didn't do it. I didn't do it, mum,' is all Joe can repeat in reply. 'I promise ya.'

'I know you didn't, son. We'll try the army again in the morning.'

And they do, but receive a familiar and empty response. 'We'll pass your message on,' they say.

Compounding everything, Joe's nan, Marie Hartley, passes away. Her death too is a half-remembered haze of mourning, of graveside grief and his broken-hearted granddad. Her widowed Arthur is melancholy, a man lost after his wife's passing. His soulmate gone, he copes through drinking by himself, spending his time cutting out photos of his life-long love to create a collage, taking sorrow-soothing sips of his favourite, Bell's Whisky.

Joe's mum, seeing her son struggle, searches in desperation to find some alternative therapy. She tells him, clinging to hope, that she's found a local reiki healing place and wants her son to try it out. *My mum's a fucking nutter*, Joe thinks at her suggestion and the prospect of her New Age nonsense, but the month in a mental health facility has failed and Joe doesn't want to disappoint his mum.

'I don't really know anything about reiki,' she confesses as they drive from Bootle. 'But someone said to me it might help. I found the place myself. It's only twenty-five quid; it can't hurt, right?'

Joe's bemused, shakes his head at his mum but goes along. They drive to the neighbouring town of Crosby and find the address of the reiki therapist, whose place is above a dingy-looking bed shop. Up the stairs is a dodgy-seeming room with half rings of orange damp around the ceiling and the deep horn-like tones of a whale song CD playing in the background.

Joe feels an horrendous awkwardness as the self-proclaimed reiki 'healer' asks him to lie down face up on the bed that's at the centre of the room.

'You're going to be okay,' Joe's mum says, to her son's continued bafflement. He's never really believed in anything in his life, especially any of these ideas.

'Just lie there, Joe, and just do it,' Lynn almost begs as the healer, a woman of middle-age in a long flowing skirt, patterned with orchids, asks her to wait outside.

This feels ridiculous, Joe muses, the sound of orcas filling the air.

Hovering over him, the woman tells Joe that his mum has explained to her over the phone that he's been going through a difficult time, struggling with depression. She says too that reiki is an ancient therapy that bases itself on Asian spiritual beliefs and practices that tap into 'ki' or vital energy. Joe listens sceptically as she tells him that she practises hands-on non-invasive body healing.

'Is it okay if I lightly place my hands on you? Would that be okay?' she asks softly.

Joe looks at the age of the woman and reminds himself it won't be that kind of relaxation in her upstairs back room.

'Aye. That's fine,' he answers after a moment.

'I'm now going to move my hands over you to facilitate the process of healing. Now, I want you to take a deep, cleansing breath in,' Joe's told.

'How do you get into this?' he asks.

The healer explains that she lost her son, a young lad and that led her to find solace in exploring life force energy healing.

Joe never feels the woman even touch him, doesn't feel anything as she brings her fingers over his body and moves around and sways like a 1960s' belly dancer. She tells him to take more breaths out and in; exhaling the anxiety and pain then inhaling life-giving oxygen. Weirdly, whatever's happening, Joe feels something, a tingling, and starts to relax. He finds himself starting to drift off, the relaxation of long-sought sleep almost enfolding him. The woman standing next to Joe seems to lose herself. With a sudden jerk, out of Joe's control, his leg shoots out, as if possessed by something. The angry wayward limb nearly strikes the woman. Shocked, Joe emerges from trance-like relaxation and sits up instantly.

'Oh my God, I'm sorry,' Joe says profusely.

The woman is quickly in streams of tears, her make-up smearing all over her face as Lynn comes back into the room.

'What have you done?' Joe's mum demands.

'He's not touched me, he's not,' the woman declares protectively. 'But your son's going through something that I can't even get at. He's got that much pain inside of him,' she continues. 'It brought the energy to his leg and that's why it shot out at me.'

Joe's mum shakes her head as if this is confirmation of all the suspicions she holds deeply.

'He's got so much negative energy, so much …' the healer says. 'I'm worried for him.'

'Oh, I know,' Joe's mum assures the middle-aged woman, then placing her hand on his back.

'It's okay love, it's okay,' she says to him, moving past him to the reiki therapist on whose cheeks tears now roll down. Joe's mum then places her arms around the woman, embracing her tightly. Joe gets up off the bed, feeling a little dazed.

'You've got some dark problems. I can't help,' says the lady to Joe. 'I'm so sorry.' she adds, her voice breaking as she parts from the hug.

'He's fought so many demons, so many demons,' Lynn chirps in. 'He fought out in Iraq. He has awful nightmares.'

'Oh, I'm really so sorry,' the healer says. 'It's never happened to me before. There's so much negative energy coming from him.' She continues, looking pale and worn. 'I can't stop crying.'

What the fuck's going on? Joe wonders, sitting up and still feeling a bit strange.

Several weeks pass and Joe receives a call from Stephen Riordan, his barrister, who tells him that he needs to attend a preliminary hearing in London. All of the accused are there, the four men each with their legal teams. Along with QC Riordan is his junior barrister, Nigel Power, and they assemble inside a complex of offices near the towering gothic Royal Courts of Justice building. The room is more like a conference room than a courtroom and Joe appears in his regimental uniform for this, his first court appearance. The pre-trial hearing feels like a formality, but allows the men a chance to hear the full charges against them and lodge their not-guilty pleas. Joe doesn't speak to the other lads, but acknowledges all but Selman with a look and a nod. At the hearing, possible trial dates are discussed for some time into 2006. It's still months away and the legal teams talk about visiting the scene where the incident happened. Basra and Iraq as a whole is still wrecked by instability, but a date is provisionally fixed for a trip just after Christmas, to allow time for the barristers to get their injections and visas and make their travel arrangements. It shocks Joe to hear these well-spoken lawyers are heading out into the dust and danger of the war-torn country. It's a place Joe's only drawn back to in terrifying flashbacks and inescapable nightmares. As they file out, Joe turns to Stephen and quietly asks him a question that's been sloshing around inside his mind.

'What am I looking at? If they decide I'm guilty?'

Riordan pauses. 'You know, it's difficult to say. I think we have a strong case.'

'Yeah, but how long. In prison?' Joe pushes.

'It could be a maximum of fifteen years.'

'Where'd they send me?' Joe asks, straining to hold back the tide of emotion.

'I have been learning a lot about the military process. For a court martial anything up to two years would be served in a military prison. Beyond that it would be a civilian prison.'

'And that could be anywhere, right?' Joe realises out loud. 'London, Wandsworth … It wouldn't be local; it wouldn't just be in Walton?' he asks, referring to the men's Category B and C HM Prison Liverpool that's barely more than a mile from Bootle.

'It's too early to dwell on that, Joe. We've got a train to catch,' says Stephen efficiently, clasping his client's shoulder. He's a tall comforting presence who's been poring through prosecution witness statements, interview transcripts and evidence to help Joe's case.

On the train back to Liverpool, these thoughts seem to saturate every part of Joe. When he's back, he heads a few streets over from Lime Street Station to Italian Kitchen, the restaurant on Queens Square where Carlos is the general manager. Inside, the man who's effectively Joe's stepdad, greets him with a warm hug. It's then that the strain seeps out of Joe. He sits down in the dimly lit bistro that's still waiting for the evening rush and wipes the streams of emotion from his face while Carlos fetches a drink. Carlos or 'Nobby' as he's nicknamed, knows the right thing to say.

'Don't go home yet,' the soft burr of his Portuguese accent calming. 'I'm worried about letting you go, Joe. We have a downstairs here. Stay awhile.'

He probably thinks that Joe will try again; this time maybe throw himself in front of a bus. Time here though is what he needs, and down below the busying restaurant Joe calms down.

Months pass, autumn recedes and a few weeks before Christmas 2005 a phone call comes. It's Stephen Riordan. He tells Joe that a court martial date has been set for April of next year and will be held at a military court in Colchester; Riordan is preparing to travel to Iraq in February as part of a site visit. The barrister wants Joe to know when the tribunal will take place so that it'll end some of the uncertainty. It helps, but the certainty of what early 2006 will bring spoils any sense of celebration at Christmas. Joe enjoys nothing, sitting sombrely, not eating, scrawny, now half the man he was. Across from Joe, his mum worries while her son takes a swig of beer and feels as though the future is a tightening noose, gripped around his neck.

Chapter 30

'Let Them Loot'

They had a noose around Saddam's neck and the Americans pulled to drag the ex-dictator into the dust. He bent first, teetered on his steel core, buckled and then was yanked off his concrete pedestal by the force of the chains tightly pulled by the US tank. They tore the effigy at his knees and finally to the ground with a bounce and a crash.

To the world, the appearance was of a small crowd of Iraqis that had swollen to many in the centre of al-Firdos Square, Baghdad. The images, transmitted through the media suggested a huge gathering had surrounded the 39ft statue of Saddam Hussein, erected only a year earlier to mark his sixty-fifth birthday. What better way to mark the Americans' arrival in Baghdad than the propaganda dream of the fallen bronze Saddam. It gave the illusion of a short easy war, rather than the heralding of a long one. Yet the toppling was carefully stage-managed and distorted to suggest a swell of local support for the Coalition action. The presence of US Marines mixed among the gathering exaggerated the numbers that made up the crowd. So too did the presence of dozens of assembled news journalists, the statue located as it was across from the Palestine Hotel where much of the world's media had stayed throughout the war. The media helped fuel the symbolism over realism, with close-ups and tight framing of groups of people helping give the appearance of mass numbers. American forces provided the sledgehammers, chains and tanks that tore down the sculpture. Some reporters tried to flag the actual thin turnout of Iraqis to their editors who dismissed the facts and wilfully omitted wide-shots that showed most of the square as mainly empty. What was called for was a perfect visual metaphor for the end of the regime: justification of patriotic action over facts.

Attention stayed tuned on the square, deflected from the reality of a Baghdad that began its unrestrained descent into violence and chaos. Much larger groups of Iraqis were gathered elsewhere in the city as they engaged in a less palatable wave of looting. A mass of the populace used trucks and taxis, horses and carts and wheelbarrows to haul away anything they could. Mobs of men trashed banks, shops, embassies, tore into the unguarded headquarters of Unicef where files on diseases and infant health were tossed aside. People took sofas, electronics, tiles, door handles, carpets, chandeliers and more. It was a mirroring of the end of the Mamluks, the Christian slaves brought by the Ottomans and converted to Islam, whose rulership dominated Baghdad during the late eighteenth and early nineteenth centuries. For them it was disease, the Bubonic plague, which led to thousands dying daily, the collapse of the administration and the local people looting anything of value. Nearly 200 years later it was the disease of war that ravaged the city.

The people of Baghdad took anything of value while the hapless American soldiers stood by and watched. They did nothing to prevent the looting across the city, with the exception of a monolithic building in the Al-Mustarisiya quarter of the city: Iraq's Ministry of Oil. Only there were US guards placed, accompanied by fifty tanks securing every entrance, while snipers watched from every angle. Elsewhere in Baghdad, which Churchill once called the Clapham Junction of the Middle East, the city was repeating the descent into chaos that had already been seen in the south.

Three hundred and forty miles away, Joe McCleary had watched similar scenes unfold days earlier almost from the moment the Irish Guards arrived in Iraq's second city. Basra, usually populated by 1.3 million people, a similar number to Merseyside, set the tone in looting and lawlessness. When the soldiers had first arrived they'd been received by hundreds of Iraqis like proper heroes. Long lines of Challenger tanks and the dusty Warriors were greeted with flowers thrown at them as the vehicles streamed down the two-lane highways that were separated with an arid central reservation sprouting tall palm trees. As the troops entered town, the convoy slowed and there was jubilation from the mostly Shiite population, long oppressed and sidelined by Sunni Saddam. Now they were finally free from being persecuted for adhering to their own branch of Islam. Passing by the people, the vehicles crawled, and the soldiers peeped through hatches at streets littered with bronze-coloured faces who spouted the few English words they knew.

'Finish! Saddam!' rose up celebratory shouts.

'Good, is very good! Free!' yelled moustached men in a staccato manner, while malnourished children in bright coloured shirts smiled at the column of passing British. The kids raised their hands and adopted thumbs-up, a sign they usually reserved for contempt and anger in this part of the world. Young people laughed freely like the cooped-up sick finally out of lockdown, while their friends wrestled playfully on the pavements. Some women watched nervously at the spectacle entering their town. Meanwhile, gunners stayed alert through their tiredness as they watched from the turrets, still nervous about remnants of the regime. Grinning 'Cheshire cat' portraits of Saddam seemed to be everywhere, painted on the sides of dusty white buildings or on billboards; some already quickly defaced. Here too, hollow statues of the former dictator were torn down by willing troops before eager Iraqis stomped on Saddam's head and battered his fallen figure with their shoes. It was that very Arab form of insult in a culture where the soles of footwear was considered unclean because of the time they spent in the dirt; the reason why shoes and sandals were removed before entering the mosques. It was with an almost religious fervour that the Iraqis here let loose their torrent of anger, rushing out to ravage not just images of Saddam but at anything that represented his state. The rage against the deposed oppressor soon shifted to a free for all.

Within hours of the soldiers' arrival in the city, the locals looted anything and everything; particularly vulnerable was government property. People ran from buildings with ransacked air conditioning units, bath taps, beds, anything of even minor value. The warmth of hospitable Arab welcome was replaced with a preoccupation to pillage.

In the beginning, the soldiers, against their nature, stood by and let the looting happen, a course that was determined by the Americans. When Baghdad fell, the order came down from the US to 'let them loot'. Their philosophy was to show the newly liberated Iraqi people that they were really free, even free to permit a redistribution of wealth and allow the self-determinism to loot if they so chose. They had democracy, they were free. Let them loot. Even the freedom to be in a free-fall of anarchy and pillaging. Bringing Democracy and freedom for the Middle East was one of the American aims, even without asking if the Arab world wanted it. The No. 1 Company sergeant major, Pat Geraghty, once pointed out that the Arabs probably looked at the West and saw the porn and 850,000 abortions a year and wondered if the West's freedom was what they wanted. In the first days in Basra, Pat was asked a question by a young Iraqi lad.

'How long you staying?' asked the Arab boy.

'I dunno,' shrugged Pat.

'We don't want Americans. British, okay,' the Baswari boy continued in broken but passable English. He pointed across to the distance.

'Oh? Why's that?' Pat asked, always digging deeper for answers.

'You see canal? British build that. Trains? British build. Americans come here? They blow things up.'

Joe agreed with Pat; the Iraqi probably had a point.

After they'd arrived in Basra, No. 1 Company set up a new base within an old gymnasium that was in a central urban area about 3 miles up from the College of Literature. There was an Iraqi man there, perhaps he had been either a squatter or a caretaker, but the soldiers told him they'd protect him and he could stay. For the Irish Guards company, just having four walls and a place to defend gave some sense of protection. The complex had a gate they could lock and guard and a big football field at the back, which meant there was somewhere to park the Warriors. It was also somewhere they could kick a football around with some local Iraqi kids who knew most of the British Premier League teams. Most of the soldiers slept in the main hall of the gym, though there were a couple of other rooms and outbuildings that the officers and sergeants slept in. They took over and tried to secure their position, but this was going to be a struggle because the gym was in an urban area and surrounded by blocks of flats. To monitor threats, the company took up positions on the roof of the gym where they set up a GPMG and nicknamed the look-out 'Position God'. Compared to the conditions that Joe and the others had been living in since they had arrived in the Middle East, being housed in the gym felt like a step up. Then Joe found out that No. 2 Company Irish Guards had made themselves at home in one of Saddam's abandoned palaces alongside the river. They were living the high life with marble-tiled floors and even having showers. For Joe, a shower involved having his mates dowse water over him.

Saddam's palace showed the huge contrast that everyday Iraqis had been living with for a long, long time. Stark were the extremes between the opulence of the palace – one of hundreds across the country where at each an evening meal was made for the dictator in case he happened to show up – and the poverty suffered by the people on the streets outside. Joe could almost sympathise with the torrent of pillaging taking place; this finally was a chance for them to even out the imbalance between the rich few and the many discriminated, mostly Shia, population. The looting though quickly became one of the worst things Joe witnessed on the tour. He was seeing a society that was collapsing in on itself. Now the chains of the dictatorship were loosened, the worst instincts of man were laid open to take for himself and the soldiers did nothing or little to control it.

Initially the looters kept away from the British and would walk to the other side of the street with their carts loaded with takings, but they soon became bolder. Looting spread to the perimeter of the gym-base compound. Two Iraqis were trying to steal the copper from the inside of cables and Joe was part of the team that had to go out and stop them. With the language barrier and just their meagre Arabic phrases their words had little impact. Joe thrust out his SA-80 toward the men, who seemed brazenly to ignore the soldiers and continued to work on pillaging the cables. Joe and another lad in his section got up in the face of the Iraqis, grabbed them forcefully by the arm and violently shook their feeble bodies. They released them after a moment, having awoken the looters to the seriousness of their presence and making them fall to the ground. The two looters picked themselves out of the grubby dirt, both backed away and sprinted off shaking, not glancing back. Joe watched the figures become smaller down the street and his heart pulsed hard inside his chest from the encounter. *This fucking mass looting going on is crazy*, he thought. He could barely cope. *But how do you cope?*

Even the company commander, Major MacMullen, was hugely frustrated. He'd been told to deal with the looting without being informed how. Things, however, changed, but this time at the direction of the British government.

'Stop the looting,' ordered Lieutenant Colonel Michael Riddell-Webster, the commander of the Black Watch, to which the Irish Guards infantry battalion was still attached. 'Guard and control and stop the stealing of cars'.

MacMullen received the orders only verbally at the daily Battle Group Orders meeting held at the Battle Group Headquarters (BGHQ) for Black Watch. The BG HQ had been set up in the Basra police college a 20-30 minute drive away north of No. 1 Company's gymnasium base, towards the river and well outside their Area of Responsibility (AOR). Many of the top brass were there. Lieutenant Colonel Riddell-Webster was the most senior, along with Major Nick Channer, the second-in-command of the Battle Group and his half dozen company commanders. All the 'higher-ups' were in attendance: Major Dougie Hay with his support staff, signal officers, the regimental sergeant major, an adjutant to take notes and MacMullen.

The change in orders telling them now to stop the looters had come down from the top because of events in Baghdad and the growing concerns about British public perception. The catalyst for the change was the first influx of looters who'd broken into the National Museum of Iraq in the nation's capital on 10 April. Since its opening in 1923, the museum had proudly built its collection of priceless artefacts, some that dated back to 9,000 BC, and that told the story of Iraq's magnificent history. As war descended, staff and curators had risked their lives to hide over 3,000 items but were powerless when the plundering began. In fear of their lives, staff had slipped away to escape the advancing American forces and, just as the rest of Baghdad imploded, the museum was quickly taken. Fifteen thousand irreplaceable objects were ransacked in the first thirty-six hours. Looted with impunity were

Abbasid wooden doors, Sumerian, Akkadian and Hatraean statues, silver and gold items, pendants, pottery and necklaces. Stolen was the headless stone statue of Sumerian king Entemena of Lagash that was from 4400 BC. Gone was the Lady of Warka vase, the alabaster vessel to the Sumerian goddess Inanna, a relic of 3000 BC and found at the remains of Uruk. Taken was the black stone duck that dated to 2070 BC and had been excavated from the ancient city of Ur. Allowing the looting was called an act of cultural genocide as priceless artefacts were pilfered; the country's historical heart ripped out.

The news became an outrage. The headlines that were due to hit the British newspapers would create a fierce political storm. The British government would be worried about the scandal that might overshadow the victorious symbol of fallen Saddam. The senior army commanders quickly received word from above that their forces must stop the looting. MacMullen and many of the infantrymen had been trained as firefighters for Operation Fresco, but here in Iraq they were fighting unquenchable fires of looters, with little training on how to do so.

Some of the senior military men had suggested a curfew. But they were reminded that this wouldn't work in Basra. With temperatures up to 50°C people rested inside during the day and then reopened their shops and business until 11.00 pm. And even if the guardsmen had tried a curfew, it could only have worked if they had been resourced with more troops. They would need to flood Basra with military personnel, but other units had headed north up to Baghdad. Instead, the soldiers settled for sending out letters and leaflets, telling locals not to go out on to the streets late at night or they'd be shot. The looting problem didn't look as though it was going to go away any time soon.

Later Pat had an exchange with Peter MacMullen.

'What are we s'posed to do? Go out and shoot 'em?' said Pat sarcastically. He knew that the Rules of Engagement (ROE) said specifically that they couldn't kill civilian looters. The exception was if they saw weapons and there was an armed threat. Only then would they be free to engage with deadly force.

'I did ask them "how",' MacMullen had said, clearly exasperated. 'Arrest them, they said,' he told his company sergeant major.

'Where do we put them?' Pat pursued. The CSM's role included processing the prisoners who were brought in, whether as looters or suspected insurgents. He knew that there were limited facilities at the gymnasium for those they'd detain. People were being arrested, prisoners were bound with plasticuffs as PoWs, and then held until the CSM determined what to do with them. But very quickly there was nowhere to keep them. All that No. 1 Company had was a caged area near the rubbish bins behind the gym that they adapted for temporary prisoner holding until they were either released or, if a serious threat, sent to a Coalition prison in Umm Qasar, 55 miles to the south. There were no prisoner toilet facilities at the gym holding area and the detainees would be out in the raw Iraqi heat. Pat knew that this was inhumane. One day, someone brought Pat four tall Arab lads who were deemed suspicious. Pat's enquiries found the four to be Palestinian basketball players, two of whom spoke English and had got caught up in the fighting.

'You'll only be here an hour or two,' Pat told them as he ensured they got bottles of water.

'This is the first clean water we've had in three days,' one of the tall players said gratefully. 'You're nicer than the Israelis,' he added.

On another day, a Warrior vehicle, from the Royal Regiment Fusiliers, brought in three generations of one family. There was a grandfather, women and children. Pat let the women and children go, but the Arab women standing at the gates wailing wouldn't leave the men. The CSM gave them bottles of water and he soon decided that there was no reason, nor space, for holding the unarmed men. The soldiers would have to find other ways and means to deal with the looters. All they could do was try and interrupt the looters' methods of robbing. They'd keep trying to usher them away. Some infantrymen shot over their heads as warnings. They took their old cars and carts away. It was something the soldiers called 'dislocation', making it difficult for the locals to carry out their pillaging.

Training on how to deal with looters wasn't something that Joe or anyone else out there ever received. Joe, like the others, was trained as an infantryman; to be a soldier not a policeman. Many in the army thought that fighting a war would last at least several months; none thought they'd be given responsibility for policing civilians in southern Iraq. Conducting combat operations could be a simple process; peacekeeping in a city this large, awakening from decades of dictatorship, was horribly complex.

Captain Niall Brennan jokingly repeated the old adage from Northern Ireland: 'What should a policeman do?' The Irish Guards had some of the best experience in dealing with complex, unstable circumstances around the world and a few of them out in Iraq also had experience in peacekeeping in Northern Ireland or the Balkans. Joe had never served there and many of the other lads were younger than him, still teenagers. Here things were very different from public order operations in Northern Ireland. They had situations with two or three soldiers in front of a thousand looters. There were two battle groups in Basra amounting to fewer than 2,500 men in total;

back in Liverpool, Merseyside Police force had twice that number. The army had gone into someone's backyard with 40 per cent of the British army and were breathtakingly swamped. It would require larger resources to keep the country in check.

Human resources weren't the only problem. The Irish Guards were still dogged by the poor state of supplies as well. There were severe supply chain problems, which meant that there was a shortage of some critical items like body armour. An Irish Guards company quartermaster sergeant (CQMS) was told by the Logistics Corps to remove the plates from the body armour of his company and send them to another unit.

'Over my dead body are they going to have the body armour,' he replied firmly to the logistics officer. The CQMS knew he was fighting to prevent dead bodies of his own company. His defiance was proved right when several members of his company came under heavy fire; if he'd followed orders he'd have been watching some of his colleagues return home early in a coffin. The CQMSs were all frustrated waiting for essential kit to arrive; even weaponry like monoculars and laser lights for their SA-80s were lacking. It was one of the many areas where there was a growing frustration at how the post-conflict operations were not well planned.

Each evening, MacMullen passed on his orders to the whole Company at the Order Group meetings where new Orders of Battle ('Orbats') were adjusted to reflect their post-conflict reality. Joe had never heard precisely when the 'war-fighting phase' ended and the 'peacekeeping phase' began. No one ever said the war was over. They were told the aim now was to restore 'normality' for the people here. Whatever that was.

Joe and his fellow infantrymen had a rotation of four activities: Platoon on guard duty of the gym base; rest (though those moments were few and far between), being ready for Quick Reaction Force (QRF) missions; and statics and patrols within their AOR. When they were on patrol the soldiers were to show their presence as boots on the ground in Basra and try to stop the looting.

The situation seemed to calm down after a few days, but Basra bore visible scars both of the conflict and the chaotic looting. When the infantrymen manoeuvred their Warriors on patrols through the narrow, dangerous city streets, those driving or in the turrets noticed the grim evidence everywhere. In Basra's commercial district, site of the half dozen or so banks, one financial institution had been found with a subterranean vault that had a small hole blown in, enough just to allow a small boy to access. His asphyxiated body was found by soldiers among the piles of paper Dinars. In the once revered

College of Literature, where Molly and Muz had lost their lives, the place was now pillaged of its rare books. Dust gathered over trampled broken desks, looters' sandal prints and samples of Keats written in perfect English in an abandoned exercise book:

> One against one, or two or three, or all
> Each several one against the other three
>
> As fire with air loud warring when rain-floods,
> Drown both, and press them both against earth's face.

On the parched streets, Captain Brennan pulled over and stopped an old man who was in the process of stealing a lamppost from a motorway. *The people seemed like termites*, he thought; they had stripped everything bare. None of the soldiers had seen anything like this tidal wave of looting that left an echo of despair over the shattered and yet still threatening city.

There were regular attacks on No. 1 Company's gym base. They came often at night, from mortars and shells. Even with the protection that the place provided, officers were concerned and exhausted. From the gym, the soldiers conducted intelligence-led raids to try and capture weapons or Ba'ath party members. Sometimes the raids took them out into suspects' run-down houses. They'd travel out in Warriors, remembering their rudimentary training for searching and handling suspects as they entered homes and forced the Iraqis on to the floor. The infantrymen carried out a search for weapons: rooting behind cupboards and stripping up floorboards. Usually the petrified people offered no resistance as soldiers detained suspects and then moved on.

There were always threats when they were on stag, doing guard duty at sites deemed valuable around the city. One night, Corporal Paul Hollander and Joe were on stag, standing outside their Warrior. It was early hours of the morning, close to 1.00 am and still hot from the day. Two of the lads were sleeping in the back, but Martin McGing was up top in his gunner's position, staying alert and keeping guard, or was supposed to be. Paul and Joe were having a smoke and chatting while leaning against the vehicle. Suddenly someone opened fire. Joe thought in a second that Paul's cigarette must have stood out in the dark of night. More bullets pinged the back wall near where they were parked up.

'Put the ciggy out, Paul!' Joe yelled. The unseen insurgent was probably using the lit end as a target. Joe switched into full alert. He quickly spied the sparks from the Iraqi's rifle. This would do as a target. Another thought occurred to Joe, *Where's fucking Gingy?* They'd had a live contact and he was supposed to be in the gunner position so should be firing by now.

'Watch my tracer,' Joe yelled. He'd seen the gunner first and needed to alert Paul to where the shooter was. Joe turned on his tracer. After every four rounds, a red-tipped bullet flew through in the ammunition, showing fellow soldiers where to target. Joe put his SA-80 rifle on automatic and let loose with burst after burst. The sky suddenly lit up with a deadly streak of little red lines as Joe unleashed a rat-tat-tat-tat of more bursts. Paul started putting some fire down. In a sudden moment the Warrior's engine roared loudly. The top-mounted 7.62mm chain gun then woke into deadly life. It erupted chaotically as if out of control. Gingy was up in the tank with his foot on the pedal trigger control, Joe realised. Thick undisciplined rounds peeled across the nearby street and tore into a parked car, ripping off its roof. The unwieldy cascade of fire continued. Shells spilled from the gun, spent casings coming down the back of Joe's neck still red hot.

'Arrrrgh! Fuck. You stupid bastard.' The noise of the Warrior up and running drowned out Joe's words. More 7.62mm bullets flew past – bububububu.

'Cease fire!' Joe yelled. More cars were sheared apart, ripped up like aluminium drinks' cans. The bullets were flying past Joe's legs, missing him by inches.

'GINGY!!!' Joe's voice going hoarse. The Warrior firing ceased.

'Gingy, fucking hell, where was ya?!' Joe demanded, angry and breathless from adrenaline.

'Mate, sorry I fell asleep,' McGing confessed, dazed and still drowsy.

'Gingy, you fooking eediot!' Joe spat ferociously.

'Sorry, sorry,' young McGing pleaded, looking shocked. There was mostly silence. They'd either hit the Iraqi gunman or he'd scarpered. Paul broke the tension by bursting into laughter at McGing and the trail of destruction his semi-conscious firing had caused.

'I nearly got shot you stupid bastard,' Joe said, his annoyance tapering off. He couldn't blame his mate for it. They were all exhausted and Martin McGing was up in the gunner position, wearing a pair of night-vision goggles that made everything dark. He had been in the heat after he'd been on his feet doing stag duty for sixteen hours. He wasn't super-human; anyone would have fallen asleep, let alone a young lad like McGing, who was one of the youngest out of the pack and a good two years Joe's junior.

'I'm sorry, I'm sorry,' Gingy said again

'Shut the fuck up. Everyone's safe,' Joe said finally, as he calmed down from the stress of the almost deadly encounter and they headed back for more duties.

The section returned to the gym for their brief rota-mandated rest times and it was during these periods that they unwound and let off the tension of the day. One night they let off the tension literally, by igniting their farts. The soldiers made it a contest and Joe ended up the winner. In the wide, square room of the gymnasium hall, darkness of the still night settled over exhausted soldiers and they passed around the fire lighter while they passed a mix of hydrogen, carbon dioxide, methane and other intestinal gases. The trick was to get the lighter close enough to the soldier's arse but not set their pants alight. With each attempt the hall would erupt into laughter and lad's cheers. Everyone was doing it. Even the officers laughed, those of refined upbringing and elocution lessons with rich mums and dads. When Joe's turn came he squeezed his sphincter and a thick leafy wave of yellow flame lit up the gym. It was ridiculous, immature and idiotic, but this and other juvenile shit broke the tension of the tour in Basra. They laughed because they needed to. A certain gallows humour was what got them through the ever-intensifying and dangerous situation.

On guard duty there were two main facilities that Joe's section had to keep secure: the Basra General Hospital and nearby a petrol station. In the land so rich in oil, petrol was a commodity. Supply lines were not yet re-established and the demand was high, not just for the tired, late-1980s cars but for those using generators because electricity was still cut. Joe was on rotation, guarding at the petrol station with his section and their Warrior, when they started taking fire. The infantrymen didn't know if the person shooting at them was a crazed looter or some angry remnant from Saddam's Ba'ath party. Whoever it was, they risked, or intended, sending the soldiers sky high if the rounds hit the fuel pumps. Along with the rest of the section, Joe took up a defensive position as a couple of bullets from the gunman pinged past his foot. They opened fire with precision shots and got their enemy fast.

There had been sporadic attacks like this since they'd arrived in the city, but otherwise a calm of sorts was descending on the country after the fighting and initial frenzy. By the middle of April, some sort of order had started to return to parts of Baghdad in the north with regular US foot patrols, shops opening and police volunteering to return to work. Aid agencies had begun to air lift humanitarian supplies and water into the country and even Sir Richard Branson had announced ambitious plans to reintroduce scheduled Virgin commercial flights to Baghdad Airport. Some forces from the south who had taken part in the initial invasion, including several RAF Tornado F-3s and ships such as HMS *Ark Royal*, had already begun their long journey home. All of the soldiers looked forward to following in their wake and heading back to the UK.

Back at the gym base one evening Pat Geraghty pulled Joe aside holding the welfare phone, a satellite phone that was reserved for calls home.

'Joey, have you phoned your mudder?' Pat said to Joe in thick Irish brogue.

'Er, no sir,' Joe replied; it had been weeks since they'd left Kuwait and he'd been able to hear his mum's voice.

'Well call her mobile,' Pat said, half scowling and half with a look of pastoral care, something that was part of the company sergeant major's role for his men.

'She doesn't have a mobile phone, sir,' the Scouser replied honestly, confused.

'Well, someone must!'

'My aunt lives a few doors down and has one.' Joe offered up.

'Well phone your aunt and let her know that you're okay!' Pat shot back.

Pat handed Joe the satellite phone, a big blocky rectangle with a pointy aerial that reminded Joe of a 1980s' mobile phone. He called the number for Carol, who was as close to an aunt without being a relative and lived over the road from Joe's mum. Carol had a mobile phone and Joe had just about memorised its number before he left for Iraq. There were the long, throaty and uncertain rings of the satellite phone as it strained to make a connection. As he waited, Joe saw the rest of his section were quickly grabbing gear again ready for another QRF run – meaning Joe had only moments left to make his call.

Suddenly there was the click of an answer and a female voice.

'Carol, it's Joe. I'm calling yer from Iraq on a satellite phone. Where's Lynn? Where's me mum?'

'Oh my God, Joe,' she replied in shock. He sensed the swell of tears as Carol told him that he'd just missed his mum; she was back at home and he had to try her there.

Shit, that was it, Joe thought frantically. He'd got barely a minute for this call.

'Listen, I'm just trying it one more time,' Joe yelled hurriedly.

Joe called the familiar number again. Too often his mum didn't pick up the phone. The throaty rings crackled again. Joe's time was nearly up. Guys were climbing in the Warrior.

Then a click of an answer.

'Helloo?'

'Mum, it's Joe,' he said weakly at the sound of Lynn's voice.

'Are you okay? Are you safe?' she said. Joe just cried for a minute, could barely speak. The sound of her voice.

'Yeah. I'm okay. I'm okay mum. I'm starving; I'm just hungry but I'm okay,' was all he could think to utter. 'I miss your Scouse stew!'

'I sent you a parcel, your favourite,' he heard back in cheerful reply through an intensifying flicker of distortion.

'Okay, mum. I haven't got it yet. I'll keep a look ...' And then the phone cut off, the line home dead. Joe cried for a moment, cradling the satellite phone in his hands.

All the boys were geared up in the Warrior vehicle with helmets on, rifles ready to go. It was time to leave again. Joe piled into the back door of the Warrior, slamming it shut as he took his seat. Everyone was staring at his red puffed eyes, a reservoir unable to prevent the stream. There were tears in the back of the tank as Joe felt it rumble down the street.

'Come on. Bring it. Just let it out, Joe,' said the lads sat around him, laughing in mock sentimentality as they put their hands on him.

'Get off me! Get off me,' Joe deflected, playing the tough soldier after having fallen to pieces the minute he heard the sound of home. It was where he desperately wanted to be more than anything in the world.

Chapter 31

Trial Begins

He desperately wants to be in Basra; it's February 2006 and this would have been the highlight of his career as an esteemed QC. Joe's barrister, Stephen Riordan, is all geared to go to southern Iraq and visit the site where the incident happened. He, along with the barristers for McGing, Cooke and Selman all have flights booked, have received their vaccinations and are going to fly into Baghdad and on to Basra via helicopter by night and then visit the Shatt al-Basra canal and Bridge Four during the day. Their trip is cancelled, however, when the degree of risk and heightened danger causes military officials to veto their plans. Iraq's chaotic breakdown is worsening, teetering on the brink of all out civil war.

The situation has been deteriorating for months with lethal insurgency intensifying week by week. After the new Iraqi Constitution is ratified in October 2005, parliamentary elections are held in December. The Shia-majority coalition wins the vote but the result leads to a surge of violence. The targets are mostly the Shia who have been facing accusations of violence and torture against the Sunni Muslims. Death squads, allegedly from inside the new Iraqi Ministry of the Interior, are targeting Sunni Arab Iraqis, their bodies often found shot dead or brutalised by electric power tools. This is said to be the Shia's favourite torture method. It is getting so that morgue doctors can identify the religion of the dead by the state of their bodies. If the victim is killed by an electric drill then they are Sunni; if they are beheaded then they are Shiite. Revenge also incites the sectarian killings; the once persecuted Shiite majority now have dominance over their minority Sunni cousins. Tyranny and religious tension fuel the power vacuum that Coalition forces have left behind on their Middle Eastern misadventure.

Further agitating the region are deadly protests that have been erupting across the Arab world. They are the result of cartoons published in *Jyllands-Posten*, a Danish magazine, at the end of September 2005 which are deemed blasphemous by many in Muslim majority lands. While the depictions of the revered Prophet ignite Western debates about freedom of speech, anger rages from Afghanistan to Yemen. Riots and killings spread in the months that follow: in Basra a Danish soldier dies when an IED explodes next to him; demonstrators in the same city march and stomp their shoes indignantly on top of the flag of Denmark; elsewhere the red and white cross emblem burns along with American, British and Israeli flags.

Anger at the West fails to unite the factions in Iraq where, in the pre-dawn hours of 22 February 2006, insurgent operatives belonging to al-Qaeda in Iraq infiltrate al-Askari mosque in Samarra. The shrine, which dates back to the tenth century, is one of the holiest Shia sites in the nation and burial place of two imams, descendants of the Prophet Mohammed. In a plan masterminded by Abu Musab al-Zarqawi, terrorists tie up the guards inside the Shia shrine and set off bombs that destroy its famed golden dome. The provocation sets off new extremes of sectarian violence between the two Islamic factions in which over a thousand perish, Shia shooting Sunni; Sunni slaughtering Shia.

Even seeking justice against the country's former dictator and his past atrocities fail to heal the broken land. At the start of April, Iraq's chief investigative judge Ra'id Juhi charges Saddam Hussein with genocide. He faces the Iraqi Special Tribunal, along with six others, for his role in the heinous Anfal campaign against the Kurdish peoples where more than 100,000 died in the late 1980s. While the dictator, whom the Americans and British deposed, faces trial for his brutal rule in Iraq, Joe and his legal team prepare for his own trial.

Joe's meetings with his solicitor John O'Leary and his barrister QC Riordan become more regular and intense. The day of the trial is getting ever closer, mere days away. They comb over details again and again, the moments of the very last days in Iraq and the tragedy that followed. The gruelling preparation and return to those memories pushes Joe sometimes over the edge. He snaps at his legal team, sometimes frustrated and angry at the way they are speaking to him; the guilt and the burden still grinding him down.

Afterwards, instead of heading home, Joe retreats to the sands not far from his home town, where harsh erosion and weathering have long done their work. He wanders the miles from Crosby Beach at the north and down past the remains of wartime sea defences, where the shoreline is a dense rocky carpet of stones coloured red, orange and grey. Along the sea front this littering of rubble, much of it local bricks from houses destroyed in the Second World War, paves Joe's path back towards Bootle. Soon the grit of sands replaces the rocks and hardened clay as he passes over the tourist beaches almost deserted now, a weekday evening late in spring. Liverpool Bay and the Mersey are to Joe's right as he walks south until he reaches the end, where beach gives way to industry. Here the asphalt suppliers, steel berths and Royal Seaforth Docks are separated by determined vertical metal railings topped with a triple row of barbed wire and big jagged boulders. Walking to the shoreline, Joe stands at the water's edge.

It's here that the hulking chunks of granite curve around into a thick seawall, grey as aged grave stones. Joe sits down on one of the harsh dark rocks, staring out to sea as he has done many times before. The only sounds he hears are those of the water swelling and ferociously beating the shore. At the distant end of the seawall stands the Seaforth Radar Tower, the almost 100ft-tall, T-shaped structure that used to monitor ships using the Mersey Channel. The structure's 1960s' architecture is a grey brick base, now graffiti-stained and with a corrugated metal-covered column stacked with two levels, the lower a square, the upper octagonal shaped. Topped off with jagged aerials, the brutal looking outline is vaguely crucifix-like on the horizon line. Joe feels as though the radar tower, although long since vacated when technology developed in the 1980s, is watching over him. It gives him a feeling of paranoia and impending judgement.

Another member of Joe's company has recently been convicted, though for crimes committed here at home. James Piotrowski, an Irish Guards lance corporal, went AWOL after stealing a pair of SA-80 rifles from Wellington Barracks in London in 2004. Police launched a manhunt and claimed that he called them up with a terroristic threat, saying he was 'going to spray' them down when he returned home to Birmingham. Piotrowski's face was projected on the side of the Birmingham police building with the word 'wanted' and his mum and teenage sister were arrested under the Terrorism Act before he was arrested.

When Piotrowski appears before the judge, the court hears about his experiences in Iraq. He tells how he saw women and children 'shot to pieces' and was close by when, in early April 2003, a teenage Fusilier named Kelan Turrington was shot dead, then the youngest Briton to die in the conflict. But these experiences and their impact are insufficient to sway the military jury at Colchester Barracks military court who hand down their harsh sentence. James Piotrowski receives seven years and four months in jail and is stripped of his rank: dismissed from the army in disgrace. He heads to prison leaving behind a girlfriend pregnant with his child and a father asking if his son was struggling with severe PTSD.

'Young men like my son are screwed up mentally,' Mr Piotrowski tells his local paper. 'When needed, he served his Queen and country with honour, bravery and pride, and yet when it comes to the aftercare of his health, where was his "adopted family", the army, to look after him? I no longer have a proud young soldier as a son, but a criminal.'

The military in turn reply. 'Each serviceman and servicewoman has the full support of the welfare and medical services provided by the army.' Joe is facing the same court in just days and an even harsher sentence could await at his trial for manslaughter.

Joe watches the ebb and flow of the sea along the Bootle coastline, the waves like the questions, memories and accusations that constantly come. His mind is wracked with the intangible image of Basra and the day he cannot undo. He pounds the rocks with his fists, allowing the built-up rage to dissipate. He punches till the backs of his fingers are red, raw then bleeding. Leftover seawater sitting on the rock stings the open cuts. The recent night's flashbacks have left Joe shattered. He sits till long after dark falls, anxiety coursing through him like a tidal surge of crawling agitation. After hours he heads inland towards town for something to take the edge off.

Joe and his mum leave Bootle at 4.00 am to drive the 250 miles south-east to Colchester for the start of the trial. Along the way, Lynn's dodgy satnav gets them lost so the difficult journey takes even longer than it should. Joe's in no hurry to get there. On the radio they hear the number one song, 'Crazy', and that's what this all feels like to them. Joe and his mum have a strange conversation while they drive through the lifting morning darkness.

'How weird is it that I've shot someone?' Joe says of being a soldier.

His mum offers the only reply she can.

'Well, they've shot at you …'

The court martial in Colchester convenes for its first day on Monday, 24 April 2006. It's been a full three long years since Joe was out beneath the oil-fire horizon of Iraq. Now the four soldiers gather under pallid cloudy skies of Essex, ordered to pose for assembled press photographers. They walk through the open gateway of ancient St John's Abbey Gate, all that remains of the eleventh-century Benedictine Abbey at Colchester. They march in a line, Martin McGing on the end, to Joe's left, James Cooke to his right and to James' right, Carle Selman. The men stride and come to a halt as instructed; dressed in dark olive-green uniforms and black regimental caps, expressionless faces severe, hiding the resentment they all feel at being there. McGing looks unsteady, his eyes narrow, like Joe, fighting to hold back the demons and fears inside him. Joe stands straight beside him, arms tightly behind his back and hands clenched; the other three men's arms hang passively by their sides. Joe hears the percussion of camera clicks shooting at them and he swallows hard as the news camera pans across their faces.

'Hold it there, guys,' instructs one of the photographers but the men are done, Cooke the first to turn on his heel and walk, crossing Joe followed by an angry Selman. They're led by officers, past skeletal yet-to-bud trees up a damp gravel path, to a thick black wooden door, behind which, in the weeks to come, their fates will be decided. The door bears the words in white lettering:

MILITARY

COURT

CENTRE

Joe feels a queasiness in his stomach and a soreness in his throat as he enters the long upstairs room with a pointed ceiling and white-painted brick walls. Along with Bulford and Catterick in Yorkshire, this is one of three Court Martial Centres in the UK. The room is divided, leaving an aisle down the middle and two rows of brown desks and matching brown chairs on either side. On the left is the prosecution and on the right is the defence. On the left-hand wall are two large rectangular flat screen TV monitors and between them is a small podium for witnesses. Opposite the podium on the right is a desk for the panel of seven officers who will act as military jury. Near the end of the room is a long, raised platform with a white seat and oak desk bearing a sign that says 'JUDGE ADVOCATE'. Behind the judge's platform, at the very far end of the room, is a small office with two blue doors and windows with white blinds. The soldiers each take their assigned places, joined by their solicitors and barristers and their junior barristers. Joe is at the back on the right-hand side with Riordan and his junior, Nigel Power; opposite them on the left is McGing and his barrister Jerry Hayes, who is a former politician, the only non-QC among the barristers, along with his junior, Robert Rinder, grandson of a Holocaust survivor. In front of Joe sits Selman and his QC, John Coffey. Cooke and his lawyers and his QC Richard Lissack sit way up front. At the very back of the long room are a few reserved places for family members, a court artist and the occasional journalist. Once everyone is settled at their desks furnished with thick lever-arch ring binders of notes, they're told to rise as the judge emerges from the back room. Vice Judge Advocate General Michael Hunter, enters looking pale-faced and terse and wearing his black robe, white neckerchief and white judicial wig – which fails to hide tufts of greying hair. He is also adorned with blue-red-blue sash over his left shoulder, the colours of the Irish Guards Tactical Recognition Flash, worn on the patch stitched on to the right arm of the Irish Guards' combat clothing. This is not Judge Hunter's first Iraq-related case; last year he presided over the case of the three soldiers of the 1st Battalion, The Royal Regiment of Fusiliers, who photographed themselves mistreating Iraqis at Camp Bread Basket. They received jail sentences and Joe is anxious about what lays ahead for him.

There's icy tension in the room, especially towards Selman, now a colour sergeant serving with the Scots Guards. They were soldiers in arms back in Basra, bonded together like mates to make it through. That all changed with the investigation. There are conflicting accounts and Joe was told by RMP Staff Sergeant Daren Jay about Selman's claims that he laughed at struggling Ahmed. Between them there is no love lost; Joe knows that McGing feels the same.

In spite of the division among the soldiers, the lawyers initially work together. Jerry Hayes belives that a golden rule in the legal profession is that if each lawyer is cut-thoat, ruthlessly disregarding the other defendants, then it's more likely that they all fail. They start the trial with a legal procedure to argue against the validity of some of the evidence used against the men. The proceeding is called *voir dire*, a French phrase that means 'to speak the truth' and is almost like a trial within a trial. The solicitors are questioning two main points of contention about the admissibility of evidence: first, that the evidence that has been properly collected is not strong enough for a reasonable jury to convict the men and second, that Selman and McGing had made statements without being given a proper police caution and that a statement given by Cooke before he was cautioned could amount to a confession. On this basis they want to try and halt the trial from the start, smother it while it's stillborn. Over the first few days, the lawyers plan to outline the circumstances under which the men were interviewed two years ago and as Joe sits and listens, he's brought back to the way he felt treated by RMP officer Jay. It still haunts him as he remembers in vivid flashback his recollection of accusatory words, 'You killed him, didn't you?! You bricked him! You killed a kid.'

That's when Joe notices him. There in the courtroom, dressed in his uniform, is Staff Sergeant Jay, watching. *That tall, horrible man,* Joe rages inside. *He's looking at me with such disgust. Does he even know what I've been through,* Joe thinks, remembering the words he heard Jay speak to him eighteen months ago: 'I'm going to make sure you go down for this.' The RMP officers are the soldiers' hate figures, their enemy; like a ghostly presence in the courtroom, still terrorising them.

Joe and his mum are accommodated in a mediocre Colchester hotel. After the assault of allegations against Joe, the day filled with legal conjecturing over manslaughter charges, obeying orders and the struggles on the ground in Iraq, he is exhausted. He feels run down and the burning in his throat has worsened throughout the day. He has a sleepless night spent staring up at the hotel-room ceiling. When morning comes Joe can hardly swallow or breathe and he hoarsely tells his mum that he has a fever along with a severe and worsening sore throat. She switches into nursing mode and examines him to find the swelling of the glands in the back of his throat. At her insistence they head to Colchester Hospital and Joe is diagnosed with quinsy, an infected abscess in the back of his throat. The treatment is a local anaesthetic while a doctor uses a scalpel to nick and drain the abscess. He'll need a brief hospital stay and a short time to recuperate.

Joe's actually relieved to miss some early days of the trial and his barrister keeps him advised of the proceedings. Despite the thorough arguments, the lawyer's application to stay the proceedings based upon their first point, that the evidence is not strong enough, is refused. On the second point, the Judge Advocate agrees that one of Selman's early statements to Jay is inadmissible and so is material relating to his subsequent interviews, but the statements and interviews of the rest of the men are considered admissible. The court case will proceed.

The stress of the impending trial is probably responsible for Joe's medical condition. When the senior consultant asks Joe what he's been going through, his patient explains about the trial and the long investigation. The consultant says he thinks that stress could have caused the onset of the quinsy infection. The physician also reveals that he was a former Royal Navy doctor.

'What an appalling situation,' he says to Joe, with Lynn at the bedside. 'These soldiers should never have been put through this,' he adds with indignation. 'He's a lovely lad,' the consultant adds, looking at Lynn.

'I know, but it's the worry and stress of it all. He puts a brave face on,' Lynn says.

'I am so sad that this is happening to you. It's awful,' the medic says. 'We've had some press who have tried to come up and they've been told to go away.' As if he's going beyond what a doctor needs to do, he makes an offer of sanctuary.

'No matter what, that bed's there for you here. You want it for six weeks, you sit in that for six weeks,' he assures the McClearys. 'We will care for you as long as it takes to recover.'

Chapter 32

Blunt Instruments

Joe was isolated in a room in the No. 1 Company gymnasium base, recovering from the most violent bout of diarrhoea and vomiting he'd ever experienced. They called it 'D and V' and it could spread quickly to any one of the lads in the camp so they put the infected soldier in quarantine until it had passed. Joe was a tough soldier, fit, strong, knew how to fight, but it took just a stomach bug to floor him. Stuff was coming up and going through him constantly. He couldn't keep anything down or anything inside. He was weak and stank of loose faeces after he'd shit himself everywhere. It had come on quickly and he felt rotten. So, too, did Guardsman McCabe.

The previous day brought the onset of D and V when McCabe and Joe were heading out to go on guard duty up on Position God, the defensive lookout at the very top of the old gym. It was where they had stationed the GPMG able to pump fire from above and where they could watch for the frequent mortar attacks on their position. Joe climbed the ladder and McCabe followed directly below when the feeling hit. *Shit, I don't feel good,* Joe realised. His bowels emptied instantly. It was uncontrollable.

'Joe!' McCabe yelled.

'Mate, I can't stop it.' By now the fabric in Joe's shorts was so worn out and thin and what was coming out of his arse was a release of almost complete fluid.

The wet excreta dripped on to McCabe as he tried to frantically descend the ladder.

'Stop it. Fuck. Stop it now.'

'I can't stop it!' Joe pleaded with him, unable to hold it in.

'Rrgh. Rrgh. It's dripping off me helmet,' McCabe muttered before he realised he'd better keep his mouth shut.

The incident got Joe quarantined for at least twenty-four hours. He needed to let the bug pass his system and rehydrate to fully recover. Joe also had to wash his own soiled, shit-stained kit. He only had one pair of pants and one top so each time the diarrhoea struck and he failed to make it to the toilet, which was most of the time, he had to stand outside with a bucket and wash them. To get himself cleaned up still required him to pour a bucket of water over his body to clean off the faeces that clung stubbornly on to him. While everyone else from his section was on duty, Joe was on lockdown mostly laid on his mat, trying to ignore his gut churning and snarling. He tried to rest, despite an almost intolerable fever and the 40° temperature outside. Between dozing he had a chance to write another 'Bluey' letter to his mum and Carlos. *'I have been to the toilet 7 times today and it's only 10 o'clock in the morning. Apart from that I am fine.'* Joe took trip number 8 before he'd finished penning the first paragraph.

> *'How's Carol can you pass on my love to her an the family. I just haven't had much time to wright the last week I will try and wright to Carol as soon as I can. The weather is hot out here. Hang on back to the bog. (9 times). Back now.'*

During their Iraq tour, many of the men took laps to the loo due to some form of gastroenteritis because the hygiene in Basra was so poor. The flies there carried disease and were everywhere. The horrific bugs especially liked to fester in the wounds of dead Iraqi bodies that littered the ground due to night after night of killings, and they'd emerge in swarms. To avoid catching diseases from the flies, the soldiers would cover their faces with their desert shemaghs in an effort to prevent them landing and crawling on them.

Food could be a problem too. For a start the men stuck mostly to military MRE rations such as packets of boil-in-the-bag pasta or beans until an Iraqi man near the gym started bringing freshly made flatbread, which some of the men hungrily ate. While Joe was on stag duty once he watched the thickly bearded man as he 'baked'. The street seller floured out a flat surface of slab beneath him and kneaded his bread dough, over and over constantly into flat rounded pieces. Joe also watched the small swarm of flies that came in and circled around him and landed occasionally on his dough. The man never seemed to let the bugs bother him as he kept on kneading his traditional *khubz tannour,* let them rise quickly out in the hot Arab sun and baked them in a clay-domed oven. He made stacks of the bread that looked like naans or pitas the lads recognised from kebab shops back home. Joe saw the man as he took a bread off his pile to eat, often pausing to pull a fragment from his mouth and flick it to the ground. It took Joe a little time to realise what the bits were. *They looked like fucking raisins,* Joe thought for a start. *But they're not, they fucking flies,* he realised in disbelief. *Is this fella fucking for real?*

'I'd be fucking starving and I'm not eating that again,' Joe had said to the guardsman who was nearby. 'Them flies have been crawling over dead bodies all week.'

Whether the company was on stag or responding to situations around the city, Basra stank. The foul smell emanated from the raw sewage that ran down the street and festered in pools along the sides of streets. Flies hovered here too, dipping in and out of the accumulating rot of human waste.

The city's still broken infrastructure – and the ongoing lawlessness that seemed as though it couldn't be controlled, continued to frustrate local people. Muggings, murders and robberies were common and people took law and punishment into their own hands. The soldiers saw Iraqis who detained a looter and wrote ALI BABA – what they called thieves – on the man's forehead in permanent Lumocolor pen, publicly shaming him as punishment. The company once stopped a man who had stolen a fridge and was trying to escape with it, using his horse and cart. Local people gathered around, surged into a mass crowd and yelled 'Hang him'. It was a fraught situation and law-abiding communities in Basra seemed to be crying out for help. The army commanders were on edge and near the end of their tether. Not knowing what to do with looters was becoming a clear problem and it was difficult for anyone to maintain the balance of force when dealing with them.

The soldiers risked being criticised when Iraqis were shot. In mid-April, British news reports accused the army of not living up to their obligations under the Geneva Convention after five suspected Iraqi looters were shot dead by British forces. The Royal Scots Dragoon Guards were investigating looting at another bank when the five Iraqi robbers who'd been caught in the act opened fire with what looked like Kalashnikovs. The soldiers returned fire and killed all five Iraqis but not before one of their own, Lance-Sergeant Bob Giles, took a round in the belly. The Iraqis were probably part of a hard-core gang, unruly elements of which were now running amok in the city. Saddam's former regime had helped unleash this blight when they emptied the prisons days before the British entered the city. Some colonels advocated that an aggressive show of force would help the soldiers' efforts. If the Iraqis knew the British were willing to open fire on lawbreakers then they'd be motivated to follow the rules.

Some tried a less belligerent type of deterrence. Looters who were apprehended by some Irish Guards were taken out of town to force them to walk back home. Sometimes it seemed as though it was for their own good. A sergeant major in No. 2 Company was out in his Land Rover doing a logistics resupply, weaving in and out of Basra's clogged roads, filled with droves of people leaving the city with whatever effects they could cram into their cars. Ahead was a commotion in sight of Bridge Four. The sergeant got out to investigate and found a fat Iraqi in traditional dishdash being kicked savagely by a braying crowd. The prone figure on the ground had one toe hacked off and a furious Iraqi was about to brutalise the man with a brick. The sergeant got among the crowd to intervene, hit a mob assailant with his rifle and got in front of the injured man. None of the crowd spoke English so an interpreter was called forward and the full story unravelled. Up on the bridge, the overweight Iraqi had tried to hijack a car using a pistol, killing the driver and throwing the body over the railing into the water below. Behind the dead driver's car was a minibus full of his extended family who all got out for some quick revenge. Mob justice had left a long tailback of cars and a fat half-dead Iraqi. The sergeant told the interpreter to tell the crowd that he was bringing the man back to the army base to be court-martialled and executed by dusk. The deception pacified the mob but something still had to be done with the fat rescued car-jacker.

'I've got a guy who allegedly committed murder. What do I do with him?' The sergeant demanded on the radio to Battle Group HQ.

'Get rid of him,' came the order. That was it. There was little capacity for dealing with the man as a prisoner. There was no functioning court of law. The country was coming apart at the seams. The sergeant made a decision. He hauled the short fat man in the Land Rover then accelerated fast from the scene. He drove 12 miles into the middle of nowhere with the bleeding Iraqi convinced he was about to be executed. The sergeant had to drag the man out of the vehicle. He was petrified, on his knees and grabbing the soldier's feet. Spinning on his heel, the sergeant jumped back in his Land Rover and left the man alone in the desert. Maybe he died there or maybe he hobbled the miles back home. The sergeant never knew the fate of the Iraqi, but at least he removed the man from the immediate life-threatening situation. Incidents like this seemed as if they were a ticking bomb ready to wreak destruction.

Elsewhere in the city, the soldiers tried to undo some of the damage of the assault on Basra. No. 2 Company attempted to diffuse an unexploded JDAM. The smart bomb was half a tonne of payload but was too dumb to detonate after it landed on Basra's Sheraton Hotel along the Shatt al-Arab riverfront. Intelligence had suggested that members of the Ba'ath party may have been holed up in the hotel so a US warplane had unleashed the weapon early on in the war. Above the many flights of stairs to the top of the building was a massive cavity in the flat roof of the hotel through which the JDAM bomb had passed; it was now lodged at the base of the building. It took trained British bomb disposal teams to drill a hole in the JDAM and diffuse the explosives. Looters had been in the hotel too, ripping out anything of value.

No. 1 Company's second-in-command captain felt that it was like the Wild West in the centre of the Middle East. Nothing was safe and nowhere was off limits.

No. 1 Company's Area of Responsibility included the Basra General Hospital, which was also being mercilessly ransacked. The hospital was on Al Joumhouria Street, part of the main road into Basra that had been called 'Red Route' by the army. The place, with limited supplies, was already struggling to cope with the wounded and dying. It was being looted of chairs, beds, mattresses. Someone brought the soldiers a looter who had even ripped incubators out of the maternity unit and so platoons stepped up guard duty there. Joe's turn soon came and, even after everything he'd seen, the hospital was heartbreaking and barbaric. It was the eye of Basra's growing humanitarian storm, the price that the city and its inhabitants were paying. Here he felt that he stopped being Joe McCleary, where he changed, lost part of himself and became entwined in the madness.

The hospital was built on a very large site and surrounded by a wall that was broken in many places. Inside, the soldiers took over a restroom on the upper floor of the hospital. They parked their Warriors at the front where a half-circle driveway allowed ambulances to pull up. The infantry patrolled in groups of four, around the trash-strewn grounds dotted with spiky bushes and occasional palm trees. They walked through the hellish halls of the medical care facility where wild and rabid dogs would run with body parts in their mouths. On one patrol, Joe opened a hospital door and saw a decaying body lying on the floor, discarded, forgotten; once human life now surrounded by flies. The face was a pitted cavity of partial flesh, rotted and with maggots coming in and out of his eye sockets. In another room was the morgue, a huge freezer containing what must have been eighty bodies of men, children, women; many with bullet holes in their heads and arms. Dead bodies of civilians who had been killed in the war-fighting, Joe presumed as he took a soon-to-be-forgotten photo. The hospital was a dangerous place. A man came into the building with a live grenade and pulled the pin out of it. The lads quickly wrestled him to the ground and threw the grenade into a skip before the man was arrested and cuffed by yelling infantryman. That was the sort of madness Joe was working in.

They were heading into summer. Temperatures were constant, around 50° C, and patrolling the hospital with the full body armour was sweaty, suffocating and exhausting. The worst part was the Neonatal-Intensive Care Unit (NICU). The ward, which was directly below the soldier's restroom, was full of babies and conditions were horrible. Incubators didn't work and it seemed to Joe as if the nurses merely kept the new-borns in there to keep the flies off their innocent faces. Even if the broken equipment had been fixed, electricity was so intermittent that nothing could be powered reliably. Any parent would have been taking their chances leaving their child there. Often there would be screaming from down the halls because a baby had just died. Grief of a parent goes beyond language barriers. Joe found it gut wrenching, scarring his senses.

He tried to help in any way he could. Each day he gave one of his two bottles of water to a young, pretty Iraqi nurse. She wore a traditional al-amira hijab, which veiled her hair, ears and neckline, and she struggled to say what little English words she knew.

'Speak with Joseph; speak with Joseph,' was about all she could say, but it was her lovely expression of appreciation in such an awful place that gave meaning to what she said.

Some of the other lads in the company acted as though they couldn't understand why Joe helped the young nurse.

'How can you fucking do that? How can you give them people ...?' one of the soldiers asked. *What some of these lads don't seem to understand is, what they've lost sight of, is we're here to save people,* Joe thought.

'You're forgetting that these are just babies, these are just people,' Joe replied.

'Oh, yeah, yeah. We know.'

'We're serving in this hospital to try and save their people,' said Joe.

'Oh, whatever, mate,' they said.

In all this mayhem, in all that fighting they'd perhaps forgotten that they'd come here to protect the people. It was as if this place had changed the other lads, made them bitter and numb. But this place changed Joe too.

Joe was on duty at the hospital when night fell. A cruel wind storm blew stinging grit and litter around in frenzied, angry swirls outside. From Joe's guard position near the front entrance he was approached by a middle-aged Iraqi man, who stumbled towards him, unsteady. His once white Arab gown was soaked through dark crimson below the waist. Joe clutched him on the arm as if to support the man and looked down to see the back of his right leg, ripped open as though he'd been savaged by a shark. The guy's blood ran down into a trail on the ground and it was clear he needed immediate help. Joe radioed the nearby Warrior and called in what he was doing.

'Look, I've got a male here. Forties. His leg's cut open to pieces. He needs medical attention now,' Joe yelled frantically.

'Okay, okay! Go take him in,' came the reply.

Joe moved quickly and helped the man's frail frame inside. It was late but the wards were still their usual busy turmoil of trolleys with the wounded lain prostrate and hallways thick with wandering battered civilians. Power failed intermittently, resulting in moments of darkness before weak emergency lights blinked on leaving dim corners hidden. Joe found a desk, and a doctor sitting over paperwork with a half-smoked cigarette hanging from his mouth, a line of ash about to crumble, but he seemed educated and spoke passable English.

'This guy needs help. His leg's all cut up,' Joe said breathlessly.

The doctor took a look up and down the wounded man, sniffed, and then flicked his hand dismissively like swatting away an annoying fly.

'I'm not seeing him. He's been drinking and it's against our religion,' he said piously. He glanced away in disgust.

The room was sweltering but the doctor's look was cold. Joe breathed hard through gritted teeth, peered down and brought his rifle up, holding it horizontally over his chest in firmly clasped hands. Next to him the wounded man swayed and reached out for a wall to support him. Joe called in over the radio but kept his eyes locked on this 'doctor'.

'They say they're not going to see him because he's been drinking ...' Joe paused his report to the Warrior and the team out front. There was a short burst of static. 'This fella's going to bleed to death, he's going to die if he doesn't get proper attention.'

The expression on the doctor's face said: just let him die. Joe thought for a moment about the cultural divide: *In my country, no matter who you were, what you'd done, we would save your life.* He waited a moment for a reply from his sergeant. It came.

'Tell the doctor that the tanks will be pulling off this ground unless he sees that fella,' came the shouted crackly response over the radio. 'That hospital will not be protected.'

Joe locked eye to eye with the doctor with a look that said: you hear that?

'Okay, okay,' the medic relented, finally standing. 'This way. Come. Bring him.'

He led Joe and the bleeding man down a corridor into a barely lit side room with a bed in the centre and a small table holding a tray of blunt scalpels, scissors and other instruments. Joe grabbed a blue Cyalume light stick and held it up to try and extinguish the shadows that lurked in the room. Surveying the place, he noticed damp mould and dried blood splashed on the walls. Nothing had been cleaned or sterilised since whatever operation had last taken place in here. Joe could tell the man wouldn't even be offering this kind of 'care' unless the soldiers were present. Joe guided the patient to the bed and the doctor leaned over and examined his leg. He was still smoking his cigarette, ash falling on the injured man with disregard. From the table the doctor grabbed a small terry cloth towel which he rolled up tightly and placed in the patient's mouth.

'Hold to that,' he said and the injured man bit down on to the cloth. With a needle and thread in one hand, the doctor pulled on the wound to close it, but Joe watched as the skin kept tearing because the gash was too wide and the skin so worn and fragile. The man made muffled howls of agony as fresh blood flowed and sprayed on the wall while the doctor worked. Tears rolled off the patient's face and he reached out to grip Joe's arm, dug his fingernails into his skin. The wound wouldn't close and the doctor seemed as though he was enjoying his treatment. He resembled the embodiment of Mengele himself. Joe had had enough. He moved forward, snapped.

'I have more medical knowledge! I'd be better at this than you,' he spat. 'I know you can understand me. Fix that fella now. Stop the bleeding,' the infantryman raged, heart racing. The gag-stifled howls were horrendous. How the old man never passed out with the pain seemed incomprehensible to Joe. He was offered neither anaesthetic nor drugs.

'What you're doing is barbaric!' the infantryman seethed.

The doctor finally pulled the stitches and closed the wound with a dozen sutures that held it in place.

Something took over Joe in those moments, altering him. Here was absolute abject horror made normal and they couldn't stop it from happening. It was as though part of his brain stopped firing the signals to say this was awful and wrong. He became numb and switched to a darker side of himself.

Joe was only peripherally aware as the doctor bandaged up the man with the wounded leg and threw him out into the Basra night. He no longer cared whether he was dead or alive. Joe wasn't himself any more. He'd become a different person, lost, changed by the events of the hospital that night.

Chapter 33

Witnesses

To Joe, it feels as though they're talking about someone else, he doesn't recognise himself in the descriptions and the allegations levelled against him. He feels as if the prosecutor is describing some other person, even as he singles Joe out. The QC highlights the claim that after the incident at the canal, Joe returned to the base in Basra and then told other soldiers in the hospital restroom that he and the others involved 'had taken looters to the river and that one of them had drowned'. These feel like things told by someone with a grudge, Joe thinks, and dredged up by an RMP investigator, eager to convict.

'He also told the others,' says the prosecutor of Joe, 'not to mention what he had told them as Sergeant Selman had told him not to say anything. McCleary was not in shock and it was as if he was telling them something normal.' The prosecutor's words go on, saying Joe's statements were a 'deliberate attempt to mislead'. He says that McGing's statement, too, is 'a pack of lies, as he was deliberately attempting to protect himself and others from the consequences of what they did'.

Court had reconvened on Tuesday, 2 May, after the Bank Holiday, though the long weekend gave Joe little break from the stress of everything. He missed most of the first week due to the hospital stay and now the prosecution fully kicks off its case. Orlando Pownall is the prosecutor's Queen's Counsel, who leads the State's charge against the men. Pownall has a revered and feared reputation as one of the best of the criminal bar, acting as either a defence lawyer or a prosecutor on a number of notorious cases. He has won the conviction of the man suspected of killing TV presenter Jill Dando, though the case was later found to be unsound and overturned on retrial; in the murder of a young black woman gunned down in London, Pownall achieved the first successful prosecution of Operation Trident which tackled gun crime in the capital; and he defended four teenagers who went on a deadly spree of violence along the River Thames.

Stephen Riordan, Joe's QC, knows that the prosecution's aim with the accusations is to show that manslaughter was as much a crime of the mind as a crime of the deed. To prove manslaughter, Pownall will have to convince the panel that the soldiers had an intentionally reckless disregard for the safety of the people they were dealing with. The prosecution will have to describe the state of the men's minds and show that what happened was intentional. The trial will have a distinct batting order. There's an indictment charge sheet and the defendants are listed in a particular order. The prosecution will question witnesses and then the defence counsel will have their chance at a cross-examination, beginning first with Cooke's QC, then Selman's, Stephen Riordan for Joe and finally Jerry Hayes for McGing. The rules are almost the same as for a criminal trial except the men's futures are being determined by a military panel rather than a jury. After the swearing in of the seven-person panel, statements are read out for the four accused affirming that they all plead 'Not Guilty'. It's then that Pownall unleashes the full body blow of the case. Even prepared for what is to unfold, his words are still savage and painful, unlike anything Joe has previously experienced.

'The prosecution will show the unlawful and dangerous activities of the four defendants acting together as part of a joint enterprise,' Pownall says. 'It is suggested that a clear picture emerges of their common design or plan to force the alleged looters into the water to teach them a lesson.'

Pownall describes to the court some of the events, construing them in such a way that lays the blame on the soldiers for what happened to Ahmed Kareem, the teenage boy in Basra who ended up in the canal with the three other boys, including Ayad, still the only witness who investigators were able to track down.

'The slope was gradual but muddy, neither he nor Ahmed could swim. Two of those who had been detained swam to the other side,' Pownall argues forcefully. 'Two soldiers from the back of the vehicle threw bricks and stones while they were in the water. Kareem was in obvious distress as he was unable to swim. His head bobbed to the surface and then disappeared.' The twisted words take Joe back to the harsh interrogation he experienced and it takes all his self-control to steel himself and not stand up and respond to what Pownall is alleging. He catches Stephen Riordan giving him a stern look, ensuring that Joe maintains composure.

'One of the soldiers who was on the bank of the canal made as if to remove his clothing in order to rescue Kareem.' Joe tries to steer a glance at James Cooke yet finds his head is turned away as the QC concludes his point. 'But then returned to the Warrior tank, which drove away,' the prosecutor says with an air of deadly finality.

'There was nothing to indicate signs of injury that might have caused his death apart from what is suggested to be an irresistible inference that Kareem had drowned.' Pownall projects his words, utterly relentless. 'All sober and reasonable people would realise that their unlawful actions must have subjected the 15-year-old boy to the risk of at least some physical harm.'

Joe's anxiety simmers, toxically. He almost believes Pownall as he lays into the men with bitter words. Joe feels every inch of the demolition of the men through the expected one-sided picture from the prosecution. Pownall goes on to attack the truthfulness of the men's statements to investigators, repeating the claim that afterwards Selman told the men 'not to say anything'.

'It might be said,' he goes on, 'as has been reported elsewhere, that the Coalition forces were ill-prepared for the occupation in Iraq and the maintenance of the peace and received insufficient guidance. There was looting of epidemic proportions,' Pownall admits.

'While no doubt the task of policing Basra and maintaining law and order would have been an onerous one, it is suggested that no soldier could have been left in any doubt as to the limits on force necessary,' he continues. 'It is the Crown's case that the activities of the four accused fell significantly and unlawfully outside what could be described as minimum necessary force. There was no need to use any force at all.'

Joe sits, taking all this in. *The Crown's case*, Joe thinks, his own country that he fought for turning against him. And still Pownall goes on.

'The looters had already been punished in that stagnant pool. They were being driven away from Basra hospital to avoid a confrontation with the crowd who had gathered. All that was needed was for them to be released and to make their way home,' he pauses for effect, allowing the military board who will judge the men to absorb his last words.

'That is not what happened and the consequences of that is that a 15-year-old died needlessly and unlawfully.'

Joe feels he's received the battering of his life and it's only just the beginning.

The next day, the prosecution calls its first witness, the only Iraqi who can tell the trial what happened at the water's edge. He is one of the four taken to the canal. The investigators have still been unable to track down the other two. Ayad Salim Hanon Khedhayyar, who reported the incident, is led into court wearing a blue and white striped shirt and jeans. The lad is 25, just a year older than Joe. Joe wonders, *what must this be like to be suddenly brought to England for this?* The Iraqi speaks only Arabic and two translators are sworn in to deliver his words. He explains to the court that he was a welder and on the morning of the incident had gone to the Baghdad Garage, near the hospital. There was no work for him so he was trying to sell things with three or four other lads, including Ahmed. He says that the British soldiers and some Iraqi police chased them from the garage, caught them and started beating them. The court sits through video, taken by the RMP, of the place where Ayad says they were made to stand, explaining to the court they were bound and beaten further before being taken in a tank to the hospital grounds. There, Ayad says, the four Iraqis were hit again while the soldiers conferred with Iraqi police. He continues, claiming that the guardsmen piled him and the others into the back of the Warrior, hitting them as they headed towards the canal. Hearing the prosecution coax the Iraqi's account of what happened that day from their star witness for the Colchester panel, feels surreal to Joe.

'We were near the water and they were throwing bricks at us and we had to cross the mud and then into the river.'

'And who was it who were throwing the bricks?' Pownall asks.

'Al Britaniu.' No one has to wait for the translation: 'The British'. The words hang like a poison in the air. Pownall prods Ayad further for his take on what happened.

'We went into the river. We had no other choice. We had to swim.'

'And what would have happened if you hadn't gone in?' inquires the prosecutor.

'I don't know. They might have killed us,' Ayad answers plainly.

Joe can barely take what's said against them.

'We could not get out of the river because the soldiers were still standing there,' the Iraqi says. 'Kareem was one yard away from me. He could not swim.' His details seem to twist the knife. 'There was mud beneath our feet, it was slippery. There was a tide. He just raised his hands but then he was under the water and then he raised them again. Both arms were stretched out of the water, but there was no sound from him. Then he vanished. There was nothing I could do because I could not swim well.'

Photos appear on the large TV monitors. They show the river and Bridge Four.

'The tide was strong and I was affected. It affected the swimming and coming down and up,' Ayad says. His sincerity seems hidden by the relay through the translator. 'After they left, I immediately came out of the river,' he goes on. 'I did nothing to find him because I couldn't swim, I waited there for two hours then went back. I stopped a taxi and he took me home. I went the next day to the British centre to make a complaint with Ahmed's father's brother. The father went to take his son's body from the river.' All the while Joe listens, suspicious, trying to fathom out where the grief was for Kareem whom Ayad was with and had drowned.

After lunch, the defence begin their cross-examination of Ayad. James Cooke's QC, Richard Lissack, goes first, beginning by trying to disassociate his client from Ayad's allegations. Cooke was driving so couldn't have assaulted the boys, he says. Lissack also starts to pick away at inconsistencies in the lad's story. He questions the claims of injuries, which were photographed less than a month after the incident. He gets Ayad to admit that he was completely wrong about a tank driving him from the garage to the hospital. He presses Ayad about what he and Ahmed were doing at the garage that morning, forcing him to concede they were looking for things to take and trade.

'I saw Ahmed inside the garage. We were both looking for something to sell,' the interpreter relays to the court. 'There was bombing by Bush at the time, there was a curfew, we could not work. It was a catastrophe, we were very hungry. It was wrong, but we had no other option.' The memory of the desperation almost seems to break through the language barrier. 'There were no jobs, no work, we were intending to take goods to sell them to support our families,' he says.

Joe sits, surrounded by his legal team, listening uncomfortably and feeling pity for the situation these Iraqis were in. Conditions in the city were terrible in the days after they'd invaded. Money to survive and keeping your family is one thing that's understandable; it motivates a lot of what people do, Joe knows.

'I was told that I would get compensation for the injuries and for the beating,' admits Ayad when Lissack asks him what he hoped to achieve by making a complaint to the British. He says it was when he'd first given his statement at Shaibah airbase that someone had told him about possibly receiving money for what he said happened to him while in British custody.

'I was paid 5,000 or 6,000 per day Iraqi dinar. Then 250,000 dinars was $100. I don't know how much compensation I'd get.' Ayad was trying to survive on a couple of dollars a day. To Joe, sitting in the dock, this whole case rests on Ayad's allegations and it seems to him as if it's all about money, but this court case is four men's lives hanging in the balance.

The next day brings a 'show and tell' with a Warrior infantry transport that's similar to the one the guardsmen had in Iraq. The armoured troop transport has been brought and is parked up on the lawn at the Colchester Barracks. It's for the accused, their legal teams and the panel's eyes only, however.

'The information I am being given,' Judge Advocate Hunter tells the court, 'is that what we are seeing is classified and for security reasons cannot be made public.' He bars disappointed family members and the press pack from viewing the Warrior. The legal teams have already examined the vehicle a month and a half earlier at a base in Warminster. Amusingly, the barristers now appear more familiar with the machine than the military top brass who make up the panel.

'Never call it a tank!' says Nigel Powell, Riordan's junior, showing his recently found knowledge of the Warrior. 'That's one thing we learned!'

'Very cramped it is too,' the taller than 6ft Riordan observes. 'I would have found it very difficult cooped up in one of those for hours on end sometimes.'

The panel examines the vehicle inside and out, seeing where each of the men were positioned on the day they drove to Bridge Four and some of the seven climb inside the back where the Iraqis, Martin and Joe would have been.

The cross-examination of Ayad resumes in the courtroom with Selman's QC John Coffey. He catches the Iraqi out on some more discrepancies in his testimony, some he admits to and others he puts down to the translator.

'There is a possibility I've given different accounts, but it might be the interpreters,' he says. 'I swore on the Koran that I would tell the truth.'

Coffey tries to establish that Selman stayed in the vehicle and was not responsible for assaulting the Iraqis.

'The tank stopped, door opened and you and the other Iraqi nationals came out?' asks the QC. 'The driver and the man in the turret stayed in?'

'No they came out,' comes the translated reply.

'All the soldiers then got in and the vehicle moved off?'

'Yes, after Ahmed drowned and then we got out of the water.'

'At no stage did the turret man have a gun?' Coffey says, referring to Selman.

'I don't think so, I didn't see,' says Ayad with uncertainty. 'But those other two did have weapons,' he adds, referring to Martin and Joe.

Stephen Riordan, Joe's QC, is up next to cross-examine Ayad, putting him on the spot over his role in the looting.

'I was one of the thieves in Basra,' Ayad finally confesses. 'All people in the area started to steal. Yes, I got the idea from them, we had no work and had to take things to sell. It wasn't a strong force, supported by the British. It was very weak.'

'Was it safe to steal?' Riordan asks.

'There was no security so it was safe to steal. I didn't think about what would happen if I got caught, it wasn't in my mind.'

Riordan presses Ayad about what happened after the soldiers drove away from Bridge Four.

'I wasn't sure if Ahmed had drowned,' says Ayad. 'I told myself, I thought there was a possibility that he knew how to swim and got out of the river from another direction.' The lad had told himself the same thing that Joe, and perhaps some of the other guardsmen had to reassure themselves after they'd left the scene.

'What did you do?' asks Joe's barrister.

'I waited for two hours for Ahmed to appear. I got a taxi to home. Once I arrived home I paid the taxi. I told my family, I told my father, he saw me beaten up, my hand and face. I told him about Ahmed.'

'And what happened next?' Riordan probes.

'My father didn't say we should go to Ali Jabbar Kareem. I was very tired and I slept.' It strikes Joe as strange that someone went straight home to sleep and waited to raise the alarm that a person they were with might just have drowned.

'And when did you see Mr Ali Jabbar Kareem, Ahmed's father?'

'I saw Jabbar on Friday in Basra at the same market,' says Ayad.

'We go there every Friday to Basra to buy and sell and there was a possibility that I would see him. I told him.'

'What did you tell him?' Riordan enquires.

'I asked him if his son came home. He said no,' recounts Ayad.

'And what did you say?'

'I said that Ahmed might have drowned.'

'How did Ahmed's father react?'

'He kept on hitting his head, then took a taxi and left. He was very angry and kept on hitting himself. He didn't blame me for what happened. He knew when the British beat us it was for stealing, it was for stealing that they beat us.' It's sad for the QC to hear a father's grief observed, but Riordan challenges the Iraqi over how seriously he was beaten.

'Is it not the case that the more badly beaten, the more the money you might receive?' he asks.

'No. I was badly beaten for a long time, I said that,' Ayad maintains.

'Is it really true that it was the British who beat you?' asks Riordan.

'How is it untrue that the British beat us? Whatever I'm saying is the truth.' Ayad replies. 'The British army, when they saw the bruises, they were really surprised.'

'I suggest it is a false allegation against the British soldiers. Was it not the Iraqi police that hit you?' contends Joe's barrister.

'I have not made false allegations against the British soldiers. I did say the Iraqi police did nothing to us,' Ayad responds.

Jerry Hayes, Martin McGing's barrister, is the last up to cross-examine the key witness. On into another day, he challenges Ayad with almost theatrical attacks.

'Who was protecting Basra at that point?' Hayes asks.

'No one was protecting the nation, not the Iraqi police; everyone was looting,' implores Ayad. 'We couldn't feed our families. I would have done anything for money.'

'And aren't you now trying to milk the British taxpayer for compensation money?' counters Hayes, almost facetiously.

'I have not come to court to lie for compensation. I did not know it would come this far. I am telling the truth.'

'You wouldn't recognise the truth if it jumped up and bit you on the nose,' retorts Hayes mockingly.

Photos and video of Ayad's injuries are put on display.

'A doctor examined me on the same day as the photo,' the Iraqi says. Hayes is having none of it.

'I put it to you that the arm scar is old,' the defence lawyer insists.

'I kept treating the injury,' replies Ayad through his interpreter. 'The knee injury is not bad, it is not old. My arm was bandaged when I went to see the army.'

'In the video of 31 May 2003, your sleeves are rolled up,' says Hayes of the image taken at Shaibah where the army police interviewed Ayad on tape. 'And there is not a bandage in sight!'

'They were only on for about five days,' claims Ayad. Hayes scoffs.

'Not since the healing of Lazarus has there been such a miraculous recovery!' he retorts. His comment is quickly withdrawn before the interpreter can attempt a translation.

'I haven't come to tell wicked lies to line my own pockets,' pleads the Iraqi. 'These are not fake allegations.'

The third week of the trial gets underway with Ahmed's father appearing to the court. Jabbar Kareem Ali El-Hamoudad describes life in Basra after the invasion, the last time he sees his son alive on 8 May 2003, and finding out that he may have drowned. It's a hard thing for Joe and the others to hear about.

'I collapsed, nervous breakdown,' the old man says through the interpreter. 'I went home, I told my brothers, we all gathered in the morning. We went immediately to Zubair, there were so many of us, not just my relatives: neighbours, friends, people from the area.'

'And then what happened?' asks prosecutor Pownall gently.

'On the 9th we waited, then on the 10th at 2.00 pm the body floated. When it floated, because the current was strong the body was taken; the man with the boat had stayed with us all the time. He went after the body. When he approached the body, he put a rope around the neck and pulled it until it was near the bank of the river. He had only his trousers. Long trousers.'

Sitting through the most gruelling of testimony, Stephen Riordan quietly thinks the father has definitely been brought in to put the knife in as much as he possibly could. There isn't a lot he can add because he wasn't at the scene and didn't know what had happened. In a murder case a prosecutor will deliberately call someone even if they've got little to say, so that the senses and emotions of the jury might be stirred up. Knowing this still doesn't make it any easier for Joe to hear.

'I was so upset I tore my clothes, I could not speak and did not speak to the doctor. I was close to my son.' says Mr Jabbar Kareem, continuing his distressing account. 'Then we took him home, stayed at home for two hours then we took the body and went to Najaf for the burial. We had to go there because that is according to our belief according to Islam.'

It is a lot for Joe to deal with, and in a room provided for his legal team he lets off steam. This is where Stephen and Nigel dress in their robes and wigs. Joe tries on the wig, joking around to hide his anxiety at how intense the case is. It's like being out in Iraq where surviving on gallows humour is the only thing that got them through. Joe has immense trust in his barrister and the joking and banter between him and Stephen helps the young defendant to cope. Riordan also sees when Joe is getting agitated at the details being presented in the court and finds a way to distract Joe's stress by prompting him to try and read some of the narrative cases of thick legal books. There are stacks and stacks of them neatly assembled on the table where the legal team sits in a row. Sometimes they'd refer to a past case from one of the books but Stephen, when he notices his client's rising anger, is strict and directs Joe to try and occupy himself by reading them. Joe, who has been trying to improve his reading recently, tackles them as though they are short stories of misdemeanours or articles of mad people and their criminal cases. Even when Joe doesn't understand all the language, it works. The mammoth volumes distract as more witnesses take their place: the Iraqi doctor who signed the death certificate, the RAF pathologist who examined the body forty days later and the British investigators who examined the crime scene.

By the end of the third week, the court begins calling some of No. 1 Company. First is Wayne Sampat who's still serving and now a lance corporal. He's taken by the prosecutor through the patrol at the hospital, the mass of looters and how they used minimum force to deal with them. Despite his foggy memory he describes being one of six in the hospital restroom when he's called to deal with looters who were near a wall outside. He tells of the four Iraqi lads being made to get into an ankle-deep swamp by local police officers in front of jeering members of the public before they were led to the hospital. He tells the court that Selman said that they were going to the Shatt al-Arab and that after seeing McGing and Joe in the back of the Warrior, Sampat went back to the restroom and slept. Sampat also says that McGing was on edge when he returned, mentioning that one of the detainees had got into difficulty and that Selman told him not to say anything about what happened. Under cross-examination, Riordan challenges Sampat on why he wasn't honest when he was questioned about what happened.

'I didn't tell the full truth at the beginning. I lied about the 8 May 2003 – saying there was nothing I could remember,' says Sampat. 'Staff Sergeant Jay identified the occasion. I knew from the beginning what he was on about. I knew something had happened, but I was determined not to say anything about it.'

'Why lie?' asks Riordan.

'They were unusual circumstances. I didn't know what anyone else had said. Loyalty to my colleagues was important.'

'What changed?'

'I cooperated,' returns Sampat. 'I wanted to get myself off the hook. There was a nightmare scenario developing of the guilty walking away and me getting the blame. I cooperated with what I knew.'

'I put it to you that you were cooperating so that the blame went to those who had been there and away from yourself,' postulates Riordan.

'You make it sound like I'm pointing the finger at people,' says Sampat, fighting to retain his cool. 'I was under pressure and had been told that two former colleagues had made false allegations against me. McCleary was not one of those people who had made false allegations.'

Robert Fleming, another member of Joe's section and still in the Irish Guards, gives evidence that follows a similar pattern to Sampat except he says Joe knew that Ahmed had drowned.

'What happened after the detainees had been taken in the Warrior?' asks prosecutor Pownall.

'An hour later McCleary came back to the restroom,' Fleming claims. 'Just said the looters had been thrown into a river, don't know by whom. One of them went under the water. He had drowned.'

That's not what happened as Joe remembers it, and Riordan catches Joe muttering with frustration under his breath as the prosecution asks what happened to detainees.

'When we detained people,' says Fleming, 'different things happened. Sometimes taken back to the gym. On a few occasions we had looters in the dismount section of the warrior.'

'Would this happen often?' asks the prosecutor.

'This was a regular occurrence, them being in the back of the warrior, if they needed to be moved to the gymnasium.'

'And where else would Iraqi detainees be taken?'

'I never took them to the river, didn't hear of that,' Fleming says. 'There were no approved methods, like putting them in the water. I know the Iraqi police had done it. I saw it done just once. Looters would be put in the rear and taken to the gym. That was it.'

In Iraq, the lowly dismount infantry soldiers knew little or nothing about the policy towards the detainees. They didn't need to; it was just their job to follow orders, not to know the ins and outs of dealing with looters. That wasn't the case for those in more senior positions.

When Daniel O'Connell, Joe's platoon commander and responsible for over a hundred men, takes the stand, he explains that he was answerable to Major MacMullen. O'Connell also says that Sergeant Selman was answerable to him.

'Where did you hear about wetting detainees?' asks John Coffey, Selman's QC, using the word that had only recently been coined to describe soaking detainees as a deterrent.

'I heard about wetting at Company O Group, which is evening orders for the next day. It was a daily occurrence,' Dan O'Connell replies.

'Who ran those meetings?'

'It is presided over by the company commander, Major MacMullen. Wetting them, that was one of the ad-hoc means by which the looters were being dealt with from time to time in early May 2003. It was a considered option available to a commander on the ground to deter looting. They'd be made to jump in water. It's a deterrent because they'd have to go home and get changed. There was no exact rule about what to do.'

For Joe's QC this a significant revelation. Riordan recognises, as does his client, that even if getting Iraqis wet was never an official policy, admission that it was common practice is important. It was also discussed at a higher level. There is evidence that it was something systemic.

'At the O Group meeting, wetting was discussed.' O'Connell continues, 'I recall it was discussed because other units in the area had used it and it was suggested as an option.'

'And who would have attended the O Group meeting?' probes Coffey.

'I would have been there. There would have been some senior ranks. Sometimes Warrior sergeants would be there. The platoon sergeant would have been there too.' Through O'Connell's testimony, Coffey is stringing out a clear line of if not approval, then passive acceptance. 'Wetting', an unorthodox method was discussed at senior meetings with senior army commanders present, it was a method that was familiar and that Selman, as a Warrior sergeant, could have been at those meetings where nothing was done to address a potentially dangerous way of dealing with looters. In his testimony, O'Connell makes a parallel with measures used at home to deal with riots.

'In crowd control water cannons are used sometimes and that's the same sort of deterrent.'

Chapter 34

Portrait of a City after Fire

Across Basra the British soldiers needed to deter the tidal wave of looters who were still destroying the city. But trying to deal with them had started to destroy some of the men of No. 1 Company as well. Towards the end of April, Martin McGing lost his eyesight and was admitted to the army hospital with his condition put down to acute stress. After three days his eyesight returned and he could see again, but by this point there was a lot that couldn't be unseen.

All over the city were the visible wounds of conflict and disorder. The dirty horizon was still a watercolour smear of hellish black smoke trails from the distant oil wells, which Saddam's forces had set fire to before they retreated in a last-ditch attempt to take the country down with him. On the dusty three-lane highways into Basra, where blue route signs hung, spent shell casings and mortar craters littered the way. Ubiquitous white Toyota cars and small Kia minibuses, most with cracked windscreens, now shared the road with horse and cart and the raw mechanised presence of Coalition war machines. Some civilians pushed their beat-up cars along while others queued up for miles for petrol in a country where a wealth of oil was buried beneath their feet. The dictator's painted image ensured he wasn't forgotten, with walls showing Saddam wearing sunglasses like a movie star, his right arm raised and a banner of Iraqi flag behind. Saddam's £25m, 400ft yacht, the Al Mansur, a name which ironically meant 'victor', lay smoking, bombed adrift by a pontoon on the Shatt al-Arab river. Nearby, the dictator's proud palace on the right bank of the river was now headquarters to Brigadier Graham Binns and his British 7th Armoured Brigade. Instead of the tyrant's notorious opulence was now the functional apparatus of war: urns of hot water and tea bags, officers coming and going, snatching phones, maps and plans, filing through rows of desks labelled with the likes of 'Royal Engineers', 'Scots DG Battle Group', '1 RRF Battle Group' and others. This was the orchestration of an occupation. Water supply was still not connected so British forces made do with supplies out of jerrycans. Generators droned and kept Coalition computers running while civilian frustration fermented at the lack of electricity in their neighbourhoods.

Inside the city, soot-stained houses that bore the brunt of the bombing campaign were covered now with cracks. Their walls were like the city's people, strained and almost buckled. Joe and his platoon patrolled streets littered with piles of brick rubble and past half-completed windowless concrete structures. New days were signalled with the 5.00 am Imam's amplified calls to prayer for the multitudes of Shiite Muslim worshippers. Arab men and boys then clustered on pavements seemingly without purpose. Without waste collection, heaps of rubbish stacked up and stunk the streets and filthy scrubland. Dead dogs lay in the open sun and flies had a field day as they feasted on the decayed flesh and fur. At nights there was shooting in the streets. Old gangs settled old scores and warlords fought for dominance.

Things seemed too slow to change after nearly a month on from the troops' arrival in Basra. There were growing tensions and the British were starting to feel like unwelcome visitors, tiring even the Middle Eastern hospitality. It had started to happen elsewhere in the country. North of Baghdad, people in the suburb of Fallujah protested and asked the Americans to leave now they'd toppled their dictator. Stones were thrown and US weapons unloaded their ammunition. Thirteen Iraqis dead one day; more the next and scores wounded. Many believed that the military effort had won the war but now they were losing the peace. Ensuring that law and order and basic services were established quickly was critical. Yet the Irish Guards, for one, were neither nation builders nor policemen.

At the Battle Group Orders meetings, plans for helping restore vital services were set and strategies for enforcing civil obedience were discussed. Royal Engineers were soon to help reconstruct demolished bridges in nearby villages, part of the infrastructure destroyed by the Iraqi militia to disrupt advancing Coalition forces. A number of NGOs were entering the city to help provide food, water and medical treatment. No. 1 Company Irish Guards were to go and paint some schools to help show their commitment to rebuilding and stabilising the region. Across Basra they had to move to a posture of focusing on the population's hearts and minds. Helmets came off, berets came on. The needs in the city were overwhelming and law and order still precarious.

Major MacMullen heard how other companies dealt with the non-serious criminal elements and looters that still plagued the city. It was complicated and fraught to find the acceptable level of force to discourage them. As the company commander he'd seen his men struggle to deal with the looters, watched some of them sometimes cross the line. There'd been exhausted guardsmen who'd screamed at Iraqis to get out of their vehicle and MacMullen had to intervene with a stern, 'Alright fellas, calm down', asserting the chain of command to diffuse tense situations. He'd seen similar things happen when he was a captain in Kosovo, but there the British went in as peacekeepers; here though, that line seemed blurred. No. 2 Company and A Company Irish Guards both faced the Shatt al-Arab river and found looters robbing a bank so they said they'd put them down in the river bank for them to have to swim back. The idea was that they would get wet, feel foolish and have to walk miserably home. Pride was a powerful motivator to Arab communities so the chastised looters would also have the stigma of shame arriving home sopping wet. To MacMullen, putting the Iraqis in water at least seemed a pragmatic solution where few other options existed and never did his brigade commander say it was a bad idea and that it had to stop. There was passive acceptance from the higher-ups. The commanders knew it happened. Major MacMullen heard that one company had caught forty looters and marched them down to the water's edge to get them wet. Captain Brennan had seen looters thrown into the Shatt al-Arab River. Humiliation and a soak seemed an acceptable way to dislocate their activities when little else worked.

The days were getting hotter and hotter, heading deeper into Middle Eastern summer. The nights were a dangerous time but were preceded by balmy warmth of beautiful sunsets: hazy mauve- and violet-painted skies. MacMullen spent one evening up in the sangar, the defensive position they'd built up around the GMPY on top of the gym roof and he listened to British Forces Broadcasting Service (BFBS) Radio. Playing over the airwaves, he heard the theme from The Archers, its merry Maypole dance of Barwick Green, while nightly enemy tracers darted overhead. *All is well with the world*, MacMullen thought to himself.

The few precious moments of downtime that the men had were spent snatching sleep or writing letters for despatch back home. When they wrote their Blueys they weren't allowed to say that much; families at home couldn't be told anything about the operations their loved ones were involved in nor the situation in Iraq. Even if it were permitted, Joe wasn't able to put into words what he was seeing. Instead, with less than two weeks left in the tour, he started to think about the future and wrote in his dyslexic hand:

I have seen some good car's for sale £1500 I se what happen when I get home. mum make sure you find out about the car as soon as you can so when I get home I know every think or wright to me about it. I have been think of buying a house when I get back. Maybe try an get a morgaaes. I have 1 year left in the army so I will put a deposit on a house. I can do it up in my last year.

The estranged veil of normality did not hide the simmering unease that was growing around Basra. Major MacMullen wasn't comfortable patrolling without his troops wearing full body armour when they walked about town. Lieutenant Colonel Riddell-Webster was clear that they wanted the locals to think that it was safe now but the speed of the transition from war-fighting to peacekeeping seemed too fast. On patrol with Pat Geraghty and others, Peter MacMullen tried his best.

'I fancy an ice cream company sergeant major. Fancy one?' said MacMullen brightly.

'No, sir. Thank you.'

'Well I do.' Peter indicated a nearby Iraqi shop. Around them tentative Iraqi markets were starting to return to business. Scattered tables were stacked with a short pyramid of home-grown green vegetables, another with shisha pipes, one with small tubs of brown spices. A bazaar stallholder, hearing British accents, looked at the soldiers, smiled and shouted the only English he knew: 'Lovely jubbly! Lovely jubbly!'

'I'll protect the perimeter, sir,' Pat stated matter-of-factly. The CSM stood outside and gave a cigarette to a nearby Iraqi man. There was no hostility, but he could tell that the mood was shifting. He sensed the change from the initial burst of optimism that greeted the troops' arrival and Saddam's fall. On patrols people started to give what he called 'the glare'. It was what military studies called 'atmospherics', how people were reacting, reading the mood and hostility of an area. Pat remembered 'the look' from serving in Northern Ireland. Tension and dust now swirled together and clogged the air.

New American policy helped hasten the crumbling of society in Basra. At the start of May, Paul Bremer took up his post as the US administrator of Iraq and ordered strict de-Ba'athification measures. This meant refusing to work with anyone who had possessed membership in the Ba'ath party and that included huge numbers of skilled former civil society employees. Near the gymnasium base one morning, two Iraqi policemen in clean pressed blue shirts had diligently returned to duty and were directing traffic. Major MacMullen, following American orders, told Pat to go and arrest the men.

'Why, sir? The way I see it they're helping,' said Pat, one of the few who could raise such a query with the company commander.

'They're former Ba'ath party members,' said MacMullen.

'But who isn't?' Pat said.

Under the old regime, any educated members of Iraqi society had to be members of the Ba'ath party simply to have jobs even if, as was often the case with the Shiite in Basra, they personally hated Saddam. Local people knew that if all those with administrative experience in their country – a teacher, a civil servant, law enforcement – were excluded, then their society would free-fall. Disbanding the Iraqi police force also meant a huge pool of men who were highly trained and had their own weapons were now bored and jobless. It was a recipe for disaster.

The soldiers were more overwhelmed than ever having to police a population that massively outnumbered them. A platoon from No. 1 Company heard about some Iraqi criminal gangs operating out of a brothel, so it was raided. They didn't find the crime bosses but the Iraqi prostitutes, wearing their Muslim veils, were furious that the soldiers had scared the male clients away. The women threw bricks in resentment as the Warriors pulled away.

On another day, a Polish water tank arrived and some NGOs started to set up a clean water distribution point. Some lads from No. 1 Company offered to lend a hand until three Australian humanitarians, typically haughty and high-minded, told them that they didn't want anything to do with the military. It was just minutes before a massive crowd of thirsty, desperate Iraqis surrounded the water tank, threatening to overcome the NGOs who quickly changed their minds about needing the infantry's help.

Joe's call sign, One Two, was called on Quick Reaction Force to respond to a hostage situation. They flew into the Warriors and headed through the dense urban side streets of the city. The section arrived to find two people being held captive in the upper floor of a building. James Cooke had just pulled up the Warrior on the street when the soldiers started taking fire from the roof down on their position. When the Warrior's door opened, two of the dismounts froze stiff, locked in place by the close zing of a mad spraying of bullets. Joe ignored them and followed Paul Hollander, his section commander, to run out with a couple of other dismounts. They quickly found cover along the building's wall before smashing in a wooden door with some well-placed kicks. Each of the men spun his head around inside, surveying for threats. No one knew what they faced as they ran in, whether insurgents or a domestic disturbance that had escalated. Hollander led the way, his rifle pointed upward. The soldiers filtered quickly through the house. They came to the second floor and smelled smoke. Someone managed to extinguish the fire while Hollander and Joe continued on. They located the room in which were a pair of Iraqi hostages: terrified civilians now abandoned. Quickly Joe had assessed that the shooter had gone. Whoever it was had run out of the back and escaped. It was another example of the instability in the city.

Throughout the exhausting and ratcheting tension of the routine in Basra, Joe was kept going by the precious letter from his granddad and was happy when a care package arrived from home. These always lifted the lads' spirits, whether Pot Noodles or sweets. It had been a couple of weeks since the phone call that Joe had had with his mum when she'd promised a package was on the way, but when an Air Mail parcel finally arrived he couldn't hold back his excitement.

Joe manically tore at the brown box and found that Lynn had posted him a tin of Princes corned beef and a box of Smash instant mashed potato. Joe was ravenous for the taste of home and clawed at the key to peel open the tin of processed beef. He yanked hard and the thin metal lid began to peel backwards to release the smell of salt-cured meat. It brought back a flash of memory, the meat his mum often used when she made her delicious Scouse, the stew that gave the name to the region's accent. Distracted for a second, Joe barely noticed as the metal key snapped, the sharp aluminium twisted and sliced through his finger.

'Fuck!' he screamed. It was his right trigger finger too.

Blood streamed down his hand but he was so ravenous. Joe licked the blood off and stuck the finger under his arm and used his left hand to claw out the meat. He ate it, unappetising though it was straight from the tin. He was desperately craving for something that wasn't from a military rations' bag.

'Mate, let me see your finger,' said the lad next to Joe.

'Ge' off!' Joe said with a mouthful of beef, ignoring the pain before allowing the lad to look at his cut. It was so severely lacerated that it needed stitching and bandaging. Later, Joe had to strip his rifle apart and take the trigger guard off so he could fit his wrapped-up finger into the trigger slot. He knew it was going to leave a hell of a scar but it was worth it for the taste of home.

The company continued its routines, working constantly, the Muezzin marking each new day with his early morning wailing. Joe's shift patterns felt exhausting. He was on duty for long days, rotating between QRF duty, stag sentry duty and patrolling of the petrol station or hospital. He became so shattered that he almost fell asleep on his feet. Out on patrol, kids were kids and hung around the soldiers, trying to find something to occupy them and seeing the foreigners as a novelty. 'Mister, mister, mister,' the olive-skinned boys would badger the infantrymen.

The guardsmen found ways to entertain the young Iraqis. Sampat got a kick out of teaching kids to swear in English. Some of the guys still kicked a football about with the young Iraqis on some land behind the gymnasium base. Joe, like other soldiers, had a small stash of boiled sweets that he shared out to the thin gangly kids.

'Alright kid, here's a sweet,' he said to one of them. 'Have a sweet,' as he passed a boiled sweet and the kid obediently put the whole wrapped thing in his mouth in a flash. Joe saw him look at him with a frown of betrayal, as if to say this is horrible.

'Ugh,' he said, universal in any language, and took the sweet out of his mouth.

Joe gave a laugh of realisation at him.

'No, no.' Joe said, as he took the wet saliva-covered plastic-wrapped sweet from his hand and peeled away the wrapper to return it to the boy. He ate all of it, smiling as he discovered its taste was nice. *He's probably never had a boiled sweet before*, Joe thought.

There was so much deprivation here. The guardsmen struggled to deal with the situation people faced and even going to the toilet was no escape. The company toilet block was located in the far corner of the camp and when Joe squatted over the simple hole in the ground he could hear the cries of local people. Distant kids called out for clean water, begged and cried while Joe squatted, trying to wipe his arse.

Trying to restore order in the city was an ongoing problem. The infantrymen were the 'boots on the ground', the ones who had to actually follow the orders and stop the looting. When they found looting suspects, they still didn't know what to do with them. Many of the lads were getting worn out by the situation and Joe saw some of the company lose it on Iraqi looters, kicking and thumping them. When the Iraqis were caught in the act of their pillaging, they were battered and sent on their way, being told: 'don't let that happen again', or threatened with 'I'll fucking smack you in the face.' Some lads took things too far, were too rough, Joe included. It wasn't long before one incident caused Platoon Sergeant Ferguson to tell the men to tone it down. There had been excessive force used at a steel yard, a man beaten up so badly that his son was crying. Two of the men in particular had led Sergeant Selman to get down from his vehicle and intervene.

'This needs to stop now,' Ferguson told the men firmly. 'These fucking attacks and fucking chasing people down.'

The men listened but were all frustrated thinking: *what could they do?*

'It just needs to stop now, because this town's gonna turn against us,' Ferguson had warned: a strict command.

Towards the end of the time in Basra Joe chatted to one of the interpreters, a Middle Eastern guy called Dave. He was young and he told Joe that his dad was a doctor and he understood his privilege of a good education. Joe had just had to deal with an old Iraqi man ransacking items in part of the town and Dave witnessed them forcefully sending the bruised Iraqi away.

'Why did you do that to that man?' Dave asked in good English as he turned to Joe.

'He looted.' Joe returned plainly.

'But what do you do, Joe?' he said slowly, really peering deeply into Joe. The way Dave asked his question made the guardsman stop for a moment. This was the Iraqi man's country. Joe was the invader. He pondered: *How would I feel if the situation was reversed and someone tried to push me around?*

Dave had made Joe sit and think: about the way they treated people, about the war and what it had achieved. And about the city they were soon to leave. The tour in Basra would soon be coming to an end. In one of Joe's last letters, his Bluey was all about how much he was looking forward to being home.

To mum an Carlos

How are you? Hope every think is ok at home. I have got all the pic you sent me. I have put them all up on the wall by my bed. mum it looks like I will be home in may . They say that the main fly's will be leaving on 17th to the 27th of may. We will go back to Germany for a week or two an then I will be home. before I came out here I was looking forward to saving money and getting a tan now I do not care about money our a tan I just want to come home. How' me nan and grandad Tell them I love them an miss them very much. Our Simon said grandad has found a local for us to wach the racing. So when I get back the first day will be checking that out so tell grandad to get the ale in. I sent our helen a letter I hope she gets it. I just wrote to say a happy birthday to here as I useally forget when it is an am useally skint. Mum when is your birthday I can never remember yours sorry. I am doing ok. O yes I cut my finger open on the tin of the cornbeef. I had to get stitches only 4. So no more tin's haha. I miss home more than word can ever say. I have seen thing out here wich I just want to forget. Looking forward to seeing you mum and carlos love you both with all my heart an soul

Joe xxx

Chapter 35

Rules of War

Joe's mum, Lynn McCleary, is there throughout the trial, Carlos too, as much as he can, their lives on hold as they come and sit at the back of the Colchester courtroom with the other families. Joe knows he can't make it through without his family's constant support, as he battles through the fourth week of the gruelling trial. Pat Geraghty, his company sergeant major who always felt like family, is next up to give evidence.

The court has heard about the wetting of looters, something that the higher-ups, and probably Sergeant Selman himself, knew about but wasn't condemned. Now the court wants to hear from Pat, who was responsible for security during the time in Basra, including prisoner handling at the gymnasium base.

'It was mayhem when it was first ended, anything that wasn't nailed down was taken,' Pat tells Orlando Pownall honestly. 'We had no facilities at all for prisoners. There was a toilet but a snake got in, then we put up an 8 x 10 in the courtyard in direct sun but we had no facilities to feed and water the prisoners.'

'What methods did you use to deal with the looters?' the prosecutor asks Pat.

'What developed was this: Avoid arrest. Remove them a couple of kilometres down the road and let them walk home. I hadn't heard of wetting,' Pat replies, his Irish accent thick and firm. Pownall immediately asks for the answer to be repeated, the prosecutor seeming annoyed because he can't fathom Pat's accent.

'We were later told that the media were very concerned by looting. We were told to stop it but not told how,' Pat continues, speaking a little more slowly for the benefit of the well-educated barrister. 'It died down a bit towards the end but even then we had situations like at the hospital where we had to stop a man with a knife threatening patients for their valuables.'

James Cooke's QC, Richard Lissack, steps up to cross-examine Pat, asking him what the orders were for dealing with looters.

'No orders or policy existed for dealings with looters apart from arrest,' Pat replies.

'And the policy of taking looters out of town, how did that come about?' Lissack asks.

'The policy of dropping looters out of town developed, rather than us processing them. We saw less because of that. Especially in the last week or so. They were moved out by military vehicles including Warriors.'

'What decisions, if any, does the driver make with regards to the moving of the vehicle?' the barrister asks Pat.

'The driver is totally controlled by the commander of the vehicle, and doesn't make any decisions with regards to its movement.' Pat knew that if the call sign had been told to be at the hospital then it shouldn't have moved from that location unless directed to by the Ops room.

'How did a lot of the soldiers experience the conditions in Iraq?'

'For young soldiers it was shocking and life-changing,' Pat answers, thinking of the lads, many still teenagers, plunged into the heat of battle, trained to fight and follow. 'Their commander could give them orders to steer them through the day. An order to drive somewhere would be followed.'

Where the four soldiers on trial had ended up, driving to the canal, annoyed and disappointed Pat when he'd found out what had happened. He thought it was a given: Don't mess about with prisoners. It saddened him that it had taken away from the soldiers' accomplishments and all they'd achieved.

'Fear took its toll on most 18-year-olds,' Pat adds sombrely.

When Stephen Riordan questions Pat, it almost moves Joe to tears.

'How long have you known Mr McCleary?' Joe's QC asks.

'McCleary became very well known to me. I worked with him on training in Senelager,' says Pat softly. 'I knew him for two years, he's always got that typical Liverpool sense of humour. In Kuwait he was talking about his family, tried to phone his aunt. He told me about his mother asking the local priest to pray after the two were lost.'

'What did you think about my client? Did you think he was brave?' Riordan asks.

'Joe always had an answer for everything. He was a good all-round soldier, well disciplined. He was certainly brave,' Pat says slowly. 'They all were.'

'No further questions,' Stephen concludes.

After Pat there are more of the lads from Joe's call sign: Paul Hollander, Jamie Wheeler, Paul Ferguson. They each give their account of Basra, its breakdown and what they claim they knew or didn't know about the devastating incident at the canal.

Pownall asks Hollander, Joe's section commander, about the looting specifically.

'I had dealings with looters, quite regularly,' says Hollander. 'They were placed in the rear of the Warrior, not very often. Not more than five times.

I don't really know how many times I arrested looters. I had arrested them before 8 May, I know that.'

'And what did you do with the looters, once you'd arrested them?' asks the prosecutor.

'We brought them back to a holding area in the gymnasium, didn't do anything else,' Hollander replies. 'We never drove them out of town, never just let them go. The policy was to take them back to the holding area.'

'Did you see any of the looters punished? Perhaps by what's been termed "wetting?"'

'Didn't see any punishment,' Hollander says. 'Knew nothing of a policy of wetting. Never heard of wetting taking place.'

There are inconsistencies in the stories. It is difficult to know who knew what and who is just covering themselves.

Joe's old mate Paul 'Fergie' Ferguson, a platoon sergeant of No. 1 Platoon, tells the court about the briefing he gave the lads about the amount of force used with the prisoners.

'I told the troops we had to treat them less aggressively. Two of our platoon were killed, the next day we were doing humanitarian work giving out water and emotions were running high,' Fergie explains. 'The young boys were worried and scared. They didn't trust Iraqis.'

'Were the looters seen as vermin of war?' puts Pownall.

'They were an annoyance,' returns Fergie diplomatically.

Jamie Wheeler, the second-in-command of the dismount section of Call Sign One Two takes the stand, reluctantly. He says he 'can't remember' to most of the questions that he's asked.

'I don't remember having them in the back of the Warrior.'

'Never dropped them off on the edge of town. Never heard of it.'

'Not heard of wetting of looters.'

His denials of memory are so much that an application is made to have him considered a hostile witness. One thing Wheeler says before he's dismissed stands out:

'Some things you choose not to remember, Iraq is one of them.'

Midway through the fourth week, the media remembers Iraq and the court case when a Lieutenant Colonel gives evidence on the planning for the war. The court martial has received little coverage, but recent bombings in Iraq have likely intensified the news media's interest. In Baghdad, close to America's ironically named Victory Base Complex, there are a series of bomb attacks on 14 May 2006. They target Shiite shrines, a bus full of civilians near the US base, and another kills two American soldiers with a roadside bomb. To the south in Basra, two British boys suffer the same fate. Privates Adam Morris and Joseva Lewaicei, a teenager and a 25-year-old, of the 2nd Battalion Royal Anglian Regiment, are killed when their armoured convoy strikes a roadside bomb. They bring the toll of British military personnel killed in Iraq to 111. Now in Britain it starts to feel as though the war itself is on trial; not just the four soldiers' actions at the water's edge.

Lieutenant Colonel Nicholas Mercer, the senior military legal adviser to the 1st Armoured Division, takes the stand to explain the state of the post-conflict planning. Mercer is a highly respected and principled man, receiving his education at a private school in Leicestershire before going on to the esteemed St Andrew's University College of Law. He qualified as a solicitor in 1990 and joined the army's legal branch the following year, rising to the rank of lieutenant colonel, with tours in Northern Ireland, Bosnia, Cyprus and Germany. In Iraq, Lieutenant Colonel Mercer was the army's top legal officer during 2003, but his involvement began well before that.

'I was involved in the planning for Telic,' he tells prosecutor Pownall, referring to the codename for the British operation. 'I was commander leader for the UK division.'

Mercer is a rational, sober individual. This gives his words almost damning weight.

'It was a belligerent occupation. It wasn't peacekeeping but an international war taking land by force.'

As the Divisional Lawyer for the military, the first Mercer had heard about a planned invasion in Iraq was at a briefing he attended in November 2002. He'd walked into the meeting and hearing Americans in the room, realised what it was about. About a month later, Mercer, who had been away at a conference, flew back to London on his birthday, 19 December, and was told by his CO to rip up his existing plans as they had a military planning meeting. After some leave around Christmas and only two weeks of planning, Mercer was deployed to Kuwait in January 2003.

'In the planning phase, what advice did you give the commanders?' Pownall asks.

'We gave guidance to commanders on treatment of prisoners. A huge number of legal issues arose. The treatment of prisoners is but one issue, there were other larger ones.'

'What issues did you find once Basra was taken by Coalition forces?'

'We found a completely imploded state giving enormous responsibility to those in the occupied state,' Mercer replies. 'There was an expectation that the Americans would take care of it, but they were massively underprepared. In one meeting the Americans produced records dating back to 1942 and 1944 for guidance.'

What emerges is a story of a quickly-convened show of force with poor forethought to the aftermath. While the soldiers were struggling with a shortage of poorly organised supplies in Iraq, Mercer was struggling to get the commanders to grasp their legal obligations after the war.

'What ensued was unique in modern post-war conflict. It was subsequently described as a strategic failure,' Mercer goes on. 'That was,' he adds, 'of course, not the fault of the troops on the ground. They all did the best with what they were provided.'

For their part, Colonel Mercer and his team of military lawyers were frantically working up every kind of legal issue from rules of engagement to dealing with PoWs. The Coalition expected 10,000 Iraqi military prisoners and the Americans wanted to build some kind of 'pen' to keep them in detention. They were told that nowhere had the facility to detain this many people so the Americans came up with a new scheme: tell the surrendered Iraqi soldiers to return and stay at their own barracks. Mercer told his general that this couldn't be done; he knew the lessons from history: Nazi soldiers had done this during the war and then ended up executing people. The Americans then turned around and told the British that they had to take care of the prisoners so a camp was opened up in the port city of Umm Qasr with capacity for 3,000 prisoners.

'In maintaining peace there's a rule of thumb: the law of armed conflict works as lethal force downwards; peacekeeping is about minimum force upwards,' says the lawyer.

'Would, do you think, the commanders have the experience and understanding of that?' Pownall asks.

'I would expect commanders to understand that basic tenet. Thirty years in Northern Ireland, ten years in the Balkans; this phrase is repeated to commanders and soldiers time and time again. The difficulty with occupations is that you are war-fighting and peacekeeping at the same time.' says Mercer emphatically. 'It was very new territory to us all. It is impossible to anticipate what you are going to find on the ground.'

When he was in Iraq, in the early days after the invasion, Lieutenant Colonel Mercer had heard that the commandant of the Umm Qasr camp had started discharging 250 prisoners a day because of overcrowding. Discharging prisoners meant that the UK wasn't fulfilling its obligations to the PoWs, so in late March 2003 Mercer visited the commandant to sort out the issue. While at the camp, Mercer saw around forty Iraqi prisoners who were bound, hooded and kneeling in a stress position next to an interrogation tent and a loud generator, something which would have been for both sensory confusion and to perpetuate fears that the noise was drowning out screams from those being interrogated. This rang alarm bells for the army lawyer as it could easily be seen as psychological intimidation. Mistreatment of detainees like hooding, stress positions, white noise, and sleep and food deprivation had supposedly been outlawed by the British since the Irish internment laws in 1975. Mercer demanded to know why he was seeing these methods being used on Iraqis. 'What the hell is going on? This is illegal,' he asked at the time. The interrogating officer responded saying, 'No it isn't. This is army doctrine. We answer to London.'

Mercer was shocked at what he saw because there was supposed to have been clear training from the army on proper prisoner handling. Nowhere were these harsh measures taught, so where had the practices come from? Mercer complained up the chain of command, writing an official memo to his general about what he saw that day. The interrogator protested saying that the way they were treating prisoners was not illegal and demanded a second legal opinion. A legal spat broke out and the government sent a one-star civil servant, someone senior, to the camp. The Red Cross had also seen the men hooded at the camp and at a meeting with the Red Cross, the government ordered Mercer to remain silent. Mercer was assured that the treatment of Iraqi prisoners, which contravened international law, would be stopped, but legal advisors' problems continued with the breakdown of law and order.

'On 7 April 2003, when Basra fell, the Commandos asked for permission to shoot looters,' Mercer tells the prosecutor, barely disguising the shock at being asked to sanction such an extreme response. 'I was away when the question came in and I'm not sure what answer was given that night, but I made it absolutely clear: non-lethal minimum force was to be used. I did not want dead looters on the streets.'

Sitting with Joe at the back of the Colchester military court, Stephen Riordan takes in the shocking testimony. To the experienced barrister, Mercer's remarks show the surprising ignorance that existed in the army in the lead up to the war when the boundaries were drawn and decisions were being made when it came to dealing with prisoners.

'Shooting them was not an option,' Mercer continues in answer to further prosecution questions. 'I advised that we did not have the legal authority to shoot looters and that in matters of law and order UK forces could only use minimum force in the prevention of crime in accordance with UK domestic law.'

'Did you find out what was happening with the suspected looters?' Pownall asks.

'I was later informed that they were simply releasing looters as they could not begin to cope with the volume of criminals.'

'What process should have taken place with regards to the looters?'

'In a perfect world, looting would have been curtailed and looters would have been removed to the military police post,' Mercer answers. 'In reality the British were massively undermanned and that was impossible. We did the best we could with the time available.'

'And what impact were the looters having on Basra at that time?' Pownall probes.

'The looters were destroying the infrastructure of everything. We had to protect the infrastructure. There was no information as to how to do it.' Mercer's description of the breakdown in Basra is finally getting to the circumstances behind why everyone is gathered there in the stuffy Colchester courtroom.

'There had to be an unorthodox approach in dealing with looters, which was fashioned to meet the situation on the ground at the time that evolved,' the army lawyer explains. 'Taken out of town, made to walk back. Something further than Bridge Four, possibly. Getting them wet and dirty. Areas of standing water where locals broke the water pipes.'

Riordan muses on Mercer's testimony. The man is saying that these unorthodox methods of dealing with looters were effectively all they could do to protect the infrastructure.

'What training did British troops receive on Rules of Engagement?' asks Pownall.

'All soldiers would have been given ROE briefings in the fortnight preceding the 19 March 2003.' Mercer, however, had a feeling from his time in Iraq that the divisional troops may have sensed a lack of unanimity over the legality of how they could treat prisoners and that the rules of engagement didn't extend to looters.

'There was no role for the British troops in punishment. There is no provision under UK domestic or international law to do that,' he says.

James Cooke's barrister, Richard Lissack cross-examines Mercer for all the defence team, asking the Lieutenant Colonel what was anticipated about the breakdown in Basra.

'It was not foreseen that Iraq would implode to the extent that it did,' Mercer answers honestly. 'Totally insufficient planning made the burden heavier.'

'What post-war planning took place by the British when it came to law and order?'

'There was no planning by higher headquarters, no planning or direction was received from the headquarters in Qatar or from Permanent Joint Headquarters in Britain,' says Mercer. 'There was scarcely enough time to prepare for war, never mind the occupation.'

'What were you told about who would be responsible for the occupation?' came the defence's question.

'I was advised that the UK anticipated that we would receive a UN Security Council Resolution prior to the invasion of Iraq and, therefore, the occupation would be the responsibility of the United Nations.'

'There was no such resolution. Which left British soldiers holding the baby?' puts Lissack.

'Yes. Correct,' answers Lieutenant Colonel Mercer pointedly.

Joe, his family, legal team and the other defendants hear how the decaying law and order in Basra became uncontrollable and mismanaged. It was the backdrop that led Joe and the others to the canal.

'It was an epidemic of looting,' Mercer continues. 'There were simply insufficient troops to carry the responsibilities of an occupying power in a belligerent occupation,' he goes on. 'I did not envisage that the army should deter looting. My solution was to hand over looters to the police. I didn't know at the time that would fail.'

'And who should have been responsible for law and order?' Mercer is asked.

'Maintaining law and order was our duty under international law. To characterise the army as the police, that means they apply the law,' the lieutenant colonel replies. 'The army corporately has a memory and training in policing. Law and order means policing and they had all been to Northern Ireland.'

'And did you hear that this plan was not working?'

'No one told me it wasn't working at that time. I can't recall when I found that out, because the divisional plan was to reconstruct the Iraqi police, there was a six-week plan to bring Iraqi police back. There was a six-week window and this incident occurred in that period.'

The court dismisses Lieutenant Colonel Mercer and he is followed by Major Peter MacMullen. Taking the stand, the company commander for No. 1 Company Irish Guards feels angry. He doesn't object to due process, but this feels a terrifying experience taking the stand and receiving no representation.

'Tell me, what was discussed as far as the rules of armed engagement after the initial fighting period,' asks the prosecutor.

'There were no briefings on occupation once the war had been won. As far as Rules of Engagement, there was no training afterwards. It wouldn't necessarily be associated with war-fighting. It was more fight control measures,' MacMullen explains, his agitation rising. 'My soldiers weren't policemen, they didn't know how to collect evidence. Things were not well planned. There was no clear direction. We discussed this at Battle Group and Company orders.'

'Let me ask you about looters being put in canals or rivers. Was that something that you were prepared to sanction?' Pownall asks of MacMullen.

'I didn't think it was something that would happen in our company,' MacMullen replies, almost frustrated by the insinuation. No. 1 Company's gym base was several miles from the canal and river. 'Geographically it didn't suit what we were doing. I wouldn't think about it either way.'

'Would you have said or done something to stop this boy dying?' Pownall puts directly.

'With hindsight, of course I would! Yes!' snaps back Peter. He loses it, his rage bubbling over. 'But it was so extraordinary, that people were doing the best they could. Every soldier under my command acted with sound moral conduct. I saw junior soldiers stopping fire at risk to themselves when civilians arrived.'

'Describe the biggest problems towards the end of your tour.' Pownall asks of MacMullen.

'It was a cumulative exhaustion,' the major answers. 'Then looting was the biggest problem for law and order which was epidemic. I can't describe it.'

For Joe it is a relief to see his company commander explain some details of the situation in Basra in those final days, after all they'd experienced. John O'Leary, Joe's solicitor, who has been dividing his time at the hearing with his junior lawyer, Grace, has heard Joe refer to Major MacMullen as his 'hero'.

'What methods did you hear were employed to deal with looters?'

'Getting them wet and dirty using a variety of mediums; standing water within Basra,' MacMullen says. 'Although it was hot, we were very low lying and the water pipes were broken by the locals so there was water about. A dyke or ditch or Shatt al-Arab river were used. Many people swam in the Shatt al-Arab. There were always people in there, sometimes hundreds in there. I know looters went into it, couldn't say if they were pushed, don't know how they were put in there.'

Giving his evidence, Peter thinks back to when he found out that Ahmed had drowned. He was raging that the four soldiers hadn't said anything and that they'd done something like that on the last day. It was such a tragic end.

'We have seen a SIB report that information strongly suggests that this wasn't a one-off occurrence, by which I mean Iraqis into the water,' puts Pownall.

'It was not a one-off event,' admits MacMullen.

'What was your feeling towards the end of the time in Basra?'

'I wanted to get out of the city, it was very demanding, I was glad we hadn't lost any other soldiers. I was glad to get out,' concludes MacMullen.

As MacMullen leaves the elevated platform from where he has been giving evidence, relief fills him. Relieved too is Joe's barrister, Stephen Riordan. *He was fantastic,* the QC thinks. His evidence is saying that these lads had no choice but to do what they did, effectively giving them the complete defence. Riordan watches MacMullen as he walks the aisle that separates the prosecution and defence and, with his back to the prosecution and to the judging panel of officers, the major gives a big wink to Joe and Martin.

The court martial heads towards the end of its fifth week and the defendants have their chance to take the stand. Stephen Riordan doesn't believe that this is a wise idea but Joe thinks otherwise. He's spent the last month hearing accusations raised against him and he's eager to speak and set his record straight. Joe's reached the point where he feels very bitter and his stubborn streak rises to the surface in the defendants' room where he and Riordan are waiting between sessions.

'I've got nothing to fucking hide. I'm telling you now I'm going up there,' Joe says aggressively.

'If you go up there, Joe, you'll be going to prison,' Riordan says with firm yet calm cadence.

'How am I going to jail?' Joe shoots back. 'I haven't done nothing wrong, Stephen. I'm telling you now I'll speak my fucking piece up there, because I've done nothing wrong!'

While the legal teams aren't working together, they adopt a common strategy over keeping their clients out of the witness box. When Riordan hears that Sergeant Selman isn't going in the witness box, he decides on the same approach for Joe. Barristers for McGing and Cooke follow suit, each of them reasoning that there's little the men could add to the record, as opposed to making an awful performance in the witness box, which might damage their chances.

'I don't want you to take the stand Joe,' Stephen returns, raising his voice an octave. 'Do not take the stand. Pownall will twist, he will tear and you'll get angry and you'll just explode.' Having said his piece, Stephen gets up determinedly and leaves Joe by himself.

Joe's still fuming a little later when his mum knocks and enters the room.

'Hey son, what's going on?' she asks and Joe explains his compulsion to share on the stand.

'What do you think?' he asks Lynn.

'Don't do it son,' she advises. 'Just do as you've been told.'

For Joe there's so much that the panel of seven, who have probably not even seen service in Iraq, don't and can't know about what happened. Calming in the presence of his mother, Joe relents, his mum always seeming to guide him to the right decisions.

'Y'right. I'll tell him no comment, I'm not going up,' Joe says. In the end, none of the four men testify. All the witnesses have given their accounts, their perspectives of that day in Iraq. The way Joe experienced 8 May 2003 is a story that the court doesn't fully hear or understand.

Chapter 36

8 May 2003

Thursday, 8 May 2003 in Basra began with news that Joe greeted with relief. The men were told that they would be pulling out of the city the next day. At the company orders meeting, MacMullen had told those in attendance to keep everything tight for the next twenty-four hours. He added a reminder to the commanders for everyone to remain professional at the end of the tour.

'Don't do anything. Just be there at your points guarding,' MacMullen said, sounding exhausted and raw. 'Don't move from your locations; don't go and do anything to the locals.' It was only a month since they'd lost Muz and Molly and had several more injured; the last thing that MacMullen wanted in their final twenty-four hours was someone else dying. He didn't want undue risks. He waved a copy of a letter that he said had been written to parents and next of kin; he didn't want to send any more. They'd almost made it and would soon be going home. Yet it did not feel like the type of 'victory in the cause of freedom' that Churchill had spoken of fifty-eight years earlier. Here Saddam was toppled but still at large, the weapons of mass destruction, too, were still elusive and the looting evidenced the perilous collapse of much of Iraqi society. The soldiers were looking forward to leaving this theatre and heading home.

Parts of the old gymnasium complex, which had been their home for the past month, was being dismantled. That morning, Danny Burton was on duty in the radio room and Richard Watkins was there as the company watchkeeper, until 10.00 am when Colour Sergeant Douglas Edwards would relieve him. The watchkeeper's responsibility was as the log keeper for the Battle Group Net, the communications system used by the battalions. If any calls came in or unusual requests about movements of call signs, then these men would receive and record them. They were based in the Ops room inside the gym, along with the signaller, intelligence officer and sometimes the company second-in-command or commander stopping by for updates. The night had been routine, at least for Basra, with various shots reported: repeated high velocity rounds in the vicinity of the bank. Sergeant Graham

Todd recorded that Call Sign One Two radioed in at 11.59 pm on the 7th May and the Warrior was instructed to crush some stolen goods as this might deter looters. The morning in the gym brought some disarray, with equipment being broken down, maps stamped 'Destroy if compromised' in red being rolled up and even items normally on hand to deal with looters, such as plasticuffs (which had all been handed back), packed away ready for leaving.

Daniel O'Connell, in charge of Platoon 1 with Call Sign One Zero, was back, after being on static patrol that night and handing over to another call sign at about 8.30 am. Several miles away from the old gymnasium, the men of Call Sign One Two were on static guard at Basra General Hospital. Sergeant Selman, and guardsmen Cooke and McGing were on stag with the Warrior at the front of the complex while Joe was up in the makeshift restroom above the NICU with the others from their section: Hollander, Sampat, Bojang, Wheeler and Fleming. Outside, dark smoke still blotted the horizon line and the nearby road rumbled with American truck convoys taking contractor supplies north. In the hospital restroom there was the whirr of the air-conditioning unit and still the sporadic screams and cries from wards below.

There was a disturbance. A thickly moustached Iraqi man, dressed in civilian clothing, entered unannounced, carrying a half-metre-long brown wooden baton. He looked like a policeman who'd lost some of his uniform and, although police were to be disbanded, he was still serving.

'Ali Baba, Ali Baba, looter,' the policeman shouted. 'You! Come,' the man said frantically in broken English.

The six soldiers exchanged weary glances, then geared up, placing their chest webbing over their desert combats and shirts and grabbing their berets (keeping helmets to their sides) and light support weapons. They followed the policeman from the hospital building, over a wall and around the back to a patch of waste ground. As they approached, Hollander was next to Joe and told them to go in firm, meaning that they'd take a fire position and cover their arcs; looking around the area in case a potential threat came running at them. They neared the barren area where there were some industrial-looking and derelict out-buildings and close by some discarded car parts. Some young-looking Iraqi lads seemed to be in the midst of taking some tyres and wires. They had a wooden cart or trolley on to which they'd piled their pilfered finds, including what looked like supplies from the hospital. Joe's blood rose at the possibility that these lads might have taken medicines or even the desperately needed incubators from the neighbouring medical centre. There were four or five Iraqi lads and the soldiers set to chase them down. Even with their heavy packs, the trained infantrymen were faster. Joe clipped one lad's ankles, caught him on the floor and pinned him down.

'Hey,' Joe shouted as he picked up a young wiry boy, hooked him under his arms and dragged him back to where the policeman was. They detained four looters and handed them over to the Iraqi police.

The man whom the soldiers assumed to be the Iraqi policeman in civilian clothes had been joined by a couple of colleagues and they waded forwards with their batons raised. The guardsmen flanked the kids and the Iraqi police moved in, yelling something angrily to them, assaulting them with batons. The elder men grabbed at their four suspects' clothing, seemingly ordering them to strip to their underwear, then bound rags around each of their prisoner's wrists. The prisoners were then herded, by prodding of batons, to a small muddy pool of water, or what could have been sewage, a couple of hundred yards from the soldiers. The men of Call Sign One Two followed the action. It looked to them as if the Iraqi police were making the underwear-clad looters roll around and get dirty as a form of punishment.

Well, this is softer than I had in my head when it comes to Muslim justice, Joe mused as the prone looters squirmed around in the stagnant puddle. *It doesn't seem as bad as having hands chopped off for stealing.* The Iraqi lads were skinny and had been wearing what looked to Joe like nighties; one who was wearing black was distinguished by wiry black hair, which to Joe, inarticulate in his experience of the world, mentally characterised as being *like an afro. The lad looks a bit like Michael Jackson or the Jackson Five,* Joe thought, as he tried not to gag at the fetid stench of the water.

For a few moments, the soldiers held their position as local people started to assemble. In the city the tide had quickly turned against looters once law-respecting Baswaris had seen how they were undermining the reconstruction. Damage from the war-fighting and air strikes was still felt around the city and locals seemed impatient with the Coalition's attempts to get the basics back up and running.

Guardsman Fleming surveyed the gathering crowd, which had very quickly become twenty or thirty strong, with people cheering and supportive of police in their hostile treatment of the looters. Sampat stared with shocked recognition as he heard the Arabic insults shouted from the jeering crowd. There was scattered applause as the 'police' roughed up their detainees to fierce yells of 'Ali Baba Ali Baba Ali Baba' from the crowd. The tension level of the mob rose quickly. The soldiers now had to hold some of the more aggressive members back and Joe saw that some had picked up rocks and chunks of broken concrete. They were getting ready. The guardsmen all knew this had gone on long enough and their section commander, Hollander stepped forward.

'That's enough!' He had to yell to be heard about the braying throng.

It was clear that the soldiers had a duty to rescue the looters from the police and crowd.

'C'mon. They're gonna get seriously attacked by the police and the crowd if we don't move them out of here,' Hollander shouted to Joe. 'Let's take 'em over to Selman. He can decide whether to release them or not.'

The soldiers cut through the assembled mass of furious bodies and grabbed the wrist-bound, near naked and now bedraggled looters who grabbed for their clothes. Wheeler clasped a couple of them by their shoulders and hustled them back through the broken wall at the side of the hospital towards the front of the building.

Sergeant Carle Selman was on stag in his seat in the Warrior's turret, maintaining radio watch as the men and looters came around to the front of the hospital. Joe could see the vehicle was parked up. Selman looked at him and Hollander from his lofty vantage point.

'What the fuck?' Joe said to the other soldiers when he realised that they'd not escaped the mob. The angry Iraqis had followed and several of them looked set to carry out 'justice' using the rocks that they had clenched in their fists. Joe noticed that the rocks were not small; they were brick-sized. *Let he who is without sin.* Some of them started to pelt and the bricks came close to Joe.

'Ali Baba, Ali Baba,' the mob shouted.

'Stop! Next person who throws …' Joe yelled as another projectile was lobbed near the looters. He drew his rifle forward and pointed it at the civilians.

'Hey, I'm gonna fucking shoot one of yous. Stop,' Joe yelled, though it was unlikely that they were words they understood. 'Stop!'

Some of the crowd, who now made a semi-circle around the back of the Warrior, were warded off slightly by Joe's posture.

'Get them in the back,' shouted an irate Selman as Sampat hovered near the rear of the vehicle. Sergeant Selman was the senior on the ground so it was his call to make. Joe ushered the wet and frightened-looking looting suspects into the Warrior. Their panic deepened, their fear evident. *It was for their own protection that we've brought them in here,* Joe reasoned. They threw them in the tank to stop them getting killed by their own people. McGing appeared next to Joe and said that he'd just been inside for a piss and was radioed to return to the Warrior.

'You two! Get in we're going ...' Selman shouted, interrupted by the growl of the Warrior as it roared fiercely to some sort of life. Selman seemed to have only the vaguest glance down toward Sampat and Joe as he tilted his head back as if to speak into his communications unit. McGing and Joe looked at each other and climbed inside the Warrior; Sampat stayed back.

'All in,' Joe shouted as the Warrior door closed, leaving the rest of the call sign, five men, on their own at the hospital. It made sense to Joe, though, that no one else came along. There were the four Iraqis, McGing and Joe, Selman and a driver, which made eight. The maximum capacity of the Warrior was nine, usually it was made up of a half-dozen infantry dismounts in the back and three crew up front and top. The regular driver, Cookie, must have been up front; Selman was up top, but that left Gingy's gunner seat vacant.

Being in the back of the Warrior with the four scared-looking Iraqis, the journey felt like an eternity. They were directly facing McGing and Joe on the bench-like seats as the vehicle rumbled along. Gingy and Joe exchanged bemused glances; unusually, McGing was seated next to Joe, on his left. His usual position was up top in the gunner's turret, which is what he'd been trained for. Perhaps Selman thought that Gingy was up in the gunner's cupola and assumed that Sampat had jumped in with Joe. As they rattled onwards though, Joe had no idea where they were going, but that was nothing unusual. He'd often headed out on QRF missions in the windowless back of the Warrior, the doors would open and he'd not know where they were. For a start Joe thought the Warrior was heading back to camp to drop the looters off for some time in the prisoner-holding cage that had been built alongside the gymnasium base. Joe was still wearing his beret and had the personal role radio (PRR) clasped to his head. He tried to speak to Selman or Cooke up front to find out what was going on but this didn't work; the radio headset seemed to have broken.

The suspected looters talked urgently among themselves in Arabic. One of them suddenly looked straight at Gingy and Joe and started shouting quick foreign words at Joe. He made to stand up.

'Aye, sit down!' Joe ordered him. The four detainees faced the guardsmen and it left Gingy and Joe a bit vulnerable. The soldiers had their rifles and kept the muzzles pointed towards the floor. The weapons wouldn't help anyway in the back of the tank because if the trigger was accidentally clipped then everyone would be injured or worse. The Iraqis were bound but there were four of them against two soldiers. The boisterous lad continued to be aggressive.

Joe pushed the agitated looter's shoulder with one hand, putting him firmly back in his seat. The lad was forced down and started to sob.

Joe looked across at the four Iraqis, the distance between them far greater than the physical couple of feet that separated soldier and looter: cultural, language, strength. Something struck Joe about the youngest of the four boys, the one with the wiry dark hair, his head hung down and a look of terror. Joe could see the fear in his eyes and he tried to reassure him, even though the guardsman didn't entirely know what was happening.

'Look, it's okay, calm down,' Joe said, hoping his tone could convey what he meant. 'Nothing's going to happen to yous.' At this point, though, Joe thought, *where the fuck are we? What are we doing? They think they're going to get shot dead.*

They'd been driving for at least fifteen minutes and still Joe and McGing didn't know what was going on. The trip seemed to have taken ages. Joe felt the Warrior bear to the left as it made a turn and then they stopped. He waited. After a moment, the Warrior's rear door opened and he saw Cooke; he'd had to get out, come to the rear of the Warrior and manually unlatch the door because the hydraulics that allowed opening from the inside had broken. Joe stuck his head out, a bit disorientated as he climbed out of the Warrior into bright sunlight and took in the surroundings. They were near water. There was a canal running close by and they had parked up on the bank, 10–15 metres from the water's edge. The size of the canal struck Joe, its great width. *It's like the fucking Mersey*, he reflected. Casting a late-morning shadow was the wide expanse of a concrete bridge that Joe then recognised as Bridge Four. They'd set up VCPs here before they'd stormed into Basra. This was where Bojang and Joe had stopped a journalist from being blown up by a mortar. *Fucking hell*, Joe realised, *we're miles away here. What the fuck did we come here for? We're in the middle of nowhere, there's no one around.* They were at least 7 miles away from the hospital and well outside the AOR for No. 1 Company. The four Iraqis were hustled out of the vehicle and Joe went to untie the rags that bound their hands. The strips of material were bound tightly and Joe struggled so Cooke lent a hand untying one boy. The lad clung on with desperation and Cooke hit the man on the head a couple of times.

'I can't get this knot undone,' Cooke was frustrated. 'Gingy, can you go in the Warrior see if you can find something to cut this?'

'Yeah, sir,' replied McGing, and headed back to the vehicle, its engine still motoring.

Joe managed to get the first two of the Iraqis' arms untied. As soon as he did, the suspected looters darted away and sprinted straight for the canal.

'Stop, stop … stop,' Joe yelled after them. In a moment the other two lads' arms were untied and they headed towards the water's edge. Joe and Cooke took a couple of steps forward; Joe wanted to let them know they were free to go. From behind, McGing reappeared.

'Looked around; checked the first aid box,' Gingy said from a few metres away. 'Couldn't find no scissors or anything,' He then headed around the Warrior and up towards his gunner's seat.

One of the remaining two Iraqi kids edged over the boulders, closer to the thick black water. They looked nervous, hesitant. Joe's rifle was slung over his back and he held up his hands, spread open in a gesture to indicate that it was ok. The Iraqi teetered at the rocky embankment and then climbed in up to his waist, then finding his rhythm, soon swam over to thick concrete support pillars holding up Bridge Four, to which the first two were clinging. The fourth boy, the younger Iraqi, the one who Joe thought looked as though he had an afro, remained near the water's edge. He'd not gone in. Joe took a step nearer to him; the closer Joe got, the more the boy backed to the brink.

'It's okay,' Joe said 'Stop there, stop.'

Joe edged closer.

The lad turned and took a look, then was in the canal. Joe saw him flounder for a minute, go under the surface and then come back up.

Cooke scrutinised the boy in the water, like a diligent lifeguard. His expression seemed to ask, should we go and get him? Is he drowning? The water was oily dark, polluted. Joe was only an average swimmer and was laden with his heavy body armour so he didn't really want to get in unless it came to it.

'Is he okay?' asked Cookie over the loud nearby groan of the Warrior. *In that split second, the boy had probably just swum under water and would pop up a little further away,* Joe thought.

'Probably gone under, just to get away from us,' Joe said.

'Yeah, maybe you're right,' Cookie replied.

Looking down on them, Sergeant Selman looked impatient and pissed off. He yelled down from the turret. 'If he comes up again be prepared to jump in.'

After a moment, the boy came to the surface, his arms flailing. Cookie started to react. He started to unbutton his outer layer of his body armour.

As Cookie was quickly getting undressed to help the lad, Joe looked behind him at Selman. He was wearing his headset and moving his arms quickly in a rotating fashion, pointing upwards. Joe understood instantly what that errant signal meant: Mount up, double time.

Complex decisions made in an instant rest on army training but here were fuelled by fear and circumstance. As the senior guardsman, Joe knew instinctively to obey his sergeant; as the senior guardsman on the ground, Joe had to make an instant decision.

The young lad may have swum away. Selman's signal meant 'Get back in the vehicle. Now.' Anything could be happening: a threat here or elsewhere. For all Joe knew, the rest of the men could be getting attacked in the hospital and there were only four of them back there at the time. *They could have been overrun. And Iraqi kids were used to water; they don't have parks, they just have water.* Joe's seen them, *it's hot and that's what they do all day*, he reasons. More than anything, Selman is Joe's superior officer and he's well trained enough to obey him; he may have a much better knowledge of what's going on than Joe does.

Joe snapped into gear.

'Let's go. We need to get in the tank now,' Joe shouted over to Cooke.

He paused and threw back a panicked look.

'Let's go. We gotta mount up now!' Urgency filled Joe's voice. 'Mount up!' And they left.

The four men drove back. Joe was alone in the back of the Warrior with his thoughts about the Iraqi boy in the water. *He would just literally doggy paddle to the side, jump back out, everyone's good,* Joe told himself. *The three others had swum over there, there's not an issue. That must have been the point,* Joe reasoned: *wet their clothes and make them walk all this way back home. The reason why the journey was so long was to take them all a long way from home.* He convinced himself.

It all happened fast, unlike the journey back. *It's good enough to stop them doing it again. Fifteen minutes in a tank is probably, on foot, an hour or two's walk.*

When the four soldiers arrived back at the hospital and the Warrior doors opened, Joe rushed out to check in with the rest of his section. He rapidly took the stairs up to the restroom and still didn't know whether an attack had happened and if they had left the lads behind to fend for themselves.

'Is everything okay?' he asked, out of breath by the time he reached the restroom.

'What's up mate? Y'right?' someone asked calmly.

The boys in the room were sitting around. They were relaxed. A couple of them were smoking ciggies, Wheeler was absorbed in reading a letter from his girlfriend, Sampat rubbed his eyes and looked as though he'd just woken from a nap, a chess board with pieces between him and Hollander.

'Yeah sound,' Joe said in reply.

'Where'd you lot bugger off to with them lads, then?' Fleming asked.

'Oh we dropped them off near the canal, like.'

'Oh right.'

'Yeah, the fuckers bolted into the river. One of them went under water.'

'Really?'

'Yeah, mate. He probably swam over to the other side,' Joe said.

'Yeah, yeah. I can swim like a length and a half of a pool under water and hold me breath,' Fleming boasted.

Joe sat down reassured, but thoughts floated to his mind again about the young lad who struggled at the water's edge. *He might have just dived under. I know he was in trouble but he might well have just swum off to a bank and climbed out*, he told himself. Like a lot of the company, Joe felt this had been an awful time and he just wanted to get out alive. This was their last full day in Basra.

The next day, Joe mostly forgot about the lad, blotted him from his mind, preoccupied as they pulled out and left the city in a long convoy of Warriors. And then they were gone, travelling the long and hard fought-for road out of Basra. It began the end.

Chapter 37

Verdict

'Yesterday I said I would stop the case versus James Cooke only,' Judge Advocate Hunter says, effectively signalling the end of the trial against James Cooke after his legal team's appeal. Richard Lissack, Cooke's barrister has put forward submissions to the court saying that the case had changed throughout the seven weeks of the court martial, that across Basra water was being used to deter looters so much that no one would say moving looters to edge of town was unlawful and, as the driver, Cooke could not be accused of acting on his own.

'Official policy was a failure,' Lissack declares belligerently. 'The instruction was to take no more looters to HQ. A range of methods were derived from shared practice, including immersion in flowing water. What my client stands accused of is no more than what was in play at the time.' At this decisive moment in the long gruelling trial the QC lays out that Cooke has no case to answer for.

'Following an order becomes a crime only when that order is palpably unlawful. That is not the case here,' concludes Lissack.

In response, Stephen Riordan, Joe's barrister, as well as lawyers for the other soldiers, try to adopt a similar position with an appeal that the Crown's case against the men is defective.

'A further application was made to stay relating to abuse. That is refused,' says Judge Hunter, refusing to halt the case against the rest of the men. 'I propose to tell the board that I have been considering a matter of law, and that I have directed them to acquit Corporal Cooke.'

Now only three remain. Joe wonders if the judge and panel of seven military officers are saving their fury for them alone? In the back of the room, Lynn McCleary sits with the handful of other family members thinking the same.

'The Crown must show evidence of the party to commit a joint enterprise not just to wet, but when viewed objectively that it was a dangerous assault,' the judge states. 'To the extent that it must have been contemplated that it was not a harmless wetting but an assault sufficient of act which would endanger death or bodily harm.' Within the density of legal terminology is a simple question: can the State prove that Joe and Martin, along with Sergeant Selman intentionally did something that they knew was harmful to Ahmed in Basra?

'First, turning to Joseph McCleary and Martin McGing, Ayad Hanon describes dismounts throwing stones and hand motions that they should swim. Evidence of forcing deeper from waist-high water must be and can only be the illegal act on which the Crown can rely,' continues Judge Hunter. 'Now turn to Selman. He was not physically participating in the alleged illegal act. On the evidence of Hanon, all four soldiers were present. Apart from his presence, there is really no evidence against Selman. There is some evidence that could be taken to say he told others not to mention it.'

Riordan and McGing's solicitor, Jerry Hayes, inform the court that neither client will be giving evidence, during which Joe bides his tongue, just as he promised his mum he would. This is one of the hardest things about the trial for Joe; being forced to listen to the prosecution paint him out as aggressive, coming at him and not being allowed to respond. The court even brings up Joe's two arrests for Drunk and Disorderly when he was stationed in Germany in 1998. The prosecution then sums up the case against the men.

'We suggest that as a matter of law, placing of looters in water was unlawful,' Orlando Pownall says. 'As to when the unlawfulness began, we say it was unlawful from the word go because they were out to punish the looters.'

The end of May bank holiday passes, marking the start of a new season as the case reaches its final week. The three remaining defence solicitors prepare to give their final speeches in the same order that they followed for their cross-examination. First to the floor is Selman's solicitor and then he is followed by Joe's own.

Stephen Riordan starts thinking about his closing speech when he's cross-examining his first witnesses for the prosecution or even long before, when he's reading case files. In his mind are the questions of how he'll present his argument to the jury and what his closing speech will sound like. He works to resolve these from the outset of the case. He never writes out a speech, speaking unscripted with only some pages of headline notes in front of him. The notes he's written articulate and clarify his thoughts and how he will present them. His strength comes not only through his arguments but the passion with which he will deliver them. His pastime as a singer, with a personal repertoire from opera to modern musicals, helps him practise and gives fierce gravity to his voice. He uses emphasis and repetition and fixes intently on the panel with his eyes; all techniques he's learned from thirty years in law. Everything is building to this one moment, his summation speech a crescendo that Riordan looks forward to. For Joe and the others, everything could hinge upon their barristers' speeches, but this is Riordan's favourite part of the trial. It's an adrenaline rush and a big fix. The speech allows Riordan to comment on the evidence, which he has not been able to do at any other time of the trial. He can highlight weak points of the prosecution's evidence that he wants the panel to dismiss. He steps up to the front and eyes each of the seven.

'I submit to you that the evidence of Hanon is so unreliable and it is credited that no reasonable board could rely upon it,' Riordan commands. 'It is also the submission that the contributions of Sampat and Fleming should be considered in the same category.'

Joe listens as Riordan takes the panel through the case and his summation makes the key arguments. He feels he's gotten close to Stephen Riordan through the trial and Joe respects and admires his barrister. He watches the tall, erudite figure as if he is a performer taking to the stage. Joe's impressed with how well he projects his voice, speaking words that can determine his future.

'It is our contention that they were acting, if not on specific instructions or orders, then at least on the understanding that what they did was acceptable to the higher command,' Riordan concludes, slowing his tempo to deliver his statements with dramatic finality. 'This then, ultimately, was a tragic accident and not a crime.'

As Riordan returns to take his place next to his client at the back of the room, he feels his speech has gone well. As he gets into his seat, giving way to Jerry Hayes' gregarious summary for Martin McGing, Riordan has the abiding feeling that he will be gravely disappointed to lose this case.

The trial is in its seventh week with Judge Hunter giving his final summation. He instructs the panel of seven who will pronounce judgement on the three soldiers.

'The burden is on the Crown,' Hunter says. 'Manslaughter is unlawful killing and the prosecution must prove that each defendant committed some act that was unlawful and dangerous so that a sober reasonable bystander would see an obvious risk of some bodily harm, and that the death occurred as a direct result of that act.' The judge goes on. 'Putting looters into shallow water in itself could not be a dangerous act. The dangerous act is the allegation that they were driven into the deeper water. The Crown alleges he died by drowning. Throwing bricks and stones causing him to go in deeper. The Crown says that they feared coming back out because at least one was holding a weapon.' The judge then turns attention to each of the three men.

'It is not suggested Selman used force. There is no evidence of that at all. He may have done something which encouraged or allowed the act.' Judge Hunter continues. 'McGing refused to answer questions in interview, but there is no adverse inference in that. McCleary gave a long and detailed explanation which is now part of the evidence in the case. You should bear in mind his good character and he is entitled to ask you to take account of that in relation to the question of credibility. This case is all about credibility.'

Tuesday, 6 June 2006 is the final day of the trial and the soldiers face their D-Day. With court summaries complete, Judge Hunter gives the final directives to the military panel. At exactly 11.04 am they retire to begin to deliberate everything they've heard these past two months and consider their verdict.

The waiting is the hardest. Each defendant remains with his legal team. Joe sits in the room below the court with Riordan and his junior legal Nigel Power. After some time, Riordan turns to Joe.

'In most cases Joe, I'm not invested in whether the client wins or loses; it doesn't become personal.' Riordan says. Joe is humbled, without words for a quiet moment. 'But you know what Joe? I've done this job twenty years, but today I really want to win this for you so much because you don't deserve to be where you're at.'

Very soon after Riordan came to the bar he trained himself to suspend all judgment about the cases he dealt with. But that doesn't mean that he wouldn't form a professional view as to whether it was a hopeless cause or a winnable case. Even in cases where he recognises that the balance of evidence is so overwhelming that the result is almost inevitable, he never gives up because that is a barrister's job, to present the best legal case for his client. In Joe's case, he deeply hopes he's done well for him and still considers this is a far more noble cause than many he's had before. Through the evidence and testimony he's come to recognise the position Joe was in and is grateful that he never had to make the same decisions in a combat zone as his client did. Riordan has a positive view of Joe but is nervous, unsure of what view this military panel of seven has taken of the young guardsman, a non-commissioned member of the infantry from a working-class background yet someone without whom the army can't function. These lads stand accused of doing something which the panel themselves would probably claim they'd never do yet would never have experienced that same position. The barrister also worries that there's a political element to all this, a collective desire to punish the soldiers for all the nation's wrongs in Iraq.

'Honestly,' Stephen adds calmly. 'In all the years I've done this, Joe, I can usually read a jury. At this point I'd tell you straight if I believed you were going to prison.' Riordan pauses. 'I can't read this panel. Sometimes a case is overwhelmingly one way or the other but this is really too hard to call. It's 50/50.' Joe feels his barrister is preparing him for whichever verdict arrives.

The afternoon of waiting wears on. Anticipation and anxiety come in waves to Joe as three hours turns to four. The jury's day will end at 4.00 pm. The marching of the wall clock starts to dominate.

'If it goes into tomorrow, I fear the verdict won't be favourable,' Riordan says sombrely. Joe watches the wall time. It is 3.50 pm.

'Look, you've still got ten minutes,' says Nigel Powell encouragingly.

Joe is sitting, shaking, clenching his fists and steeling his composure. He dwells on the prospect that he may be sent to prison. *I'll kill myself inside of a jail cell.* He holds back a pool of tears. *If that verdict comes I'll likely be remanded before sentencing. No matter what the outcome is, I'm just going tonight to get pissed. This could be my last night.* He feels defeated.

'Aye, it doesn't matter, now, eh,' Joe utters.

Another five minutes crawl by.

At 3.56 pm, the door rattles with firm knocks as a court orderly announces the jury has come out. Riordan is nervous as the panel prepares to deliver its verdict. He can't imagine how his clients handle the pressure. Joe walks up the flights of stairs and sees the swollen number of people assembling in the court. There are military officials, legal teams, family members, reporters. They're talking among themselves, but Joe sees them almost in a daze, their mouths opening but hears no words coming out of them. It feels as though his feet aren't even taking the steps up the stairs, as if he is just floating. As everyone takes their positions, Selman and McGing in their places, it is as though some force is carrying Joe. His heart thuds as silence descends on the courtroom.

'All rise,' shouts the orderly. Judge Advocate Michael Hunter strides into the room and takes his place at the front. The room sits again, Joe unsteadily and shaking.

'Has the panel reached a verdict?' Hunter asks.

'We have, sir.' The head of the panel replies.

'And how do you find the defendants?'

'In the case of the Crown versus Carle Selman: Not guilty.' There is a barrage of cheering from the back of the room.

'In the case of the Crown versus Joseph McCleary: Not guilty.' It takes a moment to register as a rain of further cheering sounds.

'In the case of the Crown versus Martin McGing: Not guilty.' Applause and cheers burst.

The judge's final words are drowned out by the explosion of celebratory screams and shouts. With all verdicts recorded, Joe's dam burst, streaming down his face as Riordan's massive hand clasps his with a hearty shake that grows into an enveloping hug.

'Yes! Yes,' he utters. 'You didn't deserve this!'

'You're dead sound, Stephen. Thank you,' Joe manages to reply.

At the back of the room, Joe's family members erupt into uncontrollable rapture.

Captain Niall Brennan and some other Irish Guardsmen reach over, pile on and hug Joe and the others. Reaching her way from the back of the court Joe's mum speaks assurance to her son.

'It's okay, it's okay, oh Joe,' Lynn says. 'It's over now. It's over.'

Outside Colchester Barracks, in the centre of the ancient Roman capital city once known as Camulodunum where Boudica's forces had bloodily overcome their occupiers, the victorious soldiers and their families emerge from the makeshift courtroom, their battleground for seven long weeks. They assemble amid the vibrancy of the green courtyard with eyes dazzling, adjusting to the bright June sunshine. A small crowd of reporters and photographers gather around the men, military officials and lawyers.

Stephen Riordan steps outside, clutching his wig and satchel in hand, as he takes in the palpable feeling of relief. He has another case that he's needed on in Birmingham and he's heading straight there. Besides, he's not one for talking to the press; he'll leave that to Jerry Hayes, he thinks with a smile. Stephen gives Joe a final look and slips away.

Jerry Hayes is pleased to publicise his part in McGing's win, quickly finding a place in the shade for interviews, his second, Rob Rinder, standing just behind him, getting a taste for fame.

'I liked your speech!' comes a comment in thick Scots that Hayes recognises as Dom McKay of the *Mirror*. 'Tell us what you think about this case.'

'If ever there was a charge which should have been strangled at birth this is it. Why are we here? This was a tragic accident,' Hayes tells the hungry journalists. 'These soldiers were the thin line between anarchy and law and order. They are decent young British soldiers doing their best to do their duty.'

Martin's solicitor, Fadi Daoud, too addresses the press. 'Whilst naturally Martin remains embittered by the decision made to prosecute him,' he says, 'nonetheless he wants to communicate his total appreciation to his regiment, the Irish Guards, for their unstinting support through a most difficult period.'

Joe finds Martin, the two clasping hands with one another in the satisfaction that comes from triumph. Still struggling to control the flooding tears of relief Joe responds to an assault of journalists, brandishing notepads, microphones and questions about how he feels.

'Justice has been served and I would like to thank everyone,' Joe says. 'I'm looking forward to going home and pleased it's all over.'

'What are your thoughts about this case against you, now it's over?' asks another journo.

'We were told to put the looters in the canal. I was the lowest rank, and we were always told we weren't paid to think. We just followed orders,' Joe vents. 'I don't know why the army went ahead with the prosecution. It was when there were reports about British soldiers mistreating Iraqis and they wanted to look like they were doing something. We were scapegoats.'

'And how does your family feel?' Joe glances over towards Lynn and Carlos, both there together for the last day of the ordeal.

'I don't know what I would have done without them all. It was so hard for them, too. I want to give something back to them.'

The reporters turn to McGing, unbuttoning the pain that's more than he feels his twenty-two years should have to handle.

'I always wanted to be a soldier. Now I have a different view because the army hung me out to dry,' his slight Brummie burr more apparent through his rage. 'I want out as soon as possible.'

'What would you say to other soldiers heading to Iraq?' poses a journalist.

'Hire a good lawyer,' he replies sharply. 'In case the army stabs you in the back.'

Off to the side, Selman's solicitor, Chris Wright, reminds the media that the sergeant has continued to serve throughout the past three years.

'He welcomes the wide-ranging support offered from across the Household Division,' Wright says. 'But above all he is relieved his innocence in this matter is confirmed.'

From above there is the whirr of a descending helicopter nearby. Moments later as the crowd of well-wishers disperses, the top brass appears. Major General Sebastian Roberts commands the Household Division and is a colonel of the Irish Guards, the regiment he's been part of since 1977.

'Congratulations!' he says beaming proudly, walking along and shaking the hands of first Selman then McGing and heading towards Joe. 'Congratulations, boys.'

'Do us a favour,' Joe says fuming with revulsion as the brigadier reaches him. The senior officer motions to shake Joe's hand who refuses the offer. *I gave you my life. I fought the war. I went above and beyond for you in loads of situations,* Joe thinks. *Yet you just fucking left me to rot.*

Over the course of its investigation and its seven-week court martial, this trial has cost the British tax payer more than £2.5m, but its cost to the soldiers and their families is inestimable.

'I'm not shaking your hand, Sir. I won't touch you.' Joe says. 'What you've done to me and my family is unforgivable.'

'I'm guessing you won't be re-joining the army?' Roberts says awkwardly.

'No sir, I won't,' Joe replies seething. 'And I'll never forgive you for this. Ever.'

Joe travels back from Colchester to Liverpool, taking off his army uniform for the final time. He then heads to a homecoming party at the Old Campfield pub in Everton, drinking away the rotting memory of the past weeks.

Joe wakes up the morning after in his home town of Bootle, with a celebratory hangover. The same day, 2,696 miles away, in a suburb north of Baghdad, there is another victory. An American air strike takes out Abu Musab al-Zarqawi, the head of al-Qaeda in Iraq. The US invasion has opened up Iraq to al-Qaeda, long since at odds with Saddam. Al-Zarqawi, who has the al-Qaeda title 'Emir of al-Qaeda in the Country of Two Rivers', managed to turn the insurgency fiercely against America and incite war between Sunni and Shiites. And Al-Zarqawi, who most probably ordered the death of Kenneth Bigley and witnessed his beheading, is dead.

'Today, we have managed to put an end to Zarqawi,' declares Nuri Kamal Maliki, the recently installed Iraqi prime minister who only three weeks ago took the reins of the first full-term government since the overthrow of Saddam. He wants the death to be a warning to other insurgent leaders.

Instead, Al-Zarqawi's blood fertilises the fanatics whose roots are in that Middle Eastern land, his adherents soon to fly black flags and terror high above Iraq.

Chapter 38

Building's Edge

He stands by the building's edge, high above the streets of Aintree, the last place the man will be seen alive if he jumps.

Joe can see as far as Bootle, the docks and the Mersey beyond from his vantage point at the top of the multi-storey car park. The parking structure is attached to the medical centre long known as Fazakerley District General, only in 1999 given its new name of Aintree University Hospital. He looks down nervously at the sprawling buildings that he knows include the emergency ward, where he once recovered from his second suicide attempt, and the grey tile roof of Stoddart House.

But this time it is not Joe who is contemplating ending his own life. It's been some time since Joe's acquittal at the court martial trial. He could never go back to the military, not after the way he feels he was treated. Instead he has a job as a security guard at Aintree Hospital and is starting his night shift when he gets the call that someone is on the top of the fifth-storey car park about to jump. Although Joe's left the army the training hasn't left him and something kicks in; he knows how to help. Joe is drinking far less now and directing his frustrations into regular gym sessions so he quickly traverses the 500 metres from his building to reach the multi-storey and powers up the stairs two at a time. Joe is the first one on the scene where a young lad is on top of a short safety barrier that's about waist high. He is looking at the murky darkness below. Joe slowly, cautiously approaches. Raw gusts whip up freezing chills in the evening air, especially this high up. There's ice forming on the roof already. It's Christmas Eve and it's possible to make out the occasional twinkling of lights in the distance. Near the entrance to the car park the flashing of blue announces the arrival of a solitary police car.

'Don't no one come near me,' the lad, who must be in his late teens or early twenties, screams frantically. He looks poised, about to leap.

'Mate …' Joe shouts across the gulf between them. 'I have stood in the same position you are. Maybe not on a multi-storey, but I'm there with you.'

Joe knows what the young man is doing; he knows how he feels, about to take his own life. It seems like second nature to talk to him.

'I was out in Iraq.' Joe tells him. 'And it messed me up …' He tells the young man what happened, building a quick rapport.

In return the lad shares with Joe his story: that he is gay, he's just come out of the closet and hasn't been accepted as who he is.

'Look, it doesn't matter who you are, no one needs to judge you,' Joe shouts. 'Do you know what I mean? You just got to accept you for who you are.' He pauses for a moment. 'So, just, come to me, come to me now.'

There is hesitation. Then the young lad angles himself away from the ledge. He takes a halting half-step back.

'Have you got a smoke?' he asks.

'I actually don't. But just a minute,' says Joe apologetically and then looks at his colleague crouching near the roof access door. 'Paul. You got a ciggy there, mate?' The other security guard fishes out a cigarette and gently tosses it and a lighter towards Joe, who uses handing over as a way to get nearer to the lad on the building's ledge.

The lad reaches out, his hand clasping the offer of the cigarette. When he does, Joe grasps his wrist and pulls him firmly away from the edge.

'C'mere,' Joe says as he embraces the lost young lad. Tears sluice from his cheeks and fall down Joe's back. Joe helps the whimpering lad to the stairs and into a ward. Later Joe's supervisor finds him still with the lad.

'What are you doing in here,' Joe's supervisor asks him. 'Ain't you got a home to go to?'

'Fucking kid's been through enough,' Joe replies. 'Told him I'd stay.' *You don't realise how fucking lucky you are*, Joe thinks bitterly, *to have not been through something so devastating that you want to end it.*

Joe stays with the young soul through the night. He sleeps by his bed until his family has been reached and arrives. Some weeks later a letter arrives from the local police, thanking Joe for his brave efforts and conduct, talking to the lad on the roof.

The conduct of Joe, the British forces in Iraq and the deaths in custody of civilians including Ahmed are receiving attention again, eighteen months after the manslaughter court martial in Colchester. A case is brought against the UK on 11 December 2007, through the European Court of Human Rights in Strasbourg, France, by six Iraqi nationals who have lost loved ones. The six named include Mr Jabbar Kareem Ali, Ahmed's father. The Iraqis' case is brought under the European Convention on Human Rights and Fundamental Freedoms (ECHR) and the applicants, who receive British legal aid, are again represented by the Birmingham-based legal firm Public

Interest Lawyers, run by Phil Shiner. Shiner is no stranger to the pain of Iraq. He was the solicitor for Pat Long, mother of Corporal Paul Long, the 24-year-old RMP who was slaughtered in Majar al-Kabir by angry Iraqis in June 2003. Shiner helped Long bring a case against the Ministry of Defence and push for an independent inquiry into the death. Shiner went on to work with a network of Iraqi lawyers and fixers in Iraq to track down people who had claims against the British for alleged abuse and unlawful death. The Iraqi relatives claim that their deceased were all under United Kingdom jurisdiction when they died and that there has not been an effective investigation into their deaths, which they say goes against Article 2 of the ECHR: the right of every person to life.

The British army conducts its own limited in scope investigation that results in a thirty-five page official army report, 'An Investigation into Cases of Deliberate Abuse and Unlawful Killing in Iraq', which is published on 25 January 2008. The Aiken Report by Brigadier Robert Aitken highlights six cases of alleged mistreatment and wrongful death of Iraqis that occurred between 2003 and 2004, including that of Ahmed Jabber Kareem. Among the report's conclusions is the assurance that:

> The great majority of officers and soldiers who have served in Iraq have done so to the highest standards that the Army or the Nation might expect of them, under extraordinarily testing conditions. There is no evidence of fundamental flaws in the Army's approach to preparing for or conducting operations.

The ECHR takes more than three years examining the Iraqi deaths before it makes its decision. On 7 July 2011, the court hands down a judgement against the UK Government, saying that its human rights obligations are not limited only to the territorial UK but can exceptionally extend overseas as well. This means the UK is accountable in regions where it had jurisdiction, such as British-controlled southern Iraq.

By July 2011, the final British forces have just vacated Iraq, with the last 170 or so mostly naval and some Royal Marine personnel departing after their mission in the south to train the fledgling Iraqi navy in Umm Qasr port. The withdrawal marks a formal end for the British presence after eight long years in the country. The recent period in Iraq has been marred by ongoing violence and instability from north to south, something which the British soldiers who fought in 2003 witness when their tour sends them back. Irish Guards' infantrymen who return to the Basra region in 2007 find it is a completely different place to the one they left behind four years earlier. Iraq's second city is massively dangerous, the soldiers seldom venture out of their compounds and when they do it's a deadly lottery with insurgents and militias and the growing threat of Improvised Explosive Devices (IEDs). Iraq's deadly deterioration had led to the US-led 'surge' strategy in summer 2007. Five fresh American brigades, more than 20,000 young soldiers, are sent to counter the insurgency mainly in the north. The British decline involvement in the surge; their troops are already committed in Afghanistan, meaning the army is already overstretched and there is enough trouble in the south of Iraq. British positions in Basra are under siege from Muqtada al-Sadr's Mahdi army for much of 2007 until the start of September, when 550 British troops make a cover of darkness retreat from their base in Saddam's Palace on the Shatt al-Arab. The British troops fall back with the remaining 5,000 personnel split between Basra International Airport and Shaibah logistical base, the appetite for their presence in the country sorely diminished.

In mid-December 2011, American forces also formally end their war in Iraq, lowering their flag at a Baghdad ceremony with the announcement that the troops leave with 'lasting pride'. As the Stars and Stripes are folded away on the December day, America's Defense Secretary, Leon Panetta in attendance, tells veterans they can be 'secure in knowing that your sacrifice has helped the Iraqi people to cast tyranny aside'. Exactly one week later 72 Iraqi civilians are killed and more than 170 are wounded in bomb attacks across the capital of Iraq, the credit for the slaughter claimed by al-Qaeda in Iraq, rising out of the ashes of Abu Musab Al-Zarqawi and its political front, a group called The Islamic State of Iraq (ISIS). With the inflamed sectarian divide between Shia and Sunni to exploit, the country moves into a new phase of heightened insurgency.

Joe is moving on with his life, into a house that he's bought with his girlfriend, becoming a stepfather to her two young boys and finding the nightmares easing off until the spectre of Iraq re-emerges. The young family are preparing for a drive to the pinewoods beaches near Formby and packing up their car with the small mountain of items they need for a toddler and a baby. Joe steps back inside after putting the elder of the two boys in his booster seat to quickly attend to the ringing of the house phone.

'Hello?' a young woman's voice says hesitantly. 'Is that Joseph McCleary?'

'Yeah, it is, yeah,' Joe tells her.

'I'm from the *Daily Mail*,' the girl says. 'My name's Larisa.'

'The paper? Why are you ringing me?' Joe asks, puzzled.

The young reporter explains down the phone line that the death of 15-year-old Ahmed is being re-examined as part of the government's investigative unit called the Iraq Historic Allegations Team (IHAT). The case against Joe is being reopened. How does he feel?

'Really? Really?' Joe says, his heart sinking, old embers of anger and anxiety beginning to enflame. Joe's girlfriend walks into the front door and looks at him, a little impatiently.

'You'll have to call me back. I need to be off this phone,' Joe tells the junior journalist.

He drops the phone to the floor.

'Oh, I can't go back through that,' he tells his girlfriend. He has a life now and can't bear the prospect that the hell of another investigation may be happening again.

The IHAT has its origins in a case of abuse and the death of an Iraqi hotel receptionist named Baha Mousa. The man had died in British custody in September 2003 and his family were also named among the six presented to the ECHR. Mousa, who was 26, had been arrested as a suspected insurgent and died having sustained ninety-three separate injuries to his body. The prosecution into Mousa's death was announced by the government in July 2005, on the same day as Joe and his fellow soldiers' court case had been publicly highlighted. At the court martial into Mousa's death, which began in September 2006, one of the accused, Corporal Donald Payne, became the first British soldier to admit to a war crime. The family of the dead Iraqi are awarded £2.83m in a damages settlement from the Ministry of Defence in 2008, but less than two years later the family bring a claim for a judicial review. As a result, the IHAT review organisation was conceived in March 2010 under Bill Rammell, a Labour MP for Harlow (a seat he won in 1997 by defeating then Conservative MP Jerry Hayes, nearly a decade before he defended Martin McGing.) Rammell, as the government's Minister of State for the Armed Forces, had been struggling to deal with a growing number of enquiries and accusations of abuse of Iraqi detainees and alleged unlawful deaths. After the Conservative-Liberal coalition election victory in May 2010, IHAT moved forward and the new Liberal Democrat Minister for the Armed Forces, Nick Harvey, announced that IHAT would start work in November. IHAT would help the government discharge its obligations under Article 2 & 3 of the ECHR, both the right to life and the prohibition of torture. The investigative body began under the leadership of Mark Warwick, a former Metropolitan Police Officer, with 165 cases relating to events that took place in Iraq between 2003 and 2008. Their caseloads were growing rapidly, due to a large number of referrals that were the work of Public Interest Lawyers and another legal firm, Leigh Day, based in London and run by Martyn Day. IHAT was known for doing a thorough job, exhuming bodies, interviewing Iraqi witnesses and inquiring about suspects.

When Joe returns to work at the Aintree Hospital the day after his call from the *Daily Mail*, he discovers that there have been questions asked about him at his place of work.

'Mate, I've just had the most weird thing.' Joe's work colleague tells him. 'Someone's been here asking me really random questions about you. I mean, proper random. Mate, is there people after you?' Joe finds his supervisor is not the only one who has had investigators asking about him and probing his character.

'Someone's been asking questions, Joe, about you,' says one of the nursing staff later.

'Are you in trouble with, like, drugs or something?'

'No, I'm not,' Joe responds defensively. 'What have they been asking?'

'It was strange. They was asking if you were aggressive and all that,' the nurse says.

'Fuck them,' Joe says.

The following day Joe calls the MoD and demands to know why he's being investigated again. They don't tell him much about the case except that there are ongoing inquiries, which are happening behind closed doors. Joe is required to write another statement, which he'll have to do with a solicitor. The new investigation prompts more nightmares. It's like the long months of Joe's struggle waiting for the court martial to be decided all over again.

The IHAT's remit originally intends it to last for two years. In July 2014, after nearly four years, the government increases the organisation's funding to more than £57m through to the end of 2019.

In November 2015, the IHAT announces the conclusion to Joe's case, IHAT/85:

> The decision has been made to discontinue any further work on the case after the investigation identified there was no prospect of gaining any new or compelling evidence to go any way to altering a previous decision made by the courts martial. All material gathered during the course of the investigation will be passed to the MOD for its decision as to whether there should be any further, non-criminal, inquiry into the circumstances of his death.

Joe feels incredible relief at the decision. He thinks it's over. But it isn't.

At the start of January 2016, Joe again receives more calls from journalists about a government inquiry specifically into deaths in Iraq called the Iraq Fatality Inquiry (IFI). The IFI is a formal judicial investigation being carried out to examine circumstances that may be considered of public concern. The new inquiry comes about because of concerns about the independence of IHAT and allegations of systemic issues relating to the treatment of detainees. In July 2010, even as IHAT had yet to get underway, Phil Shiner brought forth a new claim about IHAT's independence, but the court determined that a public inquiry was unnecessary. Shiner and his legal team appealed the decision and at the end of 2011, the court judged that IHAT's independence was 'substantially compromised' and plans were made for a separate inquiry.

When he hears of the new inquiry, Joe goes online and finds the IFI website. He reads that the inquiry promises that soldiers would not be liable for further prosecution, but that does little to reassure Joe who phones them. He gets hold of a man named Ben Dustin, who's a paralegal to the investigations and is experienced in several public inquiries, including the Al-Sweady Public Inquiry about the deaths at The Battle of Danny Boy in 2004.

'Hello?' Ben answers. Joe explains who he is and why he's calling.

'Yeah, are you trying to find me?' Joe demands.

'Oh, yes.' The paralegal explains that the IFI submissions are voluntary but they'd like Joe to attend an upcoming hearing. The man has a letter that he's yet to send to Joe. 'I haven't got your address, so I'm sorry.'

'Why am I hearing about this from the news that you're reopening an inquiry?' Joe says angrily. 'So I've got news reporters ringing my house up, ringing my house that my children are in, and you haven't done anything to let me know?'

'Well, we're sending you a letter out, can we have your address?'

'I'm not coming to your stupid inquiry,' Joe says, fuming.

'Well, you could be arrested. And then we'll go to the High Court and get you charged to bring you in.'

'Well you just told me it's voluntary,' Joe retorts.

'Yeah, it is voluntary.'

'How can it be voluntary if you're going to arrest me, you fucking idiot?'

'I don't like the way you're speaking to me,' the paralegal says.

'Mate, trust me, you're not going to like me when I get there, neither.' Joe returns angrily. 'I've just been told by a newspaper you're investigating me. Again!' Joe slams his phone receiver down repeatedly so its plastic casing shatters into a mess of broken exposed wires.

The tone of media stories covering the investigation into British soldiers' actions changes and becomes bitterly divisive. It is part of a growing souring in some towards the European Union and a movement seeking a referendum about the continued British membership of the EU, something Prime Minister David Cameron begins to discuss early in January 2013. Both the IHAT and the IFI are investigating many current and former British service personnel because of a requirement to fulfil part of the European Convention of Human Rights. It is seen as another example of European domination upon British sovereignty. After Cameron's second term victory in 2015, where he had made the EU referendum a campaign pledge, right-wing papers become suddenly ferocious in their condemnation of the cases against the soldiers. The *Daily Mail* and others run numerous critical stories in January 2016 at the same time that Cameron is renegotiating the EU Reform Bill. Joe becomes a pawn caught up amid a battle that threatens to disgrace all sides. As part of the *Daily Mail*'s ongoing series about the 'Witch-Hunt Against Our Heroes', he is featured in his own separate sidebar article: 'Nightmare of 4 probes in a decade'.

Some of the many stories regarding the investigation of British troops mention the threat that the soldiers could face charges before the International Criminal Court (ICC) in The Hague. This is the ultimate terrifying prospect for Joe and the other soldiers, which has come about because of a paradigm shift in the rules relating to war-fighting. The Iraq War was the first major conflict that Britain engaged in after new rules set by the Rome Statute of the International Criminal Court came into effect in 1998. This act expands the ICC's jurisdiction on war crimes and widens the government's responsibility to investigate allegations of abuse or else The Hague would intervene. When the government went into Iraq in 2003 they didn't realise the implications of the Rome Statute. When Joe went into Iraq neither he nor the British government realised the gruelling and ongoing trials he and others might face.

Joe travels to London to attend a meeting, along with Selman, Cooke and McGing, with the inquiry's inspector, Sir George Newman. Newman is 73 and a veteran High Court judge whose call to the Bar took place in 1965 at the esteemed London Middle Temple. In his long career Newman was a Judge of the Court of Appeal in the Bahamas and the Cayman Islands, where he dealt with constitutional settlement cases arising out of armed conflict in places like Fiji and Trinidad and Tobago. At the start of 2014, the Secretary of State for Defence called Newman out of retirement to examine Iraq's mounting number of British military fatality cases.

The four soldiers gather in Newman's chambers in London, each with new lawyers and an uncomfortable air of reluctance and resentment.

'Right, let's get all the formalities straight,' says Newman, outlining what he's looking to achieve in the case and his expectations from the men.

He's talking like he doesn't see the nights that I tried to take my own life. The battles we've all had, Joe reflects bitterly. *It's like he doesn't see that, or would he even care about it?*

'Martin here, he's been struggling so badly with his mental health,' Joe snaps angrily. 'We all have.'

'Oh, I'm sure he'll be fine,' Newman says. As Joe looks at the aged judge, his rage rises. *Do you know what, you fucking arse*, Joe thinks, *I may only be a soldier to you, I may not be a toff in the middle of London but if you're going to speak to me, and I cooperate, at least have the decency to speak to me with some respect.*

'Sure he'll be fine? Sure he'll be fine?!' Joe repeats, the judge's seeming flippancy inflaming something inside Joe. 'You have no idea what we went through. You have no idea how hard that trial was. Because if you're bringing something like this up, it's going to bring back pain. We've been through hell. You have no idea, fucking no idea what we've been through. And you turn round and tell me everything's fine? Everything's okay? I haven't fucking slept. I've fucking shed tears over this. Don't you fucking dare!'

'Joe, cool it off, right now,' says Joe's new solicitor, Simon Natas. Joe's fury burns, feeling he's being punished for a crime that he's already been found not guilty of.

'Oh yes, I understand,' says the judge, seeming to backtrack.

Joe leaves the meeting wound up, hating the prospect of the repeated investigation.

On 22 January 2016, Newman makes his first public statement in connection with his investigation into the death of Ahmed. He explains the context of his inquiry, how the IFI only receives cases through and after IHAT and the Directorate of Service Prosecutions have concluded that there is no realistic case for their prosecution and that it's a fact-finding function that he is embarking on. Several members of the press are in attendance, including Larisa Brown from the *Daily Mail*, who questions why the soldiers are not being better informed about the judicial proceedings and a *Times* reporter who suggests to Newman that 'it surely cannot be helpful for the Prime Minister to have said what he said today'. He's referring to comments from David Cameron's office that morning. 'The Prime Minister is deeply concerned at the large number of spurious claims being made against members of our armed forces.' The Downing Street source goes on to say that 'action needs to be taken and has asked the national security council to produce a clear, detailed plan on how we stop former troops facing this torment'.

The land and the people of Iraq face their own anguish as a movement of terror rises. The Islamic State in Iraq and the Levant (ISIL), an offshoot of al-Qaeda in Iraq emerges around 2011, led by Abu Bakr al-Baghdadi. Its ruthless and militant army quickly overtakes Fallujah, Samarra and Tikrit and makes its caliphate capital the city of Mosul in June 2014. The bloodshed spilled over from Raqqa in Syria amid the instability of the Arab Spring and then beyond as beastly fanatics abroad instil terror: the streets of Paris, in November 2015; coordinated bombings across Brussels the following March; and a frenetic dance of bullets at a Florida nightclub in the USA in June 2016, and elsewhere.

The veins of ISIL terror run all the way back to the heart of military action in Iraq, a connection highlighted a month after the attack in America when Britain's Sir John Chilcot unveils the conclusions of his long-awaited Iraq Inquiry. 'Blair had been advised that an invasion of Iraq was expected to increase the threat to the UK and UK interests from al-Qaida and its affiliates,' says Chilcot's report. The inquiry unearthed warnings in the months and weeks before the war from Britain's own intelligence services that told the Prime Minister his war would become a recruitment tool for extremists. 'The broader threat from Islamist terrorists will also increase in the event of war, reflecting intensified anti-US/anti-Western sentiment in the Muslim world,' read a 2003 memo. Yet the nation was led to a war 'before the peaceful options for disarmament had been exhausted', against a dictator who posed 'no imminent threat' and the conflict sold to the public on the basis of intelligence that 'had NOT established beyond doubt' that Iraq had chemical, biological or nuclear weapons. Chilcot's voluminous dissection, more than 2.6 million words over 6,275 pages, lays bare the war that cost 179 British lives and countless thousands of Iraqis.

Ahmed's death is laid bare again when IFI reveals its findings and this time Joe is the subject of reproach. After a belligerent grilling of Joe, Selman, McGing and Cooke during the summer, Sir George Newman releases his report on 16 September 2016. He condemns the four soldiers and says of Ahmed, 'the circumstances in which he died should never have occurred'. Newman ravages the men's actions:

It was a clumsy, ill-directed and bullying piece of conduct, engaged in without consideration of the risk of harm to which it could give rise and, in the event which occurred, there was a manifest failure to take action to save the life of Mr Ali ... His death ensued because he was forced by the soldiers to enter the canal, where, in the presence of the soldiers, he was seen to be in difficulty, and to go under the water.

The retired judge singles out Joe, who is under the veil of anonymity as 'SO18', for some of his harshest criticism. Judge Newman brands him 'an unsatisfactory witness', who 'exaggerated and suggested ... the journey being a form of mercy mission to avoid four looters "being bricked to death".'

Joe is bitter, angry and exhausted, like a wounded dragon, when he reads Newman's judgement of him and surmises it's only because he took on the aged Sir George over his dismissal of war's traumas. *It hurts that he can judge me*, Joe thinks. *He doesn't realise what we went through, what my family went through, what my mum went through. The nights that they had to pick me up off the floor, stone drunk, trying to kill myself. He's just judging me because I was angry in the meeting room. He's never been out on a war front; hell like he's never seen it.*

Later that day, the Ministry of Defence apologises to the family of Ahmed Jabbar Kareem Ali, the teenage boy who drowned in a canal more than thirteen years earlier. 'This was a grave incident for which we are extremely sorry,' the army's statement says. 'We are committed to investigating allegations of wrongdoing by UK forces and will use Sir George's findings to learn lessons to help ensure nothing like this happens again.'

The man who pursued and pressed the allegations against British troops, Phil Shiner, is himself condemned for wrongdoing. During a Solicitors' Disciplinary Tribunal hearing, held in Shiner's absence at the start of February 2017, the man behind his now closed-down Public Interest Lawyers firm is found guilty on twenty-two charges of misconduct, including five counts of dishonesty. Many of these charges relate to the Battle of Danny Boy and the subsequent Al-Sweady inquiry where Shiner approved encouraging unsolicited approaches to possible clients and provided financial incentives so a third party would change evidence about allegations of atrocities in Iraq. As a result of his misdeeds, Shiner is struck off as a solicitor, ordered to pay the full costs of the trial against him and then has to declare himself bankrupt.

Two months later, the government officially announces the end of its war crimes probe IHAT. With Shiner disgraced, the legitimacy of many of the cases he brought forward are thrown into doubt. Plenty of the abuse claims levelled against British service personnel and examined by IHAT were found not to be credible. Its 3,400 cases are reduced to just 20. Its £34.2m cost failed to secure a single prosecution. By the end of the summer, it will all be over. In June 2019, Sir George Newman passes away at the age of 77, his role as inspector taken over by Baroness Heather Hallett to handle the last lingering IFI cases. The sun is setting on more than a decade and a half of recriminations relating to Iraq.

For Joe, like the other four soldiers, the memory of the Middle Eastern invasion continues to haunt, more than eighteen years removed from the war. He tries to move on, he marries the love of his life, rebuilds his relationship with his father, John. Joe welcomes a new son, and gets a stable job as a bailiff.

But the lad from Bootle looks back on the years he gave to the army, gave to his country, gave to Iraq and he thinks *we should never have gone out there, we shouldn't have gone.*

Acknowledgements

The past, even a relatively recent one, is a tricky thing to reconstruct. In the summer of 2003, while investigators were putting together the tragic story of young Ahmed, I was helping reconstruct the death of British weapons inspector Dr David Kelly, the effort part of Channel 4 documentary-drama film. This began my interest in Iraq, the war and its aftermath and sets up my first thankful dedication which is due to Simon Chinn. The producer gave me my big break into television and thirteen years later brought me back to develop a potential documentary about the investigation into British soldiers involved in the Iraq war. Likewise, that gratitude is extended to Susannah Price and Kate Griffiths, collaboration with whom at Lightbox provided the genesis and introduction to this story.

As a writer I have felt surrounded by a great cloud of witnesses, the encouraging voices holding accountable to complete the journey of words – or at least tolerating my sharing this endeavour. First, my wife Amanda, and daughters C, A and E, long-suffering my immersion into this mammoth project.

Likewise, I'm grateful to Mike and Bev Ziegler for putting up with me being head down writing during the holidays and for my mother Jill for fostering my love of books.

I am grateful to the many who generously encouraged throughout: Paula Engelking, Maria Awes, Paul Woolf, Mandy Skelton, Kate Bullion for feeding back on the earliest chapters and Clementine Mortelman on the final stretch. Of special note, I'm thankful for the input, advice and commentary (often over the best of whiskies) with fellow writer, Dan Parry.

Huge thanks to Madeleine Cotter, my agent at WGM, and the ever-diligent Greg Morton. At Pen and Sword I am thankful to its commissioning editor Jonathan Wright, production assistant Aileen Pringle and of course to my editor Gaynor Haliday.

One wise veteran I spoke to noted, rightly so, the grave responsibility of writing about real people and actual events. This is something that I have taken seriously throughout approaching as many of those who were involved as I could. Despite my diligence, I was not able to track down everyone and there were some who declined to share their experiences. For those who kindly took time to speak to me, to share their stories and knowledge, I am incredibly grateful. This book would not exist without the input, discussion and deep conversations – at times through humble tears – of often hardened veterans and family members, each of whom are worthy of their own tome. Across the gamut, every serviceman I spoke to was profoundly impacted by their time in Iraq as were those who supported them. Hearing these descriptions and accounts was the highlight of this journey.

Soldiers were not the only contributors to this book and I am also duly thankful for the time and help of lawyers on this case, Iraqi witnesses and family members. Also to Bootle historian Hugh Hollinghurst, pathologist Professor Peter Vanezis and the talented military artist David Rowlands. Additional thanks to Mohamed Elezaby for translation help, Dr Mike Martin for discussing his important book *Why We Fight* and A.T. Williams at Warwick University whose *A Very British Killing* impressively tells of the Baha Mousa Iraq war trial case.

An additional note on sources is due here. Where transcripts of exchanges (such as interviews) were available these have been used. At times minor changes have been made for the sake of clarity. Excerpts from Joe's letters home from Iraq retain his original spelling. Throughout the in-depth research of this book every attempt was made to uncover the facts of events described, however where inaccuracies and errors remain they are unintentionally and apologetically mine.

While this book tells the broader story of the 2003 war, its impact is seen through the lens of one particular guardsman: Joe McCleary. I felt a connection with Joe from my first meeting and was grasped by the raw intensity of what he went through, so much so that the idea of this book would not leave me. Many times I would walk away from our long conversations stunned by the ferocity of his experiences. At times some details were slightly fragmented or muddled, which I learned was a frequent symptom of those with PTSD, and in such instances I have tried to present the available facts fairly. On repeated occasions Joe – and family members – shared honest and heartbreaking moments. I am indebted to Joe; it was a privilege to hear his story.